T0249922

RESIDENTIAL INSTITUTIONS IN BRITAIN, 1725–1970: INMATES AND ENVIRONMENTS

Perspectives in Economic and Social History

Series Editors: Andrew August
Jari Eloranta

Titles in this Series

RESIDENTIAL INSTITUTIONS IN BRITAIN, 1725–1970: INMATES AND ENVIRONMENTS

EDITED BY

Jane Hamlett, Lesley Hoskins and Rebecca Preston

Routledge
Taylor & Francis Group

LONDON AND NEW YORK

First published 2013 by Pickering & Chatto (Publishers) Limited

Published 2016 by Routledge
2 Park Square, Milton Park, Abingdon, Oxfordshire OX14 4RN
711 Third Avenue, New York, NY 10017, USA

First issued in paperback 2015

Routledge is an imprint of the Taylor & Francis Group, an informa business

BRITISH LIBRARY CATALOGUING IN PUBLICATION DATA

Residential institutions in Britain, 1725–1970: inmates and environments. –
(Perspectives in economic and social history)
1. Institutional care – Great Britain – History – 18th century. 2. Institutional
care – Great Britain – History – 19th century. 3. Institutional care – Great
Britain – History – 20th century.
I. Series II. Hamlett, Jane editor of compilation. III. Hoskins, Lesley, editor of
compilation. IV. Preston, Rebecca, editor of compilation.
361'.05'0941-dc23

ISBN-13: 978-1-138-66212-4 (pbk)
ISBN-13: 978-1-8489-3366-8 (hbk)

Typeset by Pickering & Chatto (Publishers) Limited

CONTENTS

ACKNOWLEDGEMENTS

This collection of essays results from the conference, 'Inhabiting Institutions in Britain, 1700–1950', held at Royal Holloway, University of London, in 2010. The conference and book were part of the 'At Home in the Institution' project, supported by the Economic and Social Research Council (RES-061-25-0389). We would like to thank the contributors who developed their papers for our collection and also the other delegates: Michele Cohen, Quintin Colville, Megan Doolittle, Clare Hickman, Ayla Lepine, Alysa Levene, Vicky Long, Maria Luddy, Carmen Mangion, Jane Pearson, Katherine Rawling, Maria Rayner, Anna Shepherd, Susan Skedd, Paul Tobia and Alannah Tomkins. Sandra Cavallo, Virginia Crossman, Sue Hawkins, Margaret Ponsonby and Andrea Tanner provided a very helpful summing up at the end of the day. Thanks, too to Marie Sandell for administering the conference. Recordings from the two days are available at http://backdoorbroadcasting.net/2010/09/inhabiting-institutions-in-britain-1700-1950/. We are also grateful to the anonymous reviewers of the book proposal and to our editors at Pickering & Chatto.

LIST OF CONTRIBUTORS

Jane Hamlett is Lecturer in Modern British History at Royal Holloway, University of London. Her first book *Material Relations: Middle-Class Families and Domestic Interiors in England, 1850–1910* (2010) is published by Manchester University Press. Her articles have appeared in *Cultural and Social History*, *Gender and History*, the *Journal of Consumer Culture*, the *Journal of Family History* and *Women's History Review*; she has edited special issues of *Home Cultures* and *Women's History Review*. In 2010–12 she led the ESRC-funded project, 'At Home in the Institution? Asylum, School and Lodging House Interiors in London and South East England, 1845–1914' and is working on a new book, *At Home in the Institution: Inside Lunatic Asylums, Lodging Houses and Schools in Victorian and Edwardian England*, to be published by Palgrave Macmillan in 2014/15.

Lesley Hoskins is a visiting research fellow at the School of Geography, Queen Mary, University of London. Specializing in the material culture of nineteenth- and early twentieth-century domestic and institutional interiors, she recently published 'Stories of Work and Home in the Mid-Nineteenth Century', *Home Cultures* (2011). In 2010–12, as a research fellow at Royal Holloway, working on the ESRC-funded project, 'At Home in the Institution?', she co-wrote, with Jane Hamlett, 'Comfort in Small Things? Clothing, Control and Agency in the Pauper Lunatic Asylum', *Journal of Victorian Culture* (2013) and '"A Bright and Cheerful Aspect": Wall Decoration and the Treatment of Mental Illness in the Nineteenth and Early Twentieth Centuries', *Wallpaper History Review* (2013).

Rebecca Preston is an honorary research associate in the Department of History at Royal Holloway, University of London. Her research interests and publications are on landscape and identity, and the space, use and representation of the home in nineteenth- and twentieth-century Britain. In 2010–12 she was a research fellow at Royal Holloway, working on Jane Hamlett's ESRC-funded 'At Home in the Institution?' project. Recent publications include an article in *Women's History Review* (5:18, 2009), a co-authored book, *The Picker House and Collection: A Late 1960s Home for Art and Design* (Philip Wilson, 2012) and an essay in the *London Journal* on gardens and photography in the small suburban home, 1880–1918 (2014).

Jeremy Boulton is Professor of Urban History at the School of History, Classics and Archaeology at Newcastle University. He has published widely on many aspects of London's economy, society and demography between 1550 and 1825. He is currently working on welfare and demography in Georgian Westminster. Since 2004 he has, together with Romola Davenport (University of Cambridge) and Leonard Schwarz (University of Birmingham), been leading the Pauper Lives Project (http://research.ncl.ac.uk/pauperlives), which is based on a detailed reconstruction of the lives of those who inhabited the large parish workhouse of St Martin-in-the-Fields (1725–1824). This research has been twice funded by the ESRC and also by the Wellcome Trust. Publications from the Project have been published in the *History of Psychiatry*, *Economic History Review*, *Local Population Studies* and in Joanne McEwan and Pamela Sharpe (eds), *Accommodating Poverty: The Housing and Living Arrangements of the English Poor, c. 1600–1850* (Palgrave Macmillan, 2011).

John Black is a senior research associate at Newcastle University and is currently working on the ESRC-funded project *The Origins of the Modern Demographic Regime: Infant Mortality by Social Status in Georgian London* run by Professor Jeremy Boulton (Newcastle University) and Dr Romola J. Davenport (University of Cambridge). His current interests are in all social, economic, demographic and cultural aspects of the poor in eighteenth- and early nineteenth-century London. Recent publications include work on illegitimacy amongst the urban poor and on dying poor and insane in the early modern metropolis.

Fiona Fisher is a researcher in design history in the Faculty of Art, Design and Architecture at Kingston University, where she is a member of the Modern Interiors Research Centre. Her PhD on the design and modernization of London's late nineteenth-century public houses was awarded by Kingston University in 2008. She is co-author of *The Picker House and Collection: A Late 1960s Home for Art and Design* (Philip Wilson, 2012) and co-editor, with Trevor Keeble, Brenda Martin and Patricia Lara-Betancourt, of an anthology of writings on the modern interior, *Performance, Fashion and the Modern Interior: From the Victorians to Today* (Berg, 2011). Her current research on the British modernist architect Kenneth Wood was supported by an AHRC Early Career Fellowship in 2011 and 2012.

Louise Hide is a researcher at Birkbeck, University of London, where she is working on a three-year project on the history of pain, funded by the Wellcome Trust. Her first monograph, based on her PhD thesis, *Gender and Class in Eng-*

lish Asylums 1890–1914, will be published by Palgrave Macmillan in 2013/14. She is second author, with John Falconer, of *Points of View: Capturing the 19th Century in Photographs* (2009) and co-curated a major exhibition of the same title at the British Library. Her current research interests focus on delusions and bodily pain experienced by asylum patients.

Matthew L. Newsom Kerr is Assistant Professor of History at Santa Clara University. He researches primarily in the social/cultural history of medicine and public health and is currently completing a book on infectious disease hospitalization in late Victorian London. An article on fears surrounding contagious transport appeared in the *Journal of British Studies* in 2010. A chapter on the visual culture of smallpox inoculation and vaccination is forthcoming in *Scratching the Surface: A Medical History of Skin* (Pickering & Chatto, 2013).

Michelle Johansen is a visiting research fellow at the Raphael Samuel History Centre (University of East London, Bishopsgate Institute and Birkbeck College, University of London). She completed her thesis on the professional life and identity of the late-Victorian public librarian at the University of East London in 2006. Her publications include articles in *Library History* and *Teaching History*. Her research interests are the working, social and societal lives of Londoners since about 1850. Professional and leisure associations, self-help and self-education, cross-regional networks and the relationship between different classes and groupings are particular concerns. She is currently working on suburban representations and leisure practices.

Mary Clare Martin is a social historian specializing in the history of children. She is Principal Lecturer and Programme Leader of the BA (Hons) Childhood Studies at the University of Greenwich, London, where she is also head of the Centre for the Study of Play and Recreation and co-ordinator of the London Network for the History of Children. She has published several articles and book chapters and is completing a book entitled *Free Spirits: Children and Religion 1740–1870*. Another in progress is entitled *State, Hospital and Community: Children's Experiences of Illness in Europe and North America, 1700–2000*. She is the editor of a special issue of *Youth and Policy* entitled 'Youth, Recreation and Play' (2013) and a book, *Play from Past to Present: Global Perspectives* (2013/14).

Krisztina Robert is Senior Lecturer in Modern British History at the University of Roehampton in London. Her research focuses on the social and cultural history of the First World War, including women's war participation, constructions of gender, militarism and modernity and their visual, spatial and material representations and practices. She has published articles about these subjects and is currently completing a book, *The Women's Corps: Gender, Militarism and*

Modernity in Britain during the First World War and its Aftermath (forthcoming, 2014).

Stephen Soanes completed his PhD thesis ('Rest and Restitution: Convalescence and the Public Mental Hospital, 1919–39') at the University of Warwick in 2011. He has since held an Early Career Fellowship (Institute for Advanced Study), organizing an interdisciplinary workshop on 'Getting Better' (2011). Stephen has lectured and supervised dissertations at Northumbria University on the post-1750 history of psychiatry, as well as leading seminars on modern global history at Warwick. As a research assistant during 2011 and 2012, he produced a mobile centenary exhibition on Early Women Biochemists: http://www2.warwick.ac.uk/fac/arts/history/chm/research_teaching/research/early_women_biochem/. He is working on an exhibition for Warwick University about the Nobel prize-winning discovery in 1915 of x-ray crystallography by William Bragg and his son Lawrence.

William Whyte is a fellow and tutor in history at St John's College, Oxford. He is the author of *Oxford Jackson: Architecture, Education, Status, and Style, 1835–1924* (2006) and co-editor of several other books, including *Nationalism and the Reshaping of Urban Communities in Europe, 1848–1914* (2011). Other recent publications include essays on the architecture of nineteenth-century churches and twentieth-century Oxbridge colleges, as well as on the history of publishing and popular literature. His interest in the history of town planning is reflected in editions of the 1910 International Town Planning Conference (2011) and 1913 Ghent Cities and Town Planning Exhibition (2013). Following a period of research leave funded by the Philip Leverhulme Prize, he is currently completing a monograph on the history of Britain's civic universities from the late eighteenth century to the present day.

LIST OF FIGURES

INTRODUCTION

Jane Hamlett with Lesley Hoskins and Rebecca Preston

Inhabiting Institutions: Inmates and Environments

When Brian Lunn wrote his memoirs in the late 1940s, the story of his life revealed his progress through a series of institutions. Lunn was born in 1893, the son of a wealthy businessman, and his family (whose business later became the travel firm Lunn Poly) lived in a town house in Bloomsbury, London. Lunn's first experience of institutional life was a prep school, which was swiftly followed by a scholarship to Westminster – where he fell out of favour with the other boys by boasting about his brothers at Harrow. In 1912, as was usual for young men of his background, he went up to Christ Church, Oxford. But, before he could graduate, the First World War intervened and he volunteered for the army: 'While I felt that the war was futile, I felt that it was merely a specialised or intensified form of the futility of life'.[1] According to the autobiography, in 1916 Lunn was posted from Catterick Camp in Yorkshire to Mesopotamia, where these feelings were exacerbated, and his mental health quickly deteriorated. He was moved first to the Royal Victoria Military Hospital, Netley, where his 'room overlooked a garden; the winter shrubs and trees, and the winter smell of mould reminded me of staying in some house in the English country many years before'.[2] He then transferred to Latchmere House, a military mental hospital for officers converted from a Victorian mansion, at Richmond in Surrey. There were beautiful gardens there, too. But the powerful carceral nature of the place could not be disguised and Lunn felt it natural to think of his room as a cell and the male nurses as prison warders. By this point he had spent around twelve years in institutions of various sorts and, unsurprisingly, felt distanced from ordinary life when he returned to live with his parents: 'it was rather like being back in an Oxford vacation'.[3] After a series of clerical jobs and a failed marriage, Lunn, now in his early forties, found himself trying to make a living as a writer. But he continued to yearn for institutional life and, on regular trips to use the London Library in the 1930s, he chose to stay at the Rowton House in Camden, a huge lodging house for working men, as 'the impersonal system ... appealed to me' –

despite the morning bell, which 'clanged up and down the long corridors, just like Sergeant's bell between lessons at Westminster'.[4]

Lunn's life story provides a reminder of just how many different types of residential institution existed in Britain by the first half of the twentieth century and it conveys a feeling of what it was like to live in some of these places. It was not uncommon for inhabitants to move between institutions, although most inmates had a less privileged trajectory than Lunn, and for the poor this transition might involve movement between workhouse, asylum and prison. Lunn's reminiscences therefore offer a fitting start to this collection of essays, which brings together consideration of a broad range of residential institutions in Britain, from the early eighteenth to the late twentieth century. This was a period when the expansion of the military, the relief of the poor, the punishment of criminals, the treatment of the mentally and physically ill, and the education of children and young adults in Britain were all subject to increasing charitable or governmental intervention, leading to a more systematic approach to residential provision and a huge increase in the number of individuals living in institutions. There was a movement towards the incarceration of criminals. When, in 1776, the government lost control of American convict depositories, it first confined prisoners to off-shore hulks and then to a series of penitentiaries.[5] By 1867, nine had been built across the country.[6] The chaotic local prison system was also gradually unified.[7] Increasing attention was paid to young prisoners, with the establishment of reformatory and industrial schools in the 1850s.[8] In 1834 Britain's relief system was overhauled and the New Poor Law created administrative structures that established workhouses, district schools and pauper farms. Provision diversified during the course of the nineteenth century with the sick, the old and the ill later often provided with specialist accommodation. The poor-law authorities administered entry into the increasing number of county lunatic asylums and public hospitals.[9] The Mental Deficiency and Lunacy (England and Scotland) Acts of 1913 insisted on the confinement of further categories of people. In addition to these state interventions, many independent institutions were set up, partly as a result of philanthropy; they included voluntary hospitals, convalescent homes and semi-charitable model lodging houses.[10] Long-standing educational institutions for the upper classes – public schools and universities – were reformed and expanded. Even institutions that were not specifically residential, such as department stores and libraries, sometimes created new kinds of living spaces for staff.[11] The Crimean and Boer Wars in the nineteenth and early twentieth centuries and the development of the giant military machine required for the First and Second World Wars saw the growth of temporary and permanent accommodation for the armed forces.[12]

Rather than offering a comprehensive survey of all institutional development in modern Britain, this collection offers snapshots of the lives of various estab-

lishments at different points in time. This approach allows us to bring together
a large range of the research being conducted in the field. We define institutions
as societies or organizations founded for particular social purposes – whether
philanthropic, educational, religious, reforming or penal – and residential institutions as those which provided the primary living spaces of their inhabitants
(staff, inmates or both), including sleeping accommodation and, sometimes,
space and facilities for eating, leisure and work. It is the first book to make a
comparative study of different types of modern British institution. Recent cross-
institutional comparisons have mostly been confined to similar organizations.
The county asylum and the workhouse, for example, were both administered by
the Poor Law so it has made good sense to look at them together.[13] Archaeolo-
gists' comparative work has tended to focus on institutions of confinement.[14] In
this context Eleanor Conlin Casella argues that 'to varying degrees, institutional
life can be characterized by a loss of autonomy, material possessions, individual expression, community and family life, and even basic personal security'.[15]
The recent collection of essays, *Domestic Institutional Interiors in Early Modern
Europe* (2009), edited by Sandra Cavallo and Silvia Evangelisti, stands out in
addressing a broad variety of examples.[16]

The present book makes the case that cross-institutional study is a fruitful
area of research. The same individuals could easily, like Lunn, have found themselves residing in a number of establishments during their lifetime. The gaps
between organizations are sometimes bridged in surprising ways: the early twentieth-century borstals, for example, were remodelled in the 1920s and adopted
the 'houses' and the athletics of public schools in their attempt to reform young
male criminals.[17] We are not seeking to impose a new, single, definition of the
nature of institutional life on our case studies. Rather we think that it is worth
reflecting on the similarities and divergences between institutions that were set
up for an array of purposes, at various points in time, and by different kinds of
organization. Comparing them in this way powerfully enriches our understanding of what they were and what they did, and enhances our knowledge of the
ways they contributed to the creation of collective power structures and identities in British society more broadly. The arrangement of the chapters that follow
emphasizes this. The collection opens with Fiona Fisher's discussion of the way
that a range of institutions – new and longer-established – were represented
journalistically at the start of the twentieth century. The subsequent essays are
broadly grouped according to how much choice individuals were able to exercise over their entry to the establishments in question. While there was much
overlap between these groups, the first three essays examine institutions where
there was little or no option in inmates' admission and stay; the following three
describe organizations that were usually a last resort and in which inmates had

little autonomy; and the final three essays discuss the experience of institutions where residence was voluntary.

Lunn's autobiography chimes with another significant approach of this collection: its focus on residents and how they felt and behaved in their institution. All of the organizations discussed here were more or less intentionally designed to produce a specific range of effects on the inmates, whether this was to train, reform, manage, educate or heal. And all of the essays included here discuss the experience that the various authorities intended to provide for the residents. However, while architecture, environment, rules and representation were important, they are not seen here as the only determinants of experience. Some of the essays draw attention to the discrepancy between managerial intentions and what happened to residents; others highlight the interaction between the environment and inhabitants, an exchange which itself could have an effect on the way that the institutions functioned, changed and were experienced.

In this introduction we explore how the study of institutions has developed, reflecting on major themes and points of debate, and explain how the essays in this collection bring together new, conceptually innovative, historical approaches to the process of inhabiting institutions between 1725 and 1970.

Beyond Carceral Institutions

The notion that different institutions can be defined by shared characteristics was put forward by the sociologist Erving Goffman. In *Asylums*, published in 1961, he outlined his idea of a total institution, which 'may be defined as a place of residence and work where a large number of like-situated individuals, cut off from society for an appreciable period of time, together lead a closed, formally administered round of life'.[18] According to Goffman, total institutions are often separated from the outside world by locked doors, high walls and barbed wire – and they involve sleeping, working and eating in the same place, in contrast to normal modern life, which separates these activities where possible. They work in opposition to family life and their very existence suppresses the potential households that inmates might otherwise be at liberty to create.[19] Goffman's model included a broad range of establishments, such as hospitals, army barracks, ships, boarding schools, monasteries, convents and servants' quarters in mansions.[20] Imposing a single theory on such a range of social organizations was influential but inevitably problematic. Reviewing the situation in the early 1980s, Michael Ignatieff concluded that 'in practice the concept of the "total institution" has come to be restricted to those institutions of the state – the asylum, the prison, the reformatory, the workhouse ... which have analogous functions – incarceration, deterrence and rehabilitation'.[21] But the application of the concept even to carceral institutions has now been widely challenged, mainly on the grounds that institutions were permeable – they and their inhabitants frequently maintained close connections with wider communities in the world outside. We now know, for example, that the families and friends of asylum patients often played a key role in their admission and that recovery and return to the community could be swifter than sometimes supposed.[22] Some inhabitants of workhouses, too, came and went with surprising frequency.[23] Scholars are now also turning their attention to what happened to inmates after they left institutions and the impact of this on subsequent behaviour and interaction with wider communities.[24]

By far the strongest influence on the study of carceral institutions has been Michel Foucault's *Discipline and Punish: The Birth of the Prison*, published in French in 1975 and in English in 1977.[25] Here, Foucault outlined what he saw as a revolution in the exercise of power through punishment: during the eighteenth and nineteenth centuries physical chastisement gave way to a new system in which miscreants were disciplined through periods of imprisonment, involving a precisely timetabled routine, spatial separation and complete surveillance.[26] He called this system 'panopticism' (from Jeremy Bentham's late eighteenth-century Panopticon – a prison plan designed to facilitate constant and total inspection of the inmates by the authorities) and argued that through it the individual was subject to a moral inspection that was intended to prompt self-scrutiny and conformity.[27] *Discipline and Punish* focused on the prison but Foucault argued that this method of exercising power transformed the operation of other institutions, such as factories, asylums and schools, as well as society more generally. While hugely influential, Foucault's generalist writing sparked many scholarly critiques. There have been refutations on points of evidence and chronology.[28] Local differences are seen to resist a single narrative of change.[29] Historians of the asylum and the local prison have argued that Foucault's broad-brush conceptual analysis missed the significance of the national, local and managerial politics that shaped these institutions.[30] Literary studies of the emergence of the penal system, particularly in an American context, note his failure to account for any connection with slavery or to acknowledge gender differences.[31] The architectural influence of the Panopticon was in practice limited and some doubt the usefulness of 'panopticism' in explaining nineteenth-century modes of looking.[32] Indeed, as Ignatieff puts it, Foucault's main function might be seen as 'productive provocation'.[33] His work has indeed 'provoked' much of the subsequent historical research on institutions.

This book, too, moves forward from Foucault's model, as well as that of Goffman. We argue, for example, against using a single explanation of the function of social organizations. Although we acknowledge that Foucault has identified a crucial shift in the processes of punishment, we do not believe that different institutions imposed a single model of disciplinary practice for its own sake. Even within essentially carceral establishments, such as asylums and prisons, the authorities had varied aims and disciplinary regimes. As this book will show, there were significant differences between institutions and even within the same kind of institution over time: they catered for different categories of people, in varied political, scientific and economic contexts, and proposed a range of outcomes for their residents. Some of the establishments discussed here – hospitals, convalescent homes, asylums, workhouses, prisons, care homes for children and philanthropic lodging houses – did share intentions, mostly relating to containing and managing 'problem people' of one sort or another, but others – public libraries, military quarters for women and university halls of residence – created environments that inmates entered voluntarily and that were designed to encourage self-improvement.

The impermeability of Goffman's 'total institution' has already been effectively challenged and the inmates of the establishments in this book – even those in institutions such as asylums, infectious disease hospitals and institutions for children, where the inmates were confined, sometimes against their will, were not completely sealed off from interactions with the outside world. For example, Matthew L. Newsom Kerr shows that the outraged responses of patients confined in the Metropolitan Asylum Board's Hampstead Smallpox Hospital in the early 1870s were widely reported in the public press. And Mary Clare Martin finds that the girls from the Waverley Park Home for Mental Defectives in Glasgow had a place in the civic community. Additionally, the essays here demonstrate that it is difficult to make a hard-and-fast distinction between carceral institutions and those entered willingly, but where people could be detained. Jeremy Boulton and John Black's essay on a late eighteenth- and early nineteenth-century workhouse shows that an establishment generally considered 'carceral' could be open to inmates coming and going, both with and without the agreement of the authorities.[34] Some establishments that people chose to enter, such as the convalescent homes for the recovering mentally ill analysed by Stephen Soanes, or the Women's Army Auxiliary Corps examined by Krisztina Robert, also took precautions against the unauthorized absence of their inmates. The distinction is further complicated in the libraries, university halls and large-scale lodging houses investigated here, where the residents might choose to occupy their beds for a day or a year but were nevertheless subject to significant regulation of their behaviour.

Control and Resistance

In prison studies, critiquing the idea of discipline has been an immensely productive way of developing an appreciation of the working of power relationships as well as the very nature and fabric of carceral institutions. Examination of local prisons has challenged the idea that discipline could function in a smooth and uniform way.[35] Richard Ireland takes this idea further, using an in-depth study of Carmarthen Gaol in the Victorian period to reformulate our understanding of power relations, drawing particular attention to the role of discretion in practical decision-making at a local level: 'the principal concern here is with precisely the lines of resistance, and practical problems of enforcement and with the dilemmas of discretion that the smooth lines of theoretical analysis ignore'.[36] Helen Rogers, in her imaginative analysis of the progress of the convict James Brown from Yarmouth Gaol to the penal colonies, reconsiders what discipline meant by looking at the relationship between Brown and Sarah Martin, the prison's teacher.[37] Helen Johnston's exploration of the role of nineteenth-century prison officers, meanwhile, notes that turnkeys and warders might have struggled to implement ambiguous policies.[38] By unpicking the meaning of discipline, these writers create a rich and convincing picture of everyday life in local prisons, where the silence imposed by the authorities as a means of control could be made impossible by, for example, the presence of children, or prisoners performing illicit songs, or tapping on the walls of each other's cells.[39] So both the construction of the system itself and the agency of the prisoners could disrupt the smooth operation of discipline.

In the past ten years, the idea of resistance has moved to the forefront of the study of carceral institutions and has been the subject of increasingly careful and sophisticated definitions. Alyson Brown's subtle analysis of prison disturbances across the nineteenth century considers the varied nature of disorder and whether it might be active or passive.[40] She points out that the inmate subcultures, which persisted in the second half of the century even after prison reforms, rather than undermining the prison order, actually depended on it.[41] Abigail Wills, in her study of resistance in institutions for juvenile delinquents in Britain after the Second World War, makes a similar point, arguing that institutionalized resistance took a specific form and could itself influence the boundaries and terms of institutional control.[42] Resistance now looms large in workhouse studies. Anna Clark's 'wild workhouse girls' fought back against the Poor Law in nineteenth-century Ireland.[43] David Green's analysis of London workhouses reveals how paupers resisted them, using violence and damage but also a sophisticated knowledge of their legal rights and methods of campaigning for change.[44] The idea of resistance, and the sense of autonomous agency that it implies, is complicated when applied to the lunatic asylum. It is difficult to know how to interpret patients' actions. Was their 'irrational' behaviour a symptom of illness or can it be viewed (as R. D. Laing saw it) as a valid expression of distress and therefore an act of agency?[45] In the early nineteenth century the tearing of clothes was understood by alienists as a symptom of lunacy, but Leonard Smith notes that 'For the poor, clothing was a valuable commodity; its destruction was a gesture expressing a degree of desperation close to suicide'.[46] Trying to determine the intentions behind some patients' actions is extremely difficult, but Louise Hide's recent study of Claybury and Bexley asylums in the late nineteenth century finds that small 'rational' acts of protest, such as complaints about food, were quite common.[47]

The present collection, too, reveals abundant evidence of resistance: residents and inmates escaped, misbehaved and complained. Boulton and Black find much misconduct of this kind in the St Martin-in-the-Fields workhouse, especially when it was very overcrowded. Newsom Kerr discusses the effective campaign against being treated as paupers that was mounted by patients at one of London's fever hospitals in the 1870s. Martin's investigation of a girls' home provides evidence of 'misbehaviour' of various kinds. But it also leads her to query the current tendency to valorize resistance, suggesting that it can overlook the possibilities of negative effects on other residents and inmates' positive responses to their institution, even when it was 'carceral'. Residents entered some of the institutions discussed in this book voluntarily. The London librarians and Redbrick university students described in the chapters by Michelle Johansen and William Whyte expected a positive benefit from their residential experience and it is not surprising that there was less evidence of resistance (although it was not entirely absent) in these cases. While some of the women in the Women's Army Auxiliary Corps chafed at the restrictive rules governing their conduct, Robert finds that others enjoyed the possibilities offered by a new kind of feminine identity. Looking inside London's Rowton Houses – large, highly regulated lodging houses that were designed to manage poor single men – Jane Hamlett and Rebecca Preston suggest that the residents did not so much resist as remain indifferent to the organization's aims, making themselves comfortable in institutional space on their own terms.

From the Inmates' Point of View

Residential institutions are often intended to manipulate the behaviour and mould the attitudes of their inhabitants. But how effective was this in practice? How did individuals actually respond? To what extent could they exercise personal control over their immediate environment? Were they able to maintain external connections? As these questions suggest, our analysis moves away from the issue of control as a central concept, towards a consideration of the processes of inhabiting. Rather than seeing these spaces simply as a product of design, we consider how they were shaped or fashioned by the interaction between the intentions of authorities, the activities of resident staff and the behaviour of the inmates themselves.

This approach necessitates attention to the voices of the residents (inmates and staff) – over the past decade an increasing area of interest for institutional studies. This interest is, again, partly a response to Foucault; as Rogers points out, 'inmates never speak in *Discipline and Punish*'.[48] But there have been other imperatives too. The growth in subaltern studies has encouraged historians of colonial institutions to search for inmate voices.[49] Leonard Smith, a mental-health practitioner as well as a leading expert on the history of asylums, suggests that new scholarship in this area has been influenced by 'the growing contemporary pre-occupation with gaining the active participation of mental health service users'.[50] Literary scholars have explored prison narratives, considering how prisoners challenged the cultural construction of the idea of the prisoner.[51] Jacqueline Z. Wilson, a sociologist and historian, engages with prison graffiti to recover the lost voices of Australian convicts.[52] But very few inhabitants of any institution, and especially of those which catered for the socially struggling or poorly educated, wrote the full story of their lives. Although the administrative records of public, monitored, organizations were often voluminous, they seldom allowed inmates to speak for themselves; their voices are usually transmitted, if at all, by figures of authority.[53] Nonetheless asylum scholars have had some success in sensitively reading many thousands of case records to reveal patients' behaviour and, occasionally, their own words.[54] Recent work on letters from patients and their families has added a new layer to interpretations.[55]

This collection brings together a number of different approaches to understanding the lives of institutional residents. A fundamental shared idea is that to fully understand institutions, we need to look at them from the inmates' point of view, closely examining individual biographies and carefully scrutinizing the (often limited) records of experience. Several authors analyse inmate records and other institutional data to this end. Boulton and Black argue that the systematic analysis of large numbers of admission and management records, covering a long period of time, can provide a picture of the changing regime in a workhouse and of how families and individuals engaged with it. Soanes uses previously underexploited records from the Mental After-Care Association to study the trajectories of three individual patients – showing a spectrum of reactions to convalescent homes, conditioned by differing family responsibilities. Johansen reworks the history of London's municipal libraries from the point of view of the life course of their chief librarians. Hamlett and Preston seek out the views of Rowton lodgers from inmate autobiographies and testimonies before the courts.

Institutional Environments: Space, Material Culture and the Home

As a part of the turn towards inmate voices and experiences, scholars are now paying increasing attention to institutional environments. The study of the use and distribution of space plays an important part in this. Leslie Topp and James Moran, the editors of a collection of essays on space in the asylum, note that Foucault's 'great contribution to the history of madness was to point out that it was spatial.'[56] Arguably, although some of Foucault's broader narrative has been challenged, this is the area in which his influence remains crucial. Felix Driver remarked that Foucault's 'constant recourse to the language of boundaries, location, separations, and colonisations highlights the relative neglect of questions of space and spatial strategies in questions of social policy'.[57] Driver and fellow geographer Chris Philo, an expert on the asylum, advocate a nuanced reading of Foucault, which acknowledges that his account was always intended as a theoretical outline as much as a discussion of practices.[58]

Questions of the distribution of power in space, and the results of this for inmates, remain fundamental to much of the work here and the essays explore this in the context of large-scale lodging houses, military quarters and university halls. In particular, Hide's analysis of gender, space and the patient experience in London County Council asylums between 1890 and 1910 relies on the notion that the asylum employed a spatially organized moral architecture to discipline patients. Hide's work significantly builds on this to show how such power relationships worked differently according to the gender of the patients and staff involved.

The quest to understand the institutional environment, as well as the 'material turn' in social and cultural history, has opened historians' eyes to the things that surrounded inmates. Judy Attfield wrote that people use material goods 'as vehicles of meaning through which [they] negotiate their relations with each other and the world at large' and a number of the present essays examine material culture as a means of uncovering residents' lives.[59] Those confined in asylums, often mentally ill, present a particularly difficult silence, but recent scholarship has approached the question of their experience in a variety of new and creative ways – investigating the furnishings and domestic goods in the asylum, the clothes that patients wore and the sounds that surrounded them.[60]

The essays here take this approach forward. Newsom Kerr, for example, focuses on the way that patients at the Hampstead Smallpox Hospital experienced their food – an aspect of material life that was central to social identity. Johansen reveals the importance of creating and maintaining a certain standard of living for the new professional public librarians of late nineteenth-century London. Robert considers the way that the feminized goods of the parlour and drawing room were mobilized to transform army service into a socially and culturally acceptable new option for women. Whyte's essay demonstrates that the soft furnishings of halls of residence were intended to mould students by distancing them from the inferior working-class homes it was presumed they had left. Finally, Hamlett and Preston's analysis of the material world of Rowton Houses explores how the residents were empowered and constrained by the organization of space and the furnishing and decoration of the institution.[61]

There is a growing body of research on asylum and hospital gardens. Of particular relevance to this volume is work that focuses on inmates' experience of the grounds and even of the land beyond the boundary.[62] Airing courts and exercise yards were utilitarian spaces within asylums, workhouses and prisons. Yet ornamental gardens were a striking feature of many institutions and the spaces outside the buildings could be integral to the design and purpose of the organization. Six of the chapters here show how the garden formed a vital part of the institution under scrutiny. The aesthetic and regenerative qualities associated with landscape were recognized as a method of treatment within asylums, where the gardens were ornamental and productive spaces providing exercise, work and food for the inmates (as in the London County Council asylums and the Glasgow children's home discussed by Hide and Martin in this volume). Gardens were central to the idea and representation of 'cottage homes' for convalescing patients in the early twentieth century and to Women's Army Auxiliary Corps propaganda in the First World War (as described by Soanes and Robert). More surprisingly perhaps, they were provided at some of London's new public libraries and in Rowton Houses at the turn of the twentieth century (as shown by Johansen and Hamlett and Preston). While gardens became indelibly associated with some large Victorian institutional environments, such as the asylum, they would also become a powerful factor in whether and how these and other organizations presented themselves as less like institutions and more like 'homes'.

Very recently, historians have started to think about the institutional environment in relation to familial or household domesticity. Cavallo and Evangelisti argue that early-modern social organizations were much closer to the domestic than has been thought.[63] Jane Hamlett has compared young women's student rooms at university with those in the family home, around the end of the nineteenth century.[64] Amy Milne-Smith argues that late nineteenth-century clubs in London can be seen as a parallel, extra-familial, domestic space for elite men.[65] There is a long-standing interest in the relationship between domestication and madness and, in particular, Mary Guyatt has shown how the interiors of nineteenth-century private, and some public, asylums were deliberately decorated in a home-like manner, as a part of 'moral therapy' for the patients.[66] But as yet there has been no comparative study of how ideas of home and domesticity figured in modern British institutions.[67]

In spite of the major differences between some of the institutions in this book, it is clear that the domestic home was an important common point of reference – either positive or negative – in the way they were conceived and presented. Representations of children's homes, convalescent homes, women's army accommodation and Rowton Houses were suffused with its rhetoric. Fisher discusses how, in the early twentieth century, photographic depictions of a range of residential institutions in George R. Sims's popular serial, *Living London*, often aligned them with non-institutional domestic spaces, perhaps, as with representations of Rowton Houses, to make them seem more homely and thus less threatening for the reading public. Like Robert, Fisher finds that the parlour and its furnishing were adopted for new kinds of institutional space for women (both staff and inmates) and that institutions for poor children were, like the convalescent homes described by Soanes, sometimes modelled on notions of the ideal family. Whyte, in contrast, argues that Redbrick halls of residence were constructed as deliberately different from the working-class homes of their students.

As many of the essays here also show, homely looking surroundings did not necessarily equate with inmates' feelings of being 'at home' for a variety of reasons, including the ability to exercise freedom of choice. From the inhabitants' point of view, the most successful institutional homes in this volume were probably the private apartments occupied by London's chief librarians. Johansen's findings in this respect may have wider resonance with regard to other institutional staff, such as asylum superintendents and school masters and mistresses, who had a strong enough position in the institutional power structure to exert considerable control over how they lived. Hide's study of the 'villa system' in large asylums and Soanes's analysis of the 'cottage home' indicate that a home-like environment was more readily offered for smaller groups, in institutions for less 'difficult' inmates – a method increasingly used for curable and recovering patients in preparation for their return to the community. The 'cottage homes' for convalescents from asylums certainly offered something akin to an unremarkable family environment and some patients found that they offered a supportive environment. But for others, especially those who had family and friends, the system of surveillance and quasi-parental control meant that they could not really feel 'at home'. From the point of view of the residents' experience, Martin provocatively argues that confinement in a Glasgow home for the 'mentally defective' in the early twentieth century was a positive outcome for some children, especially if they had no other home and no relatives or friends to support them. Of course, others were not so lucky, and some residents of Rowton Houses, despite the efforts made on their behalf, felt that the accommodation provided was more like a prison than a home.

Institutions and the Fashioning of Social Identities

Institutions that are not thought of as carceral, such as schools and the forces, have more often been studied individually and investigated for their specific aims and motivations. One particular area of interest for British social and cultural historians has been how such organizations helped to construct ideas and practices that reinforced particular social identities. The Marxist idea that education for the working classes was essentially designed to keep the poor in their place continues to inform some of the literature on working-class education.[68] This echoes the assumption, common in carceral studies, that the general purpose of institutions is to suppress the poor.[69] However, studies of individual establishments offer more nuanced constructions of class belonging. Christopher Hosgood, for example, in his 'Mercantile Monasteries', shows how residential accommodation for shop assistants created a particular kind of lower-middle-classness.[70] Quintin Colville has unpicked the material culture of Dartmouth Naval Training College to understand a similar, complex, process among the cadets.[71]

Our essays continue this debate. The workhouse, the asylum and the children's home made their residents identifiable, largely through clothing, but they did not seek to foster cultural or social identification with the institution. The patients at the fever hospital fiercely contested the pauperization that was forced on them for the duration of their stay. But the reverse is true of the new London librarians, who enthusiastically adopted roles and material circumstances that allowed them to improve their social position. Whyte's analysis of Redbrick university halls outlines the rules and facilities that were intended to steer students away from their former working-class culture towards the adoption and internalization of a new middle-class identity. London's Rowton Houses sought to provide a form of elite domesticity – albeit in cavernous settings – that was intended to reach across class barriers, uplifting the poor and others in temporary difficulties. But, as Brian Lunn's story at the head of this introduction shows, identity formation on an individual level was often complicated. Despite his upper-middle-class background, Lunn opted to stay at the Camden Rowton House rather than a more upmarket hotel. However, he was partly attracted to the place because of the affinity of its routine and regulation with the pattern of life he had experienced at the exclusive Westminster School.

Gender studies have also held sway among scholars of institutional life, particularly among those interested in education and the armed forces. Naturally enough, the first historians of women paid special attention to the empowering effect of educational achievement. Headmistresses and female principals are the heroines of this movement and the high schools and colleges they established challenged existing male-dominated bastions.[72] Subsequent scholarship complicated this heroic vision but remains positive.[73] Feminist historians have charted women's attempts to enter the armed forces. Scholars identified the total wars of the twentieth century as the crisis points which compelled these quintessentially male institutions to allow women to join. Their studies of female auxiliary units, however, stressed the limited and unequal terms of women's integration into the forces and the stability of traditional constructions of femininity.[74] The turn towards the study of masculinity has roused historians to scrutinize the spaces and places, often institutional, that men created for themselves outside the family home. Schools for middle- and upper-class boys, for example, have been seen as the crucible for the 'manly character' aspired to by the Victorian middle classes.[75] Initially, scholars emphasized the martial character of this manly ideal promoted by both educational and military institutions, while subsequent work on the First World War discussed how appalling conditions at the front eroded such heroic definitions of manliness.[76] In contrast, recent scholarship has stressed the more complex nature of masculinities instilled in these locations. Focusing on the residential, training and fighting sites of the armed forces, historians show that martial values mixed with domestic, familial and maternal gestures and emotions in soldiers' homosocial relations and gender identities.[77]

This book builds upon this work, showing how gender relations were contested and negotiated within institutions. Robert's essay on the provision of accommodation for female auxiliary units during the First World War reveals how the army was prepared to adjust its conceptions of gendered identities at a time of emergency. Indeed, this produced a new 'martial femininity', which challenged the way that British society understood womanhood. Hamlett and Preston show how the interior decoration and furnishing of Rowton Houses were based on an ideal of shared masculine behaviour, which, it was hoped, would diminish the 'institutional' feel of the lodging houses and encourage a quiet camaraderie among the men. Hide takes a relational approach to gender in the asylum, arguing that increasing opportunities for women as nurses around the turn of the century affected the nature of ward life and posed a surprising challenge to patients' sense of male identity.

Conclusions

From the early eighteenth to the late twentieth century, residential institutions proliferated across Britain. *Residential Institutions* argues that taking a cross-institutional approach helps us to understand and interpret their activities and their consequences for British society and culture. While the theories of Goffman and Foucault remain fundamental to this interpretation, we argue that there is no single all-encompassing definition of the operation of power in institutions and that we need to look at the different ways in which establishments operated and were inhabited. The essays here advance a number of debates that have recently engrossed scholars. We agree that resistance can be found in most institutions but some of our contributors question the wisdom of focusing on it exclusively. The essays share a concern to discover inmate voices and experiences, often focusing on the life stories of inmates or their biographical data, which may record time spent in different types of institution over a life course. We argue that paying close attention to the institutional environment is paramount to understanding the lives of inmates – and to do this we must examine the planning and use of space, the distribution of material goods and how these were imagined and used. Placing institutions side by side also allows us to think about their collective contribution to British culture and their role in constructing social identities, especially those of class and gender. Finally, we stress the importance of looking closely at the interactions between inmates and environments, and argue that it was these interactions that determined the lived experiences of inmates within residential institutions.

Acknowledgements

We are grateful to Katherine Rawling, Krisztina Robert, Helen Rogers and Susan Woodall for their constructive comments on this introduction.

1 VIEWING THE EARLY TWENTIETH-CENTURY INSTITUTIONAL INTERIOR THROUGH THE PAGES OF *LIVING LONDON*

Fiona Fisher

Living London: A Window on the Institutional Interior

This chapter examines the photographic representation of a range of residential institutions within a collection of early twentieth-century writings, *Living London: Its Work and its Play, its Humour and its Pathos, its Sights and its Scenes*, edited by George R. Sims and published by Cassell & Company between 1902 and 1903. The collection made a variety of urban environments visible to a contemporary readership for the first time and offers an opportunity to look across institutional sites and typologies to explore common aspects of their spatial, material and aesthetic organization, their status as dwelling places, and their relationship with an idealized domesticity, rooted in an understanding of the home as a moral centre for family life and a foundation of social stability. Drawing on a selection of images, it considers the visual evidence that *Living London*'s photographs offer for a relationship between the design of institutional interiors and those of private homes of the period, as well as the ways in which domestic ideals informed the representational choices of the collection's photographers and editor.

Living London, an ambitious attempt to record the panoply of metropolitan social experience at the start of the twentieth century, incorporated 175 articles and somewhere in the region of 1,500 photographs and other illustrations. The series was published fortnightly at a cost of 7 pence and in three bound volumes that sold for 12 shillings each, making it affordable to a middle-class audience and almost certainly available to a wider working-class readership.[1] In the prologue to the opening volume Sims set out the editorial aims of the publication:

> The history of London has been written, the story of its streets has been told, again and again. But the life of London in all its phases and aspects has never until now been exhaustively attempted ... With pen and pencil, with camera and snapshot, those who are associated with this work have laid every phase of London life under

contribution. Wherever photography has been practicable it has been relied upon, because no other process of reproduction is at once so actual and so convincing.[2]

Sims's desire to record London life resonates with the aims of a range of late nineteenth- and early twentieth-century literary and journalistic investigations into the city and Keith Wilson has suggested that the volumes occupy an 'inter-generic ground on which journalism, social documentary and popular literature meet'.[3] The three *Living London* volumes are also exactly contemporary with the final seventeen-part edition of Charles Booth's social survey of London, published as *Life and Labour of the People in London* – a correspondence that perhaps suggests that its publishers envisaged the collection as a popular ana-logue to Booth's study.[4] In its highly visual approach to the presentation and narration of city life *Living London* shares certain characteristics of the urban photographic survey.[5] The collection can also be situated within the context of a shift in nineteenth-century visual culture, characterized by new modes of repre-sentation and observation and by the production and privileging of new forms of visual knowledge.[6]

Although images of street and outdoor life dominate the collection, *Living London*'s volumes also incorporate a variety of interior scenes and provide an important source of information on turn-of-the-century London's domestic and public interiors, their furnishing and decoration. Approximately a third of the total visual content of the volumes – photographs and illustrations – is devoted to interior spaces, with photographs accounting for around a fifth of that total. The collection is novel in its juxtaposition of elite, middle- and working-class interiors and in the range of interior spaces depicted, which include sites of urban recreation, private dwellings and commercial, charitable, public and insti-tutional buildings. Among the residential institutions incorporated are prisons, lodging houses for the poor, workhouses, orphanages, lunatic asylums, charitable shelters and homes for immigrants. These range from buildings of modest scale, designed to accommodate a small number of occupants, to large, multi-func-tional sites of mass occupation that housed several hundred. Certain categories of institutional space, notably environments designed for sleeping, food prepa-ration and eating, work and recreation, are widely represented and this suggests a particular interest in their social use that informs the discussion here. Most of the interiors depicted were designed for use by working-class staff or resi-dents. Although many of these were intended for communal use by single-sex groups, the collection also includes a number of spaces designed for individual occupation and some for occupation by couples or children. There is little visual evidence of accommodation for nuclear or extended family units, however, at least one of the establishments – Stockwell Orphanage – employed the concept of family as a social model for institutional living.

Through the medium of photography Sims aimed to reveal 'the Londoner in his habit as he lives ... in all his moods and amid all his environments'.[7] Underpinning that aim was a belief in the affective potential of architectural design and an interest in the ways in which Londoners shaped and were shaped by their environments. In keeping with Sims's aim to capture 'every phase of London life', and in contrast to the spatial and aesthetic emphasis of architectural photography, most of *Living London*'s images of institutional interiors are populated. As David MacDougall has observed:

> Framing people, objects, and events with a camera is always 'about' something. It is a way of pointing out, of describing, of judging. It domesticates and organizes vision. It both enlarges and diminishes. It diminishes by leaving out those connections in life to which the photographer is blind, as when it imposes an explanation on events that we know to be more complex. Or it does this as a deliberate sacrifice to some seemingly more important argument or dramatic effect. Framing enlarges through a similar process. It is what lifts something out of its background in order to look at it more closely, as we might pick up a leaf in the forest.[8]

The ability of photography to elicit social responses or performances from its subjects places limitations on its exclusive use as a source of historical evidence for the lived environment, as does its tendency to omit or obscure certain spaces and social practices – the bathrooms and washing facilities of London's residential institutions are, for example, a revealing blind spot in the *Living London* collection. Nevertheless, certain common themes emerge from an examination of the diverse social settings represented and these can help further understanding of the complex relationship that residential institutions maintained with the home, as well as the gendered and classed ideals that informed their design and shaped their contemporary meanings.

The domestic interior has been understood as an important site of identity formation and performance, which was central to the emergence and consolidation of gender and class identities from the late eighteenth century onwards.[9] Studies of later nineteenth-century domesticity have demonstrated the significant role that the widening availability of manufactured goods played in allowing middle- and working-class individuals to participate in a world of consumption and to express their identities through modes of dress and through the furnishing and decoration of their homes and the display of goods within them.[10] Viewed from an architectural perspective, the development of the nineteenth-century home was, as Lynne Walker has indicated, a process through which

> dominant middle-class beliefs about 'proper' social relationships and the different roles and capacities of men and women in culture and society were coded (architecturally and linguistically) and built into the fabric of the home through the two essential elements of Victorian planning, segregation and specialization.[11]

Victorian middle-class domesticity was, as has been well-documented, culturally pervasive and not only informed attitudes towards the working-class home and its improvement, but also influenced the design and representation of late nineteenth- and early twentieth-century commercial interiors aimed at men and women of different classes, such as those of public houses and department stores, examples of which can also be found in the *Living London* volumes.[12]

Privacy and Regulation

Living London's photographs suggest that domestic ideals, expressed in generic and site-specific visual, material and spatial forms, also informed the design and representation of institutional interiors. At London's Rowton Houses, which Jane Hamlett and Rebecca Preston discuss in greater detail in Chapter 6 of this volume, turnstiles established the entrances to the buildings as spaces through which the passage of individuals was carefully regulated and closely monitored. Originally designed to inhibit the movement of livestock, turnstiles made their transition from exterior to interior in the second half of the nineteenth century, when they began to be employed to regulate human traffic in sites such as museums, fairs and sports stadia. Laurent Stalder has suggested that threshold architectures of this type highlight 'performative aspects' of the built environment, or the ways in which the fabric of a building operates on users to regulate and shape their bodies and movements.[13] As Hamlett and Preston describe, Lord Rowton wished to create a homely atmosphere and for that reason preferred that Rowton Houses be managed with 'a minimum of regulation' (see p. 99). Although anti-domestic in its authoritarian dimensions, the entrance turnstile defined the interior as a discrete social setting, replacing the entrance rituals of the private dwelling with a commercial exchange and physical transition that operated as a defence against the unwanted and guaranteed a degree of residential security and privacy to Rowton's residents.[14] *Living London*'s photograph of the entrance hall of the Rowton House in Hammersmith offered readers a view through the turnstiles to a light-filled oasis of potted plants and seated figures – a tableau of relaxed ambience that hinted at the comfort and freedom available to those admitted access.

Within the body of sociological writing that theorizes behaviour and environment, privacy is understood as a universal need, central to the construction of self and group identity, to the mediation of social relations, and to the display of status and functioning of power.[15] Irwin Altman has suggested that Western cultures place a strong emphasis on the use of physical barriers as privacy mechanisms.[16] Other photographs in the collection evidence a number of common forms of interior spatial planning, furniture types and furniture groupings, such as cubicle, dormitory and refectory layouts, which spanned institutional typologies. These determined the physical possibilities for social withdrawal or engagement within different institutional settings and suggest that the design and furnishing of the interior was not only informed by regulatory concerns, but also the perceived privacy requirements of users. Photographs of kitchens and dining rooms, for example, indicate that long communal tables were generally favoured for these spaces.[17] The refectory table was not only a practical form of furnishing for mass-occupancy institutional environments, but also reflects an understanding of the communality of working-class life that informed the design of public dining spaces. This is most evident in the case of sites frequented by the urban poor, whose shared seating arrangements can be contrasted with the 'private' model of individual tables employed by businesses aimed at a respectable middle- and working-class custom.[18]

Living London's photographs of sleeping environments offer further indication of the ways in which the design and furnishing of the interior regulated social life within different institutional settings. The collection represents a variety of accommodation including cubicles for individuals and couples and communal sleeping areas, such as shared bedrooms, open-plan and partitioned dormitories, some of which also functioned as day rooms. Certain common furnishing elements can also be found in these environments; iron bedsteads, for example, which were a feature of many institutional interiors from the first half of the nineteenth century, appear in a number of images including one of a dormitory at the Alexandra Orphanage in Hornsey Rise and one of an infirmary at Holloway Prison.[19] The latter, a sparsely furnished and unornamented interior, designed on sanitary principles, can be contrasted with other images of dormitory-style accommodation that appear in the collection, in which pictures, plants and decorative textiles lend them a homely air.[20]

The smallest units of sleeping space depicted in *Living London* were the coffin-like beds provided at Medland Hall in Limehouse, a heavily over-subscribed refuge hall for men, managed by the London Congregational Union. Still in use in 1914, and described by *The Times* as 'gruesomely suggestive', these took the form of small wooden boxes 'raised just above the floor', each with a number and a narrow crossways plank at its foot.[21] Substantially larger than box beds, sleeping cubicles also featured in a number of photographs and articles, indicating the extent of their employment at that time, as well as a contemporary interest in the cubicle as a spatial form suitable for use in a range of modern residential environments. In his examination of the historical origins of the cubicle, Tom Crook suggests that three imperatives informed its development: a concern with private space and a demand for sites of withdrawal and self-fashioning, which can be traced through the evolution of the bed and dressing chambers of the eighteenth century; a disciplinary imperative, as described by Michel Foucault, within which the individual was made docile and open to regulatory forces; and an imperative of health, concerned with overcoming moral and physical contagion.[22]

Living London's photographs of box beds and cubicles gave visual form to a set of contemporary critiques and sanitary ideals which determined that each individual be defined as an item with an exact, quantifiable requirement for space and air.[23] The London County Council's (LCC's) municipal lodging house in Parker Street, off Drury Lane, employed the well system – a form of spatial

organization in which cubicles were arranged on landings around a central opening. *Living London*'s photograph of the interior shows two well-dressed figures
inspecting the ground-floor accommodation, with a nearby worker sweeping the
floor. The sweeping figure, empty cubicles and large wall clock – the only notable object on display – signify the principles of spatial, temporal and hygienic
regulation upon which the interior was ordered and the presence of electric
lighting demonstrates its modernity. As Louise Hide discusses in Chapter 3 of
this collection, the prison often formed the model against which other institutional spaces were judged. Contemporary articles on the Parker Street lodging
house suggest that a familiarity with disciplinary forms of spatial organization
lent its interior particular meanings. An article in *The Times* made reference to
its 'prison-like arrangement' and to the iron construction of its cubicle partitions
and its clanging doors, which echoed throughout the building.[24] In his *Living
London* article, 'London's Model Lodging-Houses', T. W. Wilkinson described
Parker Street in similar terms, referring to its penal atmosphere and to the iron
cubicles that were a major feature of the interior.[25]

The ideological relationship between privacy and respectability is visually
inscribed in another *Living London* image, which depicts the interior of a couples'
lodging house in Spitalfields (see Figure 1.1). The photograph appeared in Wilkinson's article, '"Dosser"-Land in London', and shows a woman sitting and sewing
at a cubicle doorway, evoking the visual trope of the working-class woman at the
domestic boundary, a gendered domain closely associated with the codification
and performance of respectability.[26] The subject's threshold location is emphasized
through the presence of a second image on the page, depicting a group of women
and children sitting on the pavement outside a lodging house in Flower and Dean
Street in Spitalfields, one of London's most notorious streets of common lodging
houses.[27] This second image invites the first to be read in relation to the space of
the street as well as the character of the women who occupy it. As a paradigmatic
image of the performance of domestic duty, the photograph collapses the distance
between the institutional context and the private home. Through its composition
it raises questions over the extent to which gender- and class-determined socio-
spatial practices of domesticity may have been reproduced within institutional
contexts in response to the physical parameters of particular sites. The photograph
is one of several representations of women sewing within institutional settings,
an activity whose associations with domesticity, home-working and institutional
labour lent them distinct and highly contextual meanings. In this example, the
meaning of the image is complicated by the status of the couples' lodging house
as a site in which cohabiting residents were not required to prove that they were
married, to which Wilkinson's accompanying text alludes.

Although class-determined conceptions of domestic privacy informed the
provision, design and representation of sleeping accommodation in some insti-

CUBICLES IN A " COUPLES' " HOUSE
(SPITALFIELDS).

Figure 1.1: From '"Dosser"-Land in London' by T. W. Wilkinson, in G. R. Sims (ed.),
Living London, vol. 2, p. 153. Author's collection.

tutional contexts, the relationship between privacy, class and social regulation is complex. In many cases residents had no say in the matter of their sleeping arrangements, which were determined according to their status within different types of institution. In public asylums, for example, single accommodation was usually reserved for difficult patients. In contrast, within the army the provision of individual sleeping accommodation was seen as a privilege and as means of attracting a higher calibre of recruit, for whom privacy was understood as a marker of respectability and moral status.[28]

Living London's photographs and descriptions of sleeping environments draw attention to a more general feature of late nineteenth- and early twentieth-century urban development: the commodification of privacy. Several of the sites featured within the collection incorporated a hierarchy of sleeping environments that was articulated spatially, reflected in the different materials – wood, iron, zinc – used to construct them, and in the level of visual and acoustic privacy, security and comfort that they afforded to occupants. Within the context of some commercial and semi-philanthropic institutions access to different types of sleeping accommodation was determined by personal preference as well as an individual's ability to pay. The sleeping accommodation at the Victoria Home Number 2, 'a hotel for working men' that belonged to 'the pioneers of lodging-house reform', was, for example, described as follows:

> Light, airy, scrupulously clean – these are the first impressions. Here is a room full of sixpenny beds. It is split up into cubicles, the partitions of which are formed of hollow tiles. Inside each hangs a small picture, as well as a looking glass – an unusual luxury. A short walk brings us to the fourpenny quarters, where the beds are mostly four in a room, one in each corner. And, finally, here are the fivepenny cabins. They are practically the same as the sixpenny cubicles, though the partitions are of corrugated zinc.[29]

A Decorative Ideal

Other model environments that appeared in *Living London*, such as Stockwell Orphanage (founded in 1868 by C. H. Spurgeon), suggest ways in which domestic ideals provided a blueprint and moral framework for early twentieth-century institutional living. The Stockwell Orphanage laundry (see Figure 1.2) appeared in a *Living London* article by D. L. Woolmer, 'Caring for London's Children'.[30] The photograph is one of two images of older children that were included in the collection; the other shows a group of boys learning to be blacksmiths at a trades' shop run by the National Waifs Association at Stepney Causeway, established in 1870 by Thomas Barnardo. Stockwell Orphanage was an instructional environment, ordered on a model of 'family life', within which gendered roles were clearly defined.[31] The boys led 'a sort of college life' and the girls practised 'the domestic accomplishments intended to make them good servants or good housewives'.[32] As

STOCKWELL ORPHANAGE : THE LAUNDRY.

Figure 1.2: From 'Caring for London's Children' by D. L. Woolmer, in G. R. Sims (ed.), *Living London*, vol. 1, p. 377. Author's collection.

Woolmer's text describes, the work undertaken by the orphans was intended to 'cultivate the art of self-dependence'.[33] *Living London*'s photograph of the Stockwell Orphanage laundry represents it as a disciplined site of supervised labour. The two girls in the foreground of the image are observed by a member of staff as they iron, while the neatly dressed girls to the rear, with their piles of folded linen before them, are represented as an efficient and productive domestic labour force.

The Stockwell Orphanage laundry shares a number of spatial, material and aesthetic characteristics with other interiors that appear in the collection, notably working environments and the interiors of hospitals and infirmaries.[34] These include: high ceilings; large windows and skylights, designed to bring maximum light to the interior, often shown uncovered and open for ventilation; and the use of a limited palette of materials, including plain woodwork, iron, glazed bricks or tiles, employed for their durability and ease of maintenance as well as decoratively, to bring visual interest to the interior. Collectively these spaces articulate a modern and hygienic model for the interior centred on the provision of light, space and air.

The working environment of the Stockwell Orphanage laundry can be contrasted with more homely interiors that appeared in *Living London*, notably spaces designed for recreational use by a respectable female workforce. Such spaces evidence a close material and aesthetic relationship with the contemporary middle- or working-class parlour. Two examples, a communal living area at the Ayahs' Home in Hackney, a charitable home for foreign nursemaids, and a recreation room for the wardresses who were employed at Holloway Prison, incorporate characteristic visual and material markers of domesticity. 'The Wardresses' Recreation Room' seen in Figure 1.3 was one of ten photographs that illustrated Major Arthur Griffiths's article on the prison.[35] At the time of record, just before its conversion to a women's prison, Holloway housed a range of male and female detainees including 'misdemeanants of the first class, debtors, juveniles, and women', many of whom were awaiting trial.[36] The prison, a complex architectural environment that incorporated spaces informed by disciplinary, sanitary and domestic ideals, emerges from Griffiths's description as a harsh working environment for its female staff:

> An axiom holds with prison officials that women are more difficult to manage than men. Certainly it is so in Holloway: misconduct, chronic and persistent, is intensified by hysteria, and these unsexed creatures respect no authority. At times the place is like a pandemonium.[37]

The wardresses were, in contrast, described as gentle and patient:

> The female officers – the wardresses – have a life full of anxieties, even dangers, for assaults are not uncommon; yet are they mild mannered, forbearing to their troublesome sisterhood, and have strong claims to the respect and esteem of the public at

large. As Holloway is their home, the authorities, not forgetting that there should be play as well as hard work, have provided comfortable quarters for them, and a large 'recreation' room well furnished and supplied with music, games, and so forth.[38]

The wardresses' recreation room incorporated features that reflected the social status of its users and would not have been out of place in respectable working-class homes of the period: wallpaper, picture rails and pictures, a lamp, a display- or music-cabinet, easy chairs and a piano. Although homely, it is clearly a communal space and that shared identity is reflected in its furnishing and decoration – the placement of two large tables and the functional appearance of the simple, unornamented table coverings – as well as the presence of its many occupants, which together give an indication of its scale. The recreation room is less a domestic interior transplanted, than one reconfigured to meet the additional requirements of its quasi-private function within the working environment of the prison. Unlike the other spaces of the prison depicted in the article – a cell, a corridor, the kitchen and the infirmary – the wardresses' recreation room offered readers a recognizable point of identification with the sitters, who are shown reading, sewing and making music. The room also reflects values consistent with those articulated in a range of contemporary commercial settings aimed at a respectable urban custom. Taking their cue from the middle-class home, sites such as restaurants and theatres created a sense of privacy, security and comfort within the public sphere, functioning in different urban contexts to symbolize middle-class values and tastes; to create a sense of reassurance and psychological ease within unfamiliar locations; to lend respectability to problematic social sites, particularly those associated with mass leisure and consumption; and to identify certain environments as gender- or class-specific.[39] The design of the recreation room expressed its function as a private sanctuary within the wider prison setting, representing and guaranteeing the status of its female occupants, whose professional association with the 'unsexed creatures' of Griffiths's text was a threat to conventional femininity. In conjunction with the cultural values inscribed in the interior, details of the photograph – a hand draped across a colleague's shoulder and a newspaper spread across two laps – suggest a sisterly bond between the women and this relaxed sense of intimacy and familiarity directs a sympathetic reading of the subjects.

A similarly domesticated interior to that of the wardresses' recreation room is a parlour at the Ayahs' Home in Hackney that appeared in Alec Roberts's *Living London* article, 'Missionary London'.[40] Founded in the City of London in the nineteenth century, the Ayahs' Home was moved to Hackney in 1900 by the inter-denominational evangelical Christian organization, the London City Mission. The home accommodated and found employment for women from the colonies who had travelled to London as nursemaids and sought return journeys.

WARDRESSES' RECREATION ROOM.

Figure 1.3: From 'In Holloway Prison' by Major Arthur Griffiths, in G. R. Sims (ed.), *Living London*, vol. 1, p. 234. Author's collection.

The photograph depicts about a dozen women, seated around a large table, reading or sewing. The interior is less obviously institutional than the wardresses' recreation room. The decorative table covering, pictures and ornaments, and the framing of the image imply a domestic setting and scale, but the bentwood chairs on which the women sit are of a type commonly found in public interiors of the period, such as cafes and bars. The image incorporates the inhabitants within the visual frame of a respectable domesticity that reflects their role as household servants and may have functioned to normalize this group of foreign women for a contemporary readership. Yet their foreignness is in some sense magnified by the setting and by the presence of a group of small figurines on the table, which appear, like the ayahs, to be clothed in non-Western dress. Text and image reflect an interest in the customs and institutions of ethnic London that is evident in a variety of *Living London* articles, which record and map the diversity of the imperial metropolis.[41]

The wardresses and the ayahs are depicted pursuing domestic activities within appropriately feminine settings, an alignment of space and activity that was central to the structuring of their contemporary meaning. In other contexts the relationship between 'public' and 'private' spaces and activities was less clearly defined. As in the contemporary lower-middle- and working-class home, certain institutional spaces, such as kitchens and recreation rooms, fulfilled a wide range of functions and accommodated activities that extended from everyday domestic tasks to commercial pursuits. The recreation room at the LCC lodging house in Parker Street, for example, is shown in use by lodgers for the paid clerical work of 'wrapper writing' and the kitchen at a single women's lodging house in Spitalfields is described as accommodating domestic tasks, such as the repair of clothes, alongside 'vagrant industries' such as paper flower-making, which might in other contexts be represented as forms of home-working.[42]

Personalizing the Institutional Interior

In his mid-nineteenth-century study *London Labour and the London Poor*, Henry Mayhew imposed a moral distinction between 'wanderers' and 'settlers' that informed many of the subsequent descriptions and depictions of the urban poor that were published in the late nineteenth and early twentieth century, including a number of those that appeared in *Living London*.[43] Nomadism, as Anna Davin has noted, threatened to undermine the status of the home as the foundation upon which civilized society was formed: 'The home was supposed to provide essential stability in society, giving material form to the emotional comfort and moral support of the "family", with which it was inextricably linked'.[44] Home can, of course, also be an imagined or remembered space and Alison Blunt and Robyn Dowling have argued that 'one of the defining features of home is that it is both material and imaginative, a site *and* a set of meanings/emotions'.[45]

Other texts and images in the *Living London* collection suggest ways in which residential institutions may have offered possibilities for the expression of individual and familial identities at a material level, through self-determined practices of collection and display that have been historically associated with home-making within the individual family dwelling. These images raise questions about the stability of residency in different institutional contexts as well as the ways in which individuals may have mobilized the material resources at their disposal to create a sense of continuity within those environments. A description of the aged married couples' quarters that appeared in a T. W. Wilkinson article on the St Marylebone Workhouse described its 'private apartments' as 'a sort of miniature model dwelling' in which 'official furniture' was combined with 'photographs and knick-knacks' to make them 'home-like and a delight to the eye'.[46] The accompanying photograph of an 'old couple' in a common ward offers a visual comparison to Wilkinson's textual description of the more comfortably furnished private apartments and exemplifies the different conceptions and standards of comfort and decoration that informed the diverse interior schemes of large and complex institutions of this type, according to the status of their users.

Another photograph from the collection, entitled 'At Father Jay's Lodging House (Shoreditch): A Pretty Corner' (see Figure 1.4), which appeared in Wilkinson's article, '"Dosser"-Land in London', shows a highly personalized partitioned sleeping area at a charitable lodging house in Shoreditch. The extent of personalization is unusual and sets the image apart from others in the collection. However, its inclusion is worth commenting on in light of the many generic representations of a nomadic urban poor that appear in the *Living London* volumes, including images of displaced and evicted families moving their possessions. Lynn Hollen Lees has suggested that along with photographs taken by Dr Barnardo, *Living London*'s images 'captured particular visions of the destitute and fixed them in the public mind' and 'encoded late Victorian ideas of poverty, in which state and voluntary organizations took the inferior and successfully disciplined them in the public interest'.[47]

Reverend Osborne Jay's lodging house in Shoreditch incorporated a range of accommodation, including dormitories and sleeping cubicles, several of which, according to the accompanying text, had been 'tastefully decorated' by their occupants.[48] The image opens up a space in which to consider the acquisition and display of objects as an integral dimension of home-making that extended across residential domains and to re-examine the relationship between consumption and socially constitutive decorative practices within an institutional setting. The small number eight, visible on the fixed wooden partition above the occupant's head, identifies the area as one of a series and alludes to the administrative management and regulation of the interior and its occupants. The wall-mounted display lays claim to the space, animating and lending a sense of character and possession

AT FATHER JAY'S LODGING HOUSE (SHORE-
DITCH): A PRETTY CORNER.

Figure 1.4: From '"Dosser"-Land in London' by T. W. Wilkinson, in G. R. Sims (ed.),
Living London, vol. 2, p. 151. Author's collection.

to a type of interior that is represented elsewhere as anonymous or unowned. Careful scrutiny of the image suggests that among the hundred or more items on display are several photographs and a pair of what may be ships' clocks. The accompanying text refers to 'brackets, busts, looking-glasses, pictures and odds and ends innumerable'.[49] Wilkinson's text is sympathetic, describing this lodging house as an 'admirably conducted' hostel distinct from the 'typical fourpenny hotel' – the common lodging house – with its bare walls and floors and wretched occupants.[50] His comments on the interior suggest that it was not only the 'light, well appointed kitchen' that drove him to identify Father Jay's as a model example of its type, but also the evidence of tasteful decoration by its residents.[51]

Living London's photograph of the 'pretty corner' of Father Jay's lodging house invites the viewer to read the sitter as the inhabitant of the space, the duster in his hand proposing care and pride in ownership. Images of all sorts dominate the display, attesting to the availability of modern forms of print and photographic visual culture, such as postcards, playing cards, cigarette cards, popular prints and photo cards, as well as to the possibilities that they offered individuals of limited financial means to shape their living environments. Mihaly Csikszentmihalyi has suggested that domestic artefacts help objectify and stabilize a sense of self:

> For most people the home is not just a utilitarian shelter but a repository of things whose familiarity and concreteness help organize the consciousness of their owner, directing it into well-worn grooves. The home contains a symbolic ecology that represents both continuity and change in the life course and thus gives permanence to our elusive selves.[52]

Although the ephemeral nature of many of the objects suggests impermanence, the presence of fixed items, such as brackets, proposes some degree of stability of occupation. Mary Douglas has suggested that 'For a home neither the space nor its appurtenances have to be fixed, but there has to be something regular about the appearance and reappearance of its furnishings'.[53] Understood as furnishings, portable collections of this type perhaps offered possibilities for the articulation of site-responsive, modern nomadic identities.

Conclusion

Living London's three volumes represent a range of institutional typologies and residential environments that accommodated male and female occupants of different classes in diverse social circumstances and roles. The collection evidences aspects of the spatial, material and aesthetic organization of turn-of-the-century London's institutional interiors and allows certain general observations to be made about the contemporary beliefs and values that shaped their design and representation. *Living London*'s visual emphasis on rational planning, the use of hygienic materials and common interior elements, codifies a model for modern mass-occupancy building. As such it prefigures the emphasis on 'light, air and openness' that emerged as a characteristic feature of modern architecture of the inter-war period, which Paul Overy described in his book of the same name.[54] *Living London*'s photographs also reveal the spatial and material hierarchies that were central to the constitution and expression of status and identity and the regulation of privacy in a range of institutional settings, including sites within which privacy was commoditized. Informed by a contemporary, gendered ideology of domesticity that spanned public and private, domesticated interiors crossed institutional typologies and architectural environments. Visual evidence of self-determined practices of collection and display suggest that residential institutions could also offer a material context for home-making and the creation of personally meaningful living environments. Collectively, *Living London*'s photographs demonstrate the multi-faceted relationship that early-twentieth-century London's residential institutions maintained with the private home, whose diverse cultural meanings, as a real and idealized space, were mobilized visually and in contextual, site-specific forms.

2 'FRENCH BEEF WAS BETTER THAN HAMPSTEAD BEEF': TASTE, TREATMENT AND PAUPERISM IN A LONDON SMALLPOX HOSPITAL, 1871

Matthew L. Newsom Kerr

Paltry Feasts

The workhouses of London 'have their enjoyments' at least one day of the year, the *Morning Post* reported in 1872, and accordingly at Christmas patients of the Metropolitan Asylums Board (MAB) received their special feast. Imbecile inmates at the asylums were provided with roast beef, plum-pudding, beer, fruit, tobacco and snuff as well as 'other luxuries in celebration of the festival' in 'handsomely decorated' surroundings. Residents of the infectious hospitals operated by the MAB, meanwhile, made do with 'such maimed rites as the necessity of the various cases demanded'.[1] Paupers benefitted from the honoured tradition of treating the destitute to a sumptuous Christmas repast. Newspapers conventionally reported on enormous quantities of food lavished on paupers that merry day and sometimes wondered if the 'workhouse system cannot be so very bad which permits, and in fact sanctions, the annual Christmas feast for the poor'.[2] Yet, as everyone must have known, this single and circumscribed day of generosity merely marked a temporary suspension of the year-round rule of parochial austerity. The smug hypocrisy of the festivity formed a central theme in George R. Sims's very popular poem, 'In the Workhouse: Christmas Day'. In it, an old male inmate explains why 'a penniless pauper spits on your paltry feast': his wife had starved to death the previous Christmas because the parish would not allow her bread at a crucial moment.[3] Sims revived the visceral trope of degrading parochial food classically lodged in *Oliver Twist* and brought it up to date with recent changes in the Metropolitan Poor Law. Indeed, by the time the infectious inmates of the MAB hospitals enjoyed their 'maimed' holiday meal in 1872 they would be aware that, while the state now provided special institutions for the treatment of their dangerous illnesses, they were forced on all other days to perform the unsavoury rites of pauperism.

Created by the Metropolitan Poor Act of 1867, the MAB's hospitals for infectious disease represented the close association between the suppression of pauperism and the government of public health. Their operation, however, immediately placed that connection under strain.[4] While London charity hospitals were busily competing for the best reputation in comfort and liberality, rate-supported fever and smallpox hospitals of the MAB remained coloured by their legal status as workhouse establishments. Furthermore, and most crucially, the majority of infectious inmates did not consider themselves paupers; most would not have risked being associated with parish aid if not for serious illness and the panic surrounding an epidemic. Public isolation for those with infectious diseases highlights in especially dramatic ways the frighteningly uncertain status of London's sick poor. The horror and shame of pauperism was at the centre of an 1871 scandal involving the MAB's Hampstead Smallpox Hospital, where former patients did not hesitate to contest the sudden and unwelcome status of 'workhouse inmate'. The public nature of their complaints allowed patients to both articulate indignation at the status implied in their institutionalization and also to frame themselves as persons out of place. 'Workhouse gruel' had long served officially to mark the degradation of pauperism, and so it is perhaps unsurprising that the dietary at Hampstead Hospital emerged as a key measure of anger and offence. This chapter explores the various possibilities of 'taste' as a discursive signpost employed by both inmates and authorities. As Pierre Bourdieu argues, 'Taste classifies, and it classifies the classifier'.[5] Food – its appreciation and consumption – mapped respectability against institutionalization; it also allowed inmates to chart popular resistances to the workhouse regime and possibilities for contesting the pauper taint.

'A Coarser Sort of Food'

The Victorian workhouse famously epitomized the official deprivations of pauperism and provided the symbolic core of the New Poor Law's deterrent philosophy. While externally it was to exert a 'terror to the able-bodied population', internal semiotics served the same purpose.[6] The model workhouse 'should be a place of hardship, of coarse fare, of degradation and humility', the Reverend H. H. Milman explained to the New Poor Law's chief architect, Edwin Chadwick; 'it should be administered with strictness – with severity; it should be as repulsive as is consistent with humanity'.[7] Workhouse residence was the antithesis of the home and its comforts, of the family and its affections, of the family budget and the good tastes that guide responsible purchases. As seen in Chapter 5 of this volume, historians have long questioned whether these punitive principles were enforced in all, or even most, circumstances. Indeed, the reality of pauperism was always complicated, involving local variation as well as resistance.[8] Yet the emotionally powerful presence of the workhouse pauper in the Victorian imagination was far from ambiguous. The deliberateness of the stigma is hinted at in the harsh gastronomical penalty the New Poor Law intended to impose. Poor Law Commission investigator Sir Francis Bond Head maintained, for example, that the quality of relief could in no way be superior to that earned by the independent labourer (the principle of 'less eligibility'). Workhouses could allow only the 'poorest' diet – a subsistence regime, but one also deliberately starved of meaning and taste. Relief had to become 'wholesomely repulsive' and devoid of the corruptively enticing 'smell of hot joints'.[9] Paupers possessed mouths to fill, not palates to placate. Meat could only be wasted on paupers, who had already proven themselves incapable of appreciating the moral qualities of that powerful 'patriotic emblem': roast beef.[10] Workhouse dietary thus became the keynote in a chorus of pragmatic claims to 'protect the rates', but it also carried deep symbolic significance for locating and inculcating self-government.

'Pauper gruel' formed a central disciplinary tool in the model workhouse regime and continues to provide an abiding metaphor for the pauper's deprivation and debasement. Caustically ridiculed in *Oliver Twist*, the pauper meal was famed for its principled cheapness, monotony, roughness, blandness and cold efficiency of distribution. Salt was the only officially recognized flavouring. To the extent it was served at all, meat was almost always boiled instead of roasted, with exhaustive efforts to calculate the average loss of flesh in cooking and serving.[11] Consisting of mostly meatless and mushy foods, 'work'us stuff' placed recipients outside the sphere of discriminating choice and conveyed a sense of dependence and degradation.[12] Indeed, food proved a polemic cornerstone from the very inception of the new workhouse system.[13] *The Times*, reflective of conservative criticism, labelled the New Poor Law the 'Starvation Act', and William Cobbett among others was convinced it contained draconian Malthusian designs.[14] Abolitionist and factory-reform firebrand Richard Oastler prophesied that 'less eligibility' heralded an inevitable lowering of the national fare, bemoaning that 'the people of England shall, hereafter, live on a *coarser sort of food*'.[15] The popular impression of the workhouse as a site of official deprivation and degradation was surely strengthened through scandals like that at the Andover Workhouse in 1844–5, where hungry inmates resorted to gnawing bones the workhouse had contracted to crush into fertilizer with pauper labour.[16] Finally, critics worried that the workhouse regime supported a mass of 'out-door' starvation; they pointed to coroners courts' frequent declaration of deaths caused by hunger resulting from terror of parochial relief.[17] The workhouse pauper, officially forbidden from feeling 'at home' in the institution, would play a key negative role in defining Victorian notions of subsistence and taste.

Metropolitan Infirmary Reform

The ghoulish frequency of workhouse scandals gave rise to calls for civic over-sight. Concerns about the treatment of inmates, however, entered public discourse almost exclusively through the agency of middle-class reformers and humanitarians; the voices of paupers themselves were largely excluded. 'Lady visitors' organized by Louisa Twining directed attention mainly towards the plight of sick inmates.[18] Two highly publicized deaths of London workhouse inmates in 1865 prompted the *Lancet*'s ambitious 'sanitary survey' of the met-ropolitan pauper infirmaries (in reality the sick wards attached to workhouses), during which it observed sufficient examples of abuse, bad nursing, sickness, filth, inadequate space and ventilation, bad construction, and improper food and medicine to grace the journal's pages for eighteen months. The considerable attention directed to workhouse space often returned to a few common themes. First was the perceived admixture of unfortunate but decent persons (many with either infections or mental afflictions) with vicious, confirmed paupers.[19] Secondly, investigators and visitors were appalled by pauper nursing. Until the 1880s the vast majority of nurses in workhouses were themselves pauper inmates and had a worse reputation than Dickens's fictional Sairey Gamp. Their alleged brutality received special attention in the *Lancet*, which categorically stated that able-bodied pauper assistants 'are not to be trusted'.[20] Thirdly, the issue of workhouse food was a constant concern, especially with regard to sick inmates. Fixed dietaries and feeding timetables made little allowance for variation, so that a pauper may have been consistently served a tough crust although he had not a tooth to bite it. One critic wondered how

> a sick man [could] derive benefit or comfort from his food when he knows that each day brings him the same quantity of beef or mutton cooked in the same way; no change or variety by which to tempt a feeble appetite.[21]

For their part, many reform-minded doctors believed substantive food (espe-cially viands of a 'stimulating' sort, such as meat and wine) constituted the best medicine they could provide poor patients. However, penny-pinching parochial boards infamously tried to frame food orders by doctors as 'medical aid' that should come from the officer's salary. They were often successful in banning orders for consumables such as beer and champagne and insisting on tests to determine whether applicants were faking illness in order to receive free stimulants.[22]

A turning point for the London pauper population and its institutional man-agement occurred in the 1860s.[23] The Association for the Improvement of the Infirmaries of Workhouses (with the backing of reform celebrities like Florence Nightingale and Charles Dickens) observed that the 'indoor' pauper sick far outnumbered patients at the charity hospitals. London workhouse infirmaries were, for all intents and purposes, the 'real hospitals of the land', yet they were almost completely devoid of the treatments and comforts touted by modern hospital medicine.[24] Taken as a whole, too, the London workhouses had become huge aggregations of the sick and infirm poor. They provided for the residuum of unfortunate patients not accommodated by private charity: lying-in wards for poor women, black wards for venereal diseases, as well as innumerable cramped wards containing a whole range of desperate, hopeless cases that the general hospitals did not want (such as tuberculosis and cancer) or ones they deemed too dangerous to bring under the same roof (the fevers and smallpox).[25] Publically and legally, institutional care of the sick became the most disputed point of application of the Poor Law's deterrent principles.[26] As Nightingale wrote:

> So long as a sick man, woman or child is considered administratively to be a pauper, to be repressed and not a fellow creature to be nursed into health, so long will these shameful disclosures have to be made. The sick, infirm, or mad pauper ceases to be a pauper when so afflicted.[27]

Clearly, an undercurrent of criticism proposed that the workhouse sick should be looked upon not as paupers, but as patients.

The workhouse reform movement received a great boost in early 1866 as a result of James Greenwood's sensational story of infiltrating the Lambeth workhouse casual ward by disguising himself as a tramp – 'a narrative all England read and shuddered at'.[28] Attention to the institutional treatment of paupers was maintained by a new spate of deaths at the Bethnal Green workhouse (a much-criticized symbol of parochial rottenness) and by a cholera outbreak in 1866. The critical press hailed the usefulness of unofficial exposés and official investigations, but also continued to question whether inmates themselves could act as reliable judges of workhouse conditions. The *Daily News*, for instance, deprecated what it considered the inherent 'untrustworthiness of pauper witnesses'.[29] Voices of inmates, even while emanating from objects of pity, were usually disdained as disruptive and vulgar.

The Metropolitan Poor Act of 1867 capped years of worried commentary about London pauperism and workhouse conditions. It effected a metropolitan reorganization of poor-law funding, whereby the relatively low rates of the wealthy western parishes and the unduly high ones of the East End would be more equalized. A new Common Metropolitan Poor Rate funded special asylums for the separate accommodation of infectious and 'imbecile' paupers. 'The main object is to classify the inmates', explained its author, Gathorne Hardy.[30] The MAB was created and tasked with erecting and managing the anticipated hospitals, wherein these categories of paupers from across the metropolis were to receive professional treatment in conditions suitable to their recovery. Hence, the MAB did not originate as a purposive sanitary body for the general London population; rather, it was initially only intended as a safety valve to draw off workhouse inmates rendered troublesome by sickness.

Allegations and Inquiry

The first MAB infectious hospital was constructed in the northern London sub-urb of Hampstead in 1869 (currently the site of the Royal Free Hospital) and started receiving fever patients later that year. The severe smallpox outbreak of 1870–2 (the worst of the century) caused a new inrush at the Hampstead Hospital. Its medical superintendent, Dr Robert Grieve, reported that patients came primarily from 'the working classes', especially those whose work caused them to come into contact with smallpox: 'barmaids, shop men and women, 'bus- and cab-drivers, &c'.[31] Most patients were clearly from above the conventional pauper class. An internal survey listed 71 per cent of patients during the epidemic as not in receipt of poor relief prior to admission.[32] While this strengthens the image of a substantial non-pauper presence in the hospital, it is nonetheless important to remember that all inmates were legally considered paupers by vir-tue of their residence in a poor-law institution.

The metropolitan smallpox outbreak placed great strain upon the new MAB hospitals. As one officer recalled, 'every hospital was crammed'.[33] By August 1871 the Hampstead Hospital had received nearly 6,000 patients and the crowding was so great that the staff temporarily resorted to holding two patients in the same bed and housing convalescents in tents and huts on the grounds.[34] (Assum-ing that they survived the infection, smallpox patients would usually spend two to six weeks in hospital; mortality hovered around 18 per cent.) Supervision of nursing was placed in the hands of the East Grinstead Sisterhood, a lay Protes-tant order that had performed emergency nursing during the cholera crisis of 1866. Medical reformers praised the hospital as the latest in sanitary design;[35] but rumours about strange goings-on at Hampstead Hospital circulated for months. A man claimed that his wife surprised him by returning home a fort-night after he had been told she died at the hospital. Grieving relatives also published serious complaints about poor treatment and unnecessary deaths – in one case not being informed of a child's death until a week after its funeral. Another story related to a five-year-old girl who went missing at the hospital and was never found.[36] These tales easily resonated with a public already familiar with well-worn narratives of workhouse abuse and neglect. Finally, an exchange of letters in *The Times* in August 1871 seemed to confirm popular suspicions. Three recently dismissed Assistant Medical Officers (AMOs) published their own allegations of 'gross mismanagement'. This elicited harshly worded replies from MAB managers and the medical superintendent, Dr Grieve, who accused the young AMOs of insubordination.[37]

Under pressure, the government agreed to a public inquiry and quickly empanelled a commission, which would eventually sit for thirty-three sessions from September to November 1871 and hear testimony from 115 witnesses.

Several London newspapers as well as medical journals exhaustively covered the inquiry.[38] Lawyers representing the former AMOs sought to portray the chaos as directly resulting from mismanagement and the misapplication of harsh poor-law principles. Evidence for the defence came from a range of medical staff, MAB officers, current and former nurses, and also some former patients praising conditions in the hospital. Importantly, the tone of this inquiry differed from previous workhouse scandals in that former inmates were now invited to voice complaints. (Several simply showed up to give testimony after reading about the hearings in the newspapers.) Their testimony would not be dismissed as the vulgar sound of paupers. Apart from describing the awfulness of the disease, aggrieved former inmates tended to stress the carceral atmosphere of the hospital and their sense of being out of place. They also vividly emphasized the various horrors of institutional treatment, which they traced to the indignities of pauperism.

The public inquiry captivated the London reading public for some time, providing a startling glimpse into a medical institution premised on its separation from the outside world and a parochial institution modelled on the suppression of a culture of poverty. All the elements of a melodramatic script and the plebian stage were present, which perhaps helps explain the strong emotions unleashed. The *Medical Press and Circular* remarked upon 'the violent language and violent conduct used by the offended public against the nurses and the Hospital staff':

> Letters have been received by [hospital officials] frantic in the excess of vituperation and execrative expressions. The public feeling has been deeply stirred. The Government has been appealed to, and the whole press of the country have watched every phasis [*sic*] and every step of the inquiry with unabated patience.[39]

The attention of the London public, however, was also worn down by the tedium of the testimony. The inquiry proved scandalous, but monotonous. Allegations were examined in 'wearisome detail', in the words of an evidently bored *Times* reporter.[40] Nonetheless, the exhaustive testimony provides an archive of how London's first great experiment with rate-supported hospitalization in 1871 echoed the notorious troubles of the workhouse system.

Performing Degradation

Nurses bore the brunt of individual criticism by former patients. Much of this could be attributed to severe under-staffing; for example, it was not uncommon for one nurse and one sister to have charge of forty children in a single ward (and at times as many as sixty-five). Several former patients described dead bodies neglected for scandalously long periods.[41] Perhaps unsurprisingly, criticism of nursing at Hampstead Hospital solidified around a stereotype of the pauper nurse. The chairman of the hospital committee testified to the difficulty of attracting persons to take up what everyone recognized as hard work in an exceptionally unpleasant environment; they had 'exhausted every means of getting nurses, often in vain, even though we were offering the most liberal wages'.[42] As a result, most of the hospital's paid nurses were recruited from the ranks of recovered patients, even though active patients tended to view these nurses as 'true' paupers with whom they had little in common. George Tidbury, a tailor, claimed the ward nurses got drunk on the stimulants stolen from patients too ill to complain.[43] A young patient declared that a nurse called 'Frisky' shook her fist and vaguely threatened him with punishment. (The patients considered nurse Fisk – or Frisky – as literally mad.)[44] Albert Emerson Denton, a solicitor's clerk, complained that the nurses 'had them completely in their power, and patients were punished by them for complaining'.[45] Others told of not complaining because they feared being 'served out' by spiteful nurses, such as having their rations reduced.[46] Little comforts could become the currency of negotiation between inmates and nurses, but also the occasion for petty tyrannies.

Some of the most resentful testimony involved former patients who had been straightjacketed or pinned with bed linen during periods of feverish delirium – ostensibly to prevent their wandering around the ward, falling out of bed, and otherwise injuring themselves or others. James Henry Wills, a clerk, deposed that during his residence nurses had tied him to the sharp edges of a bedstead, as the marks on his legs still showed.[47] Stories of patients suffering under mechanical restraint clearly fascinated London newspaper readers. Bondage of a sort already occupied a thoroughly theatrical place in mainstream Victorian narrative culture (and its preoccupation with scenarios of dungeon-like confinement), the straight-waistcoat especially serving as a signpost of antiquated madhouse cruelty or a reminder of the possibility of wrongful confinement under the lunacy laws.

A large proportion of Hampstead patients were convalescent at any one time, meaning they were through the most dangerous part of the disease but not free of infection or well enough to leave. These patients were required to help the nurses in ward work, such as emptying slops and commodes, sweeping floors and making beds. Labour had long been required from able-bodied workhouse inmates, but in this hospital patients were expected to assist the operation of the institution. Those who graduated to the convalescent wards could expect extra rations of beer and meat in return for their labour and could wear little stars to distinguish themselves.[48] Several former patients recalled that they willingly and happily did what they were asked. Yet smallpox was particularly gruesome. James Henry Wills related that he refused to help lay out the body of a fresh corpse because it was in 'such an offensive condition'.[49] Inmates risked being disciplined as refractory paupers if they failed to perform certain tasks. Arthur Partridge, a bootmaker, complained at the inquiry that his beer was cut off when he declined to assist in scrubbing a ward.[50] In these and other ways, the hospital exactly resembled a workhouse (which it legally was) and conformed to the shame-inducing pauper regime.

Many complaints dealt with the Hampstead Hospital's lack of cleanliness and sanitation. One witness felt insulted by being required to share four or five towels among 113 patients.[51] Another common grumble was about persistently bug-ridden linen.[52] The strain upon the laundry caused a lack of clean sheets and clothes, meting out another stigmatizing sign of destitution. Edward Wilson, a chairmaker, claimed that upon admission to the hospital he had 'served out to him a "lady's nightgown" for a shirt', and he 'made shift' with it for some time.[53] Some patients were placed in beds directly after another left. William Charles Peters testified that 'the bed allotted to him was in such a disgusting condition, from the sheets being defiled with "gore, matter, and lice," that he preferred walking about all night to sleeping in it'.[54] Elizabeth Fowle, a watchmaker's wife, stated that her dress was not changed nearly often enough, and when she was transferred to a convalescent ward after the death of her child, her dress was 'stiff up to her arms with filth'. She also recalled disgusting tubs of water almost black with the grime of previous washers.[55] All of these allegations were more reminiscent of previous workhouse scandals than any complaints that had been levied at hospitals.

Unwholesomely Repulsive

Former patients complained most persistently and emphatically about the poor quality of the Hampstead Hospital diet. Numerous individual objections stand out. It was 'impossible to distinguish the tea from the coffee'.[56] The potatoes were usually bad, mouldy or spotty (patients used to joke that the 'taturs' had the smallpox like the patients).[57] The butter was rank (one witness asserted 'he would not grease a cartwheel with it').[58] While still in hospital, several patients had signed a petition to Dr Grieve regarding the tea, coffee, meat and short measure of beer. They testified that the food improved shortly, but soon fell back into its bad state.[59] Miserable hospital food clearly resonated with the indignity of pauper gruel, yet some patients challenged its suitability under even poor-law standards. James Henry Wills, a clerk, very deliberately said that he thought the food was 'vile' and 'not fit for paupers' (persons he evidently thought far below his station). He had 'what was called boiled mutton handed to him on an ice cold plate, and potatoes not fit for a pig'.[60] This theme of inhuman consumption paralleled the degradation of pauper consumption. The petition sent to Dr Grieve contained a statement that the meals were not fit for a dog, and not enough for a dog.[61] And indeed, comments of this sort marked practically every session of the inquiry, with former patients seemingly very eager to devise ever more evocative culinary condemnations.

Meat served as a potent symbol of the Hospital's daily institutional fare, which left patients hungry, uncomfortable and indignant. For some, its disagreeableness could be traced to a lack of care in preparation, which itself was resonant with pauperism: interminably boiled and unseasoned, either repeatedly inferior beef or repeatedly low-grade mutton. One witness deposed that the meat, though over-boiled, could not be made tender;[62] others grumbled that the nurses and officers received roasted meat whereas the patients only got boiled.[63] Some believed the fare was good in quality but always badly cooked. A butcher, Thomas Owen, remembered the meat 'stewed as if the goodness was stewed out of it'. The plate-meat also contained 'stickings' (inferior parts of the carcass suitable only for making beef-tea or soup).[64] Meat could convey a sense of degradation like few other foodstuffs. A variety of witnesses, almost entirely men, rained down abuse on the tough, coarse, indigestible meat, with more than a few remembering occasions when it was 'distinctly decomposing'.[65] Once, fourteen patients refused to consume their dinner until the medical officer had seen the meat.[66] A bootmaker, Arthur Partridge, claimed to have sometimes opened a window and thrown the disappointing stuff out.[67] The relative absence of fleshy viands had long marked the deprivation and degradation of the pauper meal, yet its presence in an offensive form could convey that ignominy just the same.

Several male patients pointedly insisted that the 'very middling meat' was 'unfit for sick men'.[68] Historians have noted that meat consumption was strongly gendered within Victorian patterns of consumption and representation.[69] The pauper regime at Hampstead Hospital was therefore also an insult to the manly culture of meat-eating and the chops of British citizenship. William Charles Peters, a wine and commission agent, stated that he did not admire Parisian beef, 'yet he would say that French beef was better than Hampstead beef' (evidently a cosmopolitan yet also very damning patriotic assessment).[70] Patients like Elizabeth Fowle, the watchmaker's wife mentioned above, were also insulted by the degraded domesticity of the hospital and had grown indignant at bad meat. It was 'served out in coarse and vulgar-looking pieces; it was like cats'-meat', she testified. Perhaps cognizant that this was a typically masculine complaint, Fowle added quite emphatically that they were 'certainly not "ladylike-looking" pieces'.[71] The crudity of pauperism was boiled into this coarse fare, but it was a humiliation that had to be expressed differently by men and women. The variety of complaints about hospital meat is one indication that this was an important public means of asserting self-respect and, at the same time, of bringing the complex politics of private consumption into what was intended to be a highly normalizing institution.

In addition to (and perhaps in spite of) the distasteful dietary, patient after patient also deprecated the small portions allowed by hospital authorities. Many ruefully assumed it was part of the 'starvation diet' stipulated by the Poor Law

Board. John Channon related a strange mixture of repulsion and attraction, as there were always hungry patients ready to snatch what others had left on plates in disgust.[72] Another witness concurred that there were 'always plenty of candidates to eat it', since no one could get enough; patients got 'about four good mouthfuls [of meat], and if more was supplied it was an accident'.[73] Several former patients, all men, deposed that they received far less than the official dietary's stipulated 6 ounces of meat. Thomas Johnstone, a machine maker, drew laughter from the court when he estimated his average cut of meat at about ⅟₁₆ of an inch thick.[74] The butcher, Thomas Owen, stated to his AMO that he was doing pretty well in the hospital except that he was 'nearly starved', to which the doctor replied that it was out of his power to give more to eat. Receiving food from outside was apparently against the rules, but Owen wrote to his relatives and had them send parcels of bacon, cheese, cakes, biscuits, anchovies 'and cetera'. He testified to frizzling the bacon in the ward during the doctors' rounds expressly to show that there was not enough to eat, and this reportedly became the 'talk of the hospital'.[75] The official dietary also could be undermined in other ways. One patient confessed that he could trade postage stamps for milk – indicating something of an authority-defying underground barter system within the hospital.[76] Disobediences of this sort and the somewhat embellished nature of complaints serve to emphasize how sick inmates portrayed themselves as inappropriate subjects of workhouse discipline and austerity.

Invalid Dietary

Former patients who appeared at the Hampstead Hospital inquiry sought to stress how out of place they had felt. They testified that during their hospitalization they pined for homely comforts, especially those requisite invalid foods such as beef-tea, arrowroot and milk. Peters, the wine agent who did not like French roasts, said he could not 'make out' the beef-tea and accounted for its bad taste by the rumour that it was made from Liebig's meat extract (an imported South-American condensed beef jelly).[77] In home-nursing, the preparation of beef-tea was an honoured craft of womanly attentiveness and was supposed to derive from actual joints of meat stewed into thick broth. The hospital, however, provided cheap, industrially processed 'slop'. Decent milk and arrowroot (traditional invalid foods) were also scarce and dearly missed, due, patients presumed, to workhouse restrictions on wholesome victuals. Each drink held a place in the *habitus* of sickness and therefore also carried the burden of representing social respect. Henry William Clicker, a foreign tailor, claimed he did not get enough milk. He did testify to having been offered water, but amused the court by stating that he 'never drank water in his life'.[78] These preferences should not be passed over as mere petulant grumbling. The Hampstead patients were asserting claims to the domestic comforts expected by sick persons of the 'decent class'. They placed these 'medical comforts' before and against what they saw as their superficial and artificial – yet official – status as paupers.

Scanty food provisions for patients formed part of the original complaints to *The Times* that had prompted the inquiry. Albert Kynaston, one of the dismissed medical officers, explained that during his casual visits the wards 'would be like a Babel, from a lot asking for food at once'.[79] He and his colleagues testified to their persistent inability to get the amount of eggs, milk and wine they deemed necessary for the recovery of specific patients – a malprovision they traced to the hospital's poor-law status.[80] Until June 1871, the Hampstead Hospital operated under emergency powers granted by the Poor Law Board, meaning that the institution had not received orders governing its conduct. Cautioned about expenditure, Dr Grieve drew up three standard patient dietaries: low, ordinary and full. Many patients complained of being kept on the 'low' diet and noted the rarity of the 'ordinary' diet. Apparently Grieve did not authorize full diet at any time, though he justified this as a medical measure in smallpox treatment.[81] The distribution of the austere dietary was even more rigorously enforced after the hospital received its poor-law orders in June, with Grieve now reserving the right to nullify food prescriptions given by the junior officers. Kynaston testified that up to that time he could order port, sherry, brandy, whisky, extra bread, milk and beef-tea, but henceforth it was stipulated (as in all workhouses) that no 'extravagances' would be tolerated.[82] The AMOs had great difficulty getting the one item they previously could prescribe in abundance: eggs. Forbidden to intervene in any matters not strictly 'medical', the junior officers maintained that smallpox treatment was essentially a question of diet and comfort.[83] So, while ample food was considered a luxury under the Poor Law, the ward-level doctors saw it as a therapeutic necessity. They went so far as to argue that the high mortality amongst child patients could be traced to insufficient nursing and nourishment. Kynaston heatedly argued with Grieve that deaths in the hospital would be halved if the dietary (principally milk) were doubled.[84]

Classification and Validation

Patients' ability to link their complaints to issues of sustenance, taste and civility illuminate the ways they were compelled to negotiate the official gulf between deservedness and pauperism. Several former patients corroborated the statements of Charles M'Laren, a bricklayer, who claimed he was told not to complain because 'while he was there, he was only a pauper'.[85] A mechanical draughtsman, Thomas Jones, testified to only taking the beef-tea once, and 'he never tasted such a cup of nastiness in his life'.[86] He also objected to the condescending conduct of the medical superintendent:

I told Dr Grieve that I wanted to know under what authority he opened my letters, and he asked me what I thought I was. I told him I was a draughtsman, that was what I was, and I would see when I got out all about it. He told me I was a refractory pauper. It was the general feeling in the ward that it was no use to complain to Dr Grieve.

Upon cross-examination, Jones admitted that he had entered the hospital 'on the parish' (St Pancras) and had not reimbursed the parochial authorities for the costs of his maintenance. The MAB's legal counsel maintained that he was therefore a pauper. While Jones insisted that he was in the hospital through having small-pox, the attorney explained that others had paid and suggested that non-payers like Jones had less ground from which to voice complaints.[87] (In fact, only a few patients paid anything towards their costs, and those that did received absolutely the same treatment.) The defence lawyers challenged the testimony of James George Palmer – who had complained that hospital meals were not fit for dogs – by tracking his movements after being discharged from the hospital. They showed that Palmer had immediately visited the Newport Market Refuge for the Destitute and received clothes from this charity for the homeless.[88] The implication was clear: paupers could not legitimately talk about taste or judge discomforts. Other MAB witnesses cast complainers as undependable and their complaints as the result of roguish temperaments. Miss Harrison, a Hampstead nurse who *The Times* noticed as having the 'manners and speech of a well-cultured person', testified that 'this hospital was one of the places provided for those who could not be treated in their own homes when smitten with this disease; it followed that there were many brutal, blasphemous, and violent persons in the wards at times'.[89] The MAB's main defence was to imply that the aggrieved were an indolent, incorrigible, malcontented lot – morally indistinguishable from true paupers.

Some complaining former inmates expressed a complicated attitude towards their confinement, both criticizing the conditions of their treatment and expressing their begrudging appreciation. For example, Edwin James Barter, a bank clerk who talked in detail of revolting sanitary conditions and unpalatable food, had also pleaded with Dr Grieve to be allowed to stay a few additional days because his father had expressed fear of infection.[90] Similarly, Thomas Hatcher, a waiter who had complained bitterly about the food and vermin in the hospital, also stayed longer than necessary because 'with the marks on my face I could not get work, and I stayed to get rid of the marks'.[91] The hospital could have been seen as a comparably safe shelter for those with the taint of dreaded smallpox. This seems to have been the case with James George Palmer, the man exposed by MAB attorneys as essentially homeless following his hospital stay, who expressed significant anxiety about going out before his face had healed.[92] Palmer's sad predicament highlights the potential for a tarnished appearance to mark an irretraceable step towards actual destitution. Public hospitalization provided a private benefit, but most inmates clearly believed that this should not be purchased through their degradation and abasement. For the complainers, residence at the Hampstead Hospital imparted a frightening sense of the fluid and unpredictable boundary between the vulnerabilities of sickness and the stains of pauperism.

As the MAB took its turn to present evidence at the inquiry, assessments of conditions at Hampstead Hospital more openly involved estimates of witnesses' characters – especially as they suggested relevant markers of taste. James Salmon, a cabman described in *The Times* as a 'respectable man of his class', was called to state that there was sufficient and good food and patients had 'no cause whatever for complaining of anything'. He further claimed that the dirty habits of the patients themselves contributed to the 'sloppy state' of bathrooms and other parts of the hospital.[93] Indeed, a procession of working-class witnesses expressed satisfaction and gratitude for their hospital stay. Stephen Wakefield, who could earn 24 shillings per week as a bricklayer's labourer, deemed the food in the hospital 'quite as good as he got out of doors, and as good as a working man could wish for'. Similarly, Charles Alderson – 'a respectable man of the artisan class' – found the bread and beer especially good, the latter much better than could be had in public houses.[94] Masoah Walker, a former patient now employed as the hospital's coachman, swore that 'everything was done in the hospital for the comfort of the patients'.[95] Much of this type of exonerating testimony was weakened by the fact that it came from former patients who were now employed by the MAB. However, perhaps by distancing themselves from the stereotype of the ungrateful rascal, these witnesses (not all of whom had subsequent contact with the MAB) were also pursuing a different personal strategy for refuting the accusation of pauperism. Flowers Allpress, a master saddler, maintained that he could not have been more kindly or better attended to at the hospital if he had been a child cared for by his mother. He blamed all discontent on a 'dirty lot – the kind of men one saw at public-house corners'.[96] With clearly contradictory evidence in play, it is no surprise that final assessments of the scandal turned to a scrutiny of the subjective qualities of individual taste. Nevertheless, the MAB's witnesses appeared on the stand after newspapers had generally shifted attention from the inquiry. Its wearisome monotony had evidently taxed the London public's patience for details about bedbugs and boiled mutton.

Conclusion

By the time the official report of the inquiry into conditions at Hampstead Smallpox Hospital was issued in January 1872, the scandal had slipped from public attention. On the whole, the report dismissed the charges brought against the hospital's senior management and made a point of regretting that allegations had been 'based upon such slight and insufficient grounds'.[97] While most casual newspaper readers had undoubtedly received a detailed confirmation of the predictable horrors of London workhouses (especially when allowed the unpleasant addition of a loathsome illness), public narrative following the scandal was more nuanced than suggested by the official report. First, subsequent commentary was convinced that the majority of inmates had been paupers in title only. The *Morning Post* typified this explanation, writing that 'not one of these complainants was of the pauper class'. More conjecturally, it concluded that true paupers 'not only did not grumble at their fare, but expressed themselves as highly delighted with the luxury in which they had been maintained'.[98] In other words, Hampstead inmates had successfully presented themselves as patients, not paupers. Confirming this narrative of persons out of place, the *Medical Times and Gazette* reasoned that the average treatment at the institution would not

> suit the requirements of persons who had been accustomed to the comforts with which the lower middle-classes surround themselves in this country. The Hospital may have been fairly good for a pauper Hospital, but it was not suited for the reception of patients of various grades of society.[99]

Therefore, just as it cast smallpox patients as unsuitable subjects of pauper deterrence, this explanation also normalized workhouse degradation. Secondly, this recollection of the scandal served to negate and undo discussions concerned with objective measures of discomfort and deprivation. As the *Lancet* recalled some years later, the inquiry had 'showed very many well-to-do people coming forward as witnesses about tough meat and other things which real paupers would hardly have cared much, or as much, about'.[100] Taste, in other words, spoke of the individual and the quality of appreciation conferred by social class. Food, especially, remained within the orbit of relational assessment, and therefore these misplaced persons were essentially disqualified from passing judgement upon pauper treatment.

Thirdly, the Hampstead scandal introduced disturbing questions about pauperism's ability to compromise the public health. The *Morning Post*, while praising the 'triumphant acquittal' of the MAB, conceded that most patients had been admitted 'not in charity to themselves, but in order to prevent their infecting others'.[101] The *Borough of Marylebone Mercury* editorialist worried that for unpleasant revelations at Hampstead to drive Londoners from the public hospitals 'would be the greatest public calamity. The isolation of infectious diseases is a necessary sanitary precaution for the welfare of the state'. Indeed, in the coming years, the pauper hospitals would remain the only reliable site for the separation of London's dangerously sick. Those who were 'removed from their homes for the good of others on sanitary grounds', the editorialist maintained, 'should have secured for them efficient medical attendance, food and nursing, and not be subject to horrors of uncleanliness worse than that expected by the amateur casual'.[102] The Hampstead inquiry had begun as a deposition upon the 'rottenness of the poor-law arrangements', which had made London workhouses infamous for 'harsh and even cruel treatment'.[103] It ended with an anxious new discourse on the importance of good taste in public services. MAB hospitals were legally 'depauperized' in 1883, largely as a consequence of these lingering concerns and immediate worries about an impending cholera epidemic. Nationally, all forms of parochial medical assistance were depauperized two years later amidst the implementation of the Third Reform Bill.[104]

The 1871 Hampstead Hospital scandal, relatively brief and unremembered, is a vivid illustration of the clashes between poor-law philosophy and new attitudes towards public medicine. For patients, the inquiry afforded new opportunities to resist the ignominy of pauperism – and in some cases challenge the Poor Law itself. Given the workhouses' reputation for calculated gastronomical degradation, 'taste' emerged as an important register by which to measure whether inmates might be treated as penal subjects of poor-law discipline or medical subjects deserving of courteous treatment and clean civil status. The scandal established homely comforts as an appealing standard by which inmates sought to assert respectability. For all involved, the gloomy history of London workhouses assured that the metropolis's first public health hospitals would be strongly steeped in the politics of 'coarser food'.

3 FROM ASYLUM TO MENTAL HOSPITAL: GENDER, SPACE AND THE PATIENT EXPERIENCE IN LONDON COUNTY COUNCIL ASYLUMS, 1890–1910

Louise Hide

'The Modern Asylum has Long Passed the Prison Workhouse Stage, and its Work Demands Recognition as a Mental Hospital in Every Sense of the Word'[1]

In February 1901, the eminent asylum architect George T. Hine presented a lengthy paper titled 'Asylums and Asylum Planning' to the Royal Institute of British Architects. Asylum construction was, he contended, 'a special branch of architecture' because 'asylums are built for people who cannot take care of themselves, and who have to be watched, nursed, and provided with employment and recreation under conditions inapplicable to sane people'.[2] He cited plans for the East Sussex Asylum when outlining his vision for a new type of public asylum which, in this case, included an acute hospital for eighty patients that would be nearly half a mile from the main asylum building (itself holding 840 patients of all classes); four detached villas containing thirty patients each; and 'a block for sixty idiot and imbecile children'.[3] This indicated a distinct move towards an approach that was ostensibly more patient-centric, away from the old style of building, which accommodated patients according to the institutional resources required to manage them (for example, more attendants worked on refractory wards for disturbed patients than on those for 'quiet and chronic' patients). Previously, patients admitted for disorders that were believed to be curable might live beside those who had chronic and congenital conditions. Hine now wanted 'new cases' – meaning patients who were not diagnosed as being 'hopelessly incurable' – to be treated in a separate acute hospital that was situated well away from the main building.[4] The villas in the plan comprised small units that provided a less institutionalized existence for groups of patients who displayed similar behaviours, or who were at the same stage of their treat-

– 51 –

ment, such as convalescence. In addition to architectural changes, the modern asylum was increasingly incorporating practices appropriated from general hospitals, aligning itself more closely with general medicine. The shift from asylum to mental hospital was gathering speed.

These changes did not, however, herald the death of the Victorian asylum, which was a custodial institution. Indeed, both asylum and mental hospital co-existed during this period, with new hospital practices adding an extra layer of control and surveillance to a system known as 'moral management', which contrived to employ space and routine to control patients' behaviour. Michel Foucault analysed these processes in three of his most important works: *Madness and Civilisation* (1961), *The Birth of the Clinic* (1963) and *Discipline and Punish* (1975).[5] In these publications, Foucault set out to disabuse his readers of any notion that moral management and certain other emerging medical discourses had been anything other than pernicious methods of social control. These practices, he argued, dehumanized patients by subjecting them to the 'medical gaze', reducing them to little more than objects of knowledge and making them complicit in their own regulation. Space played an important role in this process.

Since Foucault, much has been written about the role of moral management in nineteenth-century asylums. Historical sociologist Andrew Scull developed the social control theme by linking the incarceration of the insane to capitalism, claiming that families who were required to live in densely populated areas and work outside the home could no longer care for their non-productive siblings, children or parents. Scull also attributed a growth in lunacy numbers during the nineteenth century to, among other things, efforts by the inchoate psychiatric establishment to expand the boundaries of insanity by upholding it as a distinct pathology in need of treatment that only the medically qualified could provide.[6] Roy Porter, who challenged some of Foucault's historical claims, has made a significant contribution to the history of madness, urging historians to tackle 'history from below' in order to understand madness and its treatment from the patient perspective.[7] Elaine Showalter introduced a feminist perspective, elements of which have since been contested, in *The Female Malady* (1985) where she argued that a patriarchal medical establishment increasingly linked women with mental disorder from the nineteenth century.[8] Over the past two decades more nuanced micro-histories have been produced, which seek to understand the wider effects of socio-political and cultural factors on the lived experience of asylum inmates, often analysing them through the prisms of class, gender, 'race' and religion. Most notable are works and edited collections of essays from Joseph Melling and Bill Forsythe, David Wright, Jonathan Andrews and Anne Digby and, providing an Australian perspective, Catharine Coleborne and Dolly MacKinnon.[9] Finally, design and architectural historians such as Lindsay Prior, Barry Edginton and Jeremy Taylor have provided invaluable insights into how discourse was embedded in the structures, space and material culture of nine-teenth-century asylums.[10] More recently, Carla Yanni has explored the use of 'therapeutic architecture ... to cure social ills' in American asylums.[11] And a collection of essays edited by Leslie Topp, James E. Moran and Jonathan Andrews brings fresh interdisciplinary scholarship to the changing nature – social, cultural and medical – of asylum spaces from the early modern period to the late twentieth century across a wide geographical spread.[12]

This chapter aims to build on this rich body of work by exploring the role of space as a technology of control, as contended by Foucault, focusing in particular on its gendered nature. Drawing on annual reports, committee minutes and case books from the London County Council's (LCC's) first two asylums – Claybury and Bexley – built in the 1890s, it explains how shifts in medical epistemology, together with wider changes in women's working practices, began to transform asylum structures and processes, and examines the impact of these changes on patients. But first, a very short history of madness in the late nineteenth century is needed.

Accommodating the Rise in Lunacy

Along with other institutions, such as prisons and workhouses, the asylum was at the centre of the movement to form and reform character, which began in the late eighteenth century.[13] An unprecedented rise in the number of 'known persons of unsound mind' took place in England and Wales during the second half of the nineteenth century, growing from over 31,000 in 1859 to more than 128,000 in 1909.[14] Vast, purpose-built asylums were constructed by local authorities in every county across the country to accommodate pauper lunatics whose care and treatment was managed by poor-law authorities and funded through the public purse. By 1910, ninety-one county and city asylums each contained an average of 1,072 patients;[15] many housed well over 2,000 each. Most asylums contained more female than male patients, reflecting the gendered make-up of the population as a whole, due mainly to women living longer both inside and outside the institution.[16] The function of asylums remained fairly constant during the century, even though the emphasis shifted over the latter decades. Earlier, their purpose had been to provide a refuge for lunatics where it was hoped they might be cured through the system of moral treatment. But this spirit of optimism began to falter from mid-century as treatments failed and asylums became 'silted-up' with people suffering from chronic mental and physical conditions, often brought about by extreme poverty and social deprivation. The other role of the asylum was to lock away some of society's most 'undesirable' and problematic members, safely sequestering them out of sight and mind. The Victorian public asylum was, therefore, a temporally specific institution. Protecting society and its inmates from each other, it combined prison, workhouse, home and curative functions in one enormous, sprawling institution.

Rates of lunacy were higher in densely populated urban areas such as London, where they exceeded those of any other county in England and Wales.[17] This phenomenon was partly attributed to the increasingly popular notion of degeneracy, which purported that mental, physical and social pathologies such as insanity, criminality and prostitution were biological 'taints' that could be passed from one generation to the next. Adverse environmental circumstances such as overcrowding, overwork, poverty and excessive alcohol consumption were believed to trigger these conditions. To cope with burgeoning numbers, the LCC Asylums Committee launched an ambitious asylum-building programme.[18] By 1905, 16,539 patients were accommodated in nine LCC asylums, while a further 900 were boarded out in other asylums around the country.[19] In 1906, there were reported to be 55.5 lunatics per 10,000 of the population in London compared to 35.7 across the country.[20] Not only were there proportionately more lunatics in London, but a higher percentage were housed in asylums. By 1909, 98 per cent of the insane in London were detained in asylums, compared to 85 per cent in the rest of England and Wales.[21] Eight out of the ten LCC asylums in operation by this time each contained close to 3,000 patients and staff.

Claybury and Bexley Asylums

Claybury was the first asylum to be built by the LCC and opened in 1893. The architect was George Hine, mentioned above, who was also commissioned by the LCC to design Bexley, Horton and Long Grove asylums. Situated at Woodford in Essex, Claybury was built on 269 acres of land located around nine miles from the City of London.[22] The *London* journal described the main Claybury building as a 'magnificent institution – perhaps the finest asylum in the country' and as having a 'stately and substantial character'.[23] Such opulence for a publicly funded, pauper institution inevitably drew its critics, including the LCC which had not been involved in the original planning and protested that it was too 'ornamental and sumptuous'.[24] The Heath Asylum (renamed the Bexley Asylum in 1905) in Bexley in south-east London was the first asylum to be both planned and built by the LCC. A far more modest and much cheaper affair, it was opened in 1898.[25] Yet, despite the differences between Claybury and Bexley, both asylums were massive institutions designed to accommodate 2,000 patients – 800 male and 1,200 female – together with around 400 staff.[26] Like most other public asylums, they were intended to be as self-sufficient as possible, with their own farm, laundry, needlerooms and workshops. Patients were strongly encouraged to work for two reasons: first, to contribute to the asylum economy, for example by growing food and making asylum clothes; and secondly, because work was considered to be therapeutic.

Asylum spaces were segregated by sex and the level of management and care a patient needed. At Claybury, the male and female 'sides' were separated by the administrative block, recreation hall, kitchen, stores and laundry;[27] here some staff and patients of different sexes might come together within a controlled environment. Areas that were initially out of bounds for the opposite sex were the wards; in 1898, two Commissioners in Lunacy reported that no men should be given keys to the female side except for the medical officers and the chaplain.[28] Until the turn of the century, women were not permitted to enter the male wards or men-only working spaces. Claybury even had different mortuaries for male and female patients.[29] Where space could not segregate the sexes, routines were imposed. For example, both male and female patients attended services in the chapel at Bexley, but at different times.[30] Yet, in large institutions with their labyrinthine corridors and extensive grounds, it was almost impossible to keep men and women apart. Time and again the Commissioners in Lunacy, who were responsible for inspecting asylums and reporting their findings to the Lord Chancellor, revealed that they had found workmen and male artisans with keys to the female side.[31] When male patients were drafted in from other LCC asylums to work at the all-female Manor Asylum at Epsom, the superintendent reported the situation to be 'a constant source of worry and anxiety'.[32]

The other main form of segregation was based on the degree to which patients needed nursing assistance and management. For example, infirmary wards provided intensive nursing care, usually for physical conditions, whereas chronic wards for 'quiet and harmless' patients, often located near workplaces such as the laundry, required very little staffing. Each ward contained at least sixty patients, usually many more, and had at least one dormitory, a day room, a dining area and an outside space called the 'airing court' which functioned as an exercise area and was often surrounded by unclimbable fencing, making it resemble a prison exercise yard.

Space as a Technology of Control

Having set out above how asylum inhabitants were intended to populate different areas of Claybury and Bexley, this section explains how space was employed to regulate and control their behaviour through moral management – an approach based on 'moral treatment', which had been introduced earlier in the century. A psychological system of regulation and surveillance that was unwittingly internalized by patients, moral treatment was designed to subtly coerce them into policing their own behaviour. It was embedded into every aspect of an asylum's structure and processes: the material environment and surroundings, the daily routine and timetable, work and leisure activities – all were encoded with discourses that were intended, in the words of historian J. K. Walton, to 'resocialize the patient into behaviour patterns acceptable to those in authority'.[33] And while moral treatment itself required no specialist medical knowledge as such, early alienists, as psychiatrists were then called, insisted that its success was contingent on the finely calibrated relationship between physician and patient. This, according to Scull, was part of the strategy adopted by the fledgling medical fraternity to ensure that the care and treatment of the insane remained within its discipline.[34]

Focussing on the individual, moral treatment became increasingly impracticable as asylum populations grew.[35] However, similar techniques were applied to larger numbers of people from mid-century through moral management, which was still considered an important method for both treating and controlling large numbers of patients at Claybury and Bexley by the end of the century. 'Extended exercise, real work and occasional diversion are none of them matters to be considered of secondary importance in the proper treatment of the insane', commented two Commissioners in Lunacy in 1896.[36] In 1908, the superintendent of Claybury, Dr Robert Jones, described how the morning routine on the men's side was carried out with near military precision:

> After breakfast is finished, things are cleared, cleaned and put away, the men are booted, cloaked, entered on lists, counted, sorted, and taken out under the care of various groups of attendants numbering nine on to the farm and one in charge of the workshop patients – who are handed over to the heads of the shops. The remaining patients are taken to lavatories, dressed for the courts, hatted and booted by the staff left in the Wards, and they get out into the airing courts by 9.30am ... the patients must get back to their Wards by 12 o'c. having to be collected, counted, undressed, unbooted, slippered and washed before their dinner hour at noon.[37]

It was, therefore, incumbent on architects, including Hine, to take every detail of asylum life into consideration when drawing up plans for new buildings. Spatial arrangements and architecture, material culture such as clothing, interior decoration and furniture, work routines, exercise regimes, amusement programmes and religious instruction were all contrived to control behaviour, circumscribe movement, reinforce class and gender identities, punish and reward, cure and reform. Indeed, these practices were considered to be treatment.[38] And, as such, they came within the jurisdiction of the medical superintendent who was involved in all decisions, however minor. To this end, philanthropist and hospital reformer Henry Burdett insisted that new asylums should not be erected until the medical superintendent had been appointed as he believed it essential 'to have his trained intelligence brought to bear upon every detail of the design'.[39] The medical superintendent at Bexley, Dr T. E. K. Stansfield, who had previously worked as an assistant medical officer under Jones at Claybury, chose the wallpaper for certain day rooms and went so far as to recommend 'Monkey Brand' soap to clean the door brasses.[40] At Claybury, it was left to Jones and the asylum steward to decide on the length of the fall of the bed valances.[41] Jones reported that 'nurses keenly enjoy making their own fresh tea in the Wards and prefer it in small tea pots to great urns full of tea made for all', commenting that it was 'quite daintily served'.[42] Advice on tea-making was, however, unlikely to have been recommended to attendants working on the male wards. Moral management was intended to intensify gender identities, so much so that conforming to normative gendered behaviour was interpreted as a sign of recovery.

The notion of 'gendered spaces', as advocated by moral management, had a significant impact on patients' lived experiences and chances of recovery. Fresh air and outdoor areas such as the asylum grounds and farm were valued for their therapeutic and calming influence on patients' minds. Jones advocated systematized walks for as many patients, both men and women, as possible, commenting that 'Apart from motives of health and cheerfulness, I would urge this as a matter of economy for less clothing would be destroyed, fewer windows broken and there would be more contentment and quietude in the wards'.[43] Yet only male patients could work in the grounds, gardens and on the farm since these spaces were difficult to police in terms of keeping the sexes apart, but also because outdoor work was seen as 'men's work', making them 'more tractable indoors', according to Jones.[44] A similar practice took place at Bexley where the Commissioners reported in 1900 that 70 per cent of male patients were able to walk freely beyond the grounds, most likely meaning the 'airing grounds'. Yet 'no women', they added, 'had this privilege ... being entirely confined to the airing courts for exercise'.[45]

Outside spaces were used for sporting activities that were becoming increasingly popular during the late nineteenth century. Games such as football and cricket were advocated for the lower social classes due to their health-giving benefits and because they instilled into participants the value of discipline and rules;[46] these were exactly the qualities asylums sought to cultivate in their patients. Both male and female patients turned out as spectators at Bexley, where they would have watched from different vantage points.[47] Indeed, Stansfield reported that at Bexley in 1911, around 800 male patients were on the recreation ground every Saturday afternoon, and occasionally during the week 'from 2.30 until about 7 o'clock'.[48]

What, then, of the female patients who accounted for the majority of the asylum population? Which physical therapies were available to them? According to Dr D. Thomson, they were not interested in pursuing such activities: 'women hated exercise, staff and patients alike', he commented.[49] Nevertheless, it was reported in 1903 that Swedish gymnastics with a musical accompaniment had been organized for some of Claybury's female patients.[50] Elaine Showalter has suggested that the action of pounding, wringing-out, hanging and ironing were 'thought to be a useful and effective outlet for the superfluous nervous energy (or anger) of women patients in the laundry'.[51] Efforts to make life in the asylum reflect that which was taking place in the community outside were made, but to a very limited degree. At Claybury, some women were allowed out of the asylum and into the surrounding locale on supervised walks, picnics and shopping trips, as were some male patients. And selected women patients were encouraged to call on friends and neighbours in other wards on Sundays and when the weather was too wet to go outside.[52] There is also evidence that, within limits, new working opportunities were made available to female patients, thus reflecting shifts that were taking place outside the institution. Again, only a few women were offered alternatives to cleaning, needlework, laundry work and, in some institutions, kitchen work. Stansfield reported in 1904 that 'a number of female staff have been employed in working stocking-knitting machines and as tailoresses'.[53] Interestingly, he used the word 'shop' for the tailoresses' workplace, a term normally employed when referring to men's work spaces – for example, workshop, upholstery shop, carpentry shop.[54] In 1908, women patients at Horton were employed to carry out the haymaking in the farmland surrounding the asylum, which the superintendent stated was 'much to their pleasure'.[55] Otherwise, women were confined to their wards, working areas or the prison-like airing courts; the latter of which Jones complained about in 1895, writing that 'It cannot be conducive to mental composure and recovery for patients to pace a bare railed area, with men and women in uniform keeping guard over them at fixed points ... many patients complain of the want of ... distractions'.[56] By 1897, the courts were still surrounded by unclimbable iron fencing but had been planted and contained kiosks with teak seats where patients could sit.[57]

While outside spaces were believed to calm the minds of inmates, asylum interiors were designed to stimulate them, or at least to make the dreary surroundings a little more tolerable. Many alienists were keen to move away from the prison-like environment and, wherever possible, removed features such as bars on the windows. In 1886, attendants as well as medical staff were exhorted to 'render the wards interesting, beautiful, comfortable and home-like'.[58] Jones struggled to create a stimulating environment at Claybury, claiming 'I should like the wards to be a little brighter, the walls are not coloured or painted, nor are there any pictures, birds or plants about'.[59] Clearly funds were found, as three years later he described the wards as 'light, airy, clean and ... eminently comfortable for patients'.[60] Both Bexley and Claybury had carpets on the wards, which at Claybury were transferred to the 'refractory' wards for destructive patients when they became worn.[61] Other proposed 'improvements' included lift-up pedestal closets to replace the male urinals, which were reported to be 'always objectionable'. Similar measures were recommended at Bexley.[62]

The New Mental Hospital

Despite attempts at improving the asylum environment, alienists did not succeed in treating mental disorder on a large scale, which, according to Scull, was conveniently attributed to the scourge of degeneracy.[63] Many doctors were discouraged and disheartened by this failure, their discipline sullied by the stigma of the asylum, which was seen by so many as a place of last resort. The increasing medicalization of mental disorders gathered momentum during the latter decades of the century, renewing the enthusiasm for physical therapies that were devised to act on the mind through the body.[64] In 1909, J. R. Lord, superintendent of Horton Asylum who had previously worked with Stansfield at Bexley, wrote:

> There is a tendency at present to minimise even to adversely criticise the work done in asylums as compared with those institutions more fortunately known as hospitals or infirmaries. The modern asylum has long passed the prison workhouse stage, and its work demands recognition as a mental hospital in every sense of the word.[65]

As people with mental disorders were urged to seek early treatment in order to enhance their chances of being cured, the LCC asylums began to explore how they could prevent those with more acute conditions from being absorbed into the asylum back wards. A separate admission hospital with procedures based on general hospital practices appeared to be the answer. Hine explained: 'With a hospital as a separate and distinct institution, and which does not share in the popular stigma attaching to a lunatic asylum, there will be less reluctance ... to enter a building which by its very name holds out a prospect of cure'.[66]

One such acute hospital for all new female cases was opened at Bexley. Figure 3.1 shows a ward in transition from the old style of asylum with its plants, pictures and rugs, to a new clinical environment, complete with nurses in starched uniforms. In 1902, Stansfield described the building as follows:

> It is conducted strictly on hospital lines: The patient is put to bed on her arrival and remains there until her case has been exhaustively taken and full observations made and recorded as to her various bodily functions and mental habits, when, usually at the expiration of about one week she is got up and, unless the case is recognised as irretrievably hopeless or the patient manifests particularly obnoxious traits ... is gradually given an increasing amount of outdoor exercise until she ultimately, weather permitting, lives in the open air during the day, her meals frequently being served on the lawn ... The non-recoverable ... are transferred to suitable wards in the main building as soon as their condition has been thoroughly gone into.[67]

In 1903, Bexley's sub-committee began to consider the construction of a similar Hospital Villa for male admissions.[68]

Figure 3.1: Ward in Hospital Villa, Heath Asylum, Bexley, c. 1905. Note that this has every appearance of a hospital ward but includes many domestic features such as plants and pictures. Reproduced with permission of the Wellcome Library, London.

According to Hine, the acute hospital was one of the two most important architectural developments to emerge during this period.[69] The second was the villa system. Architectural historian Leslie Topp has described it as being built to embody 'the architectural features of the home, while at the same time breaking up patient populations into smaller units that could be classified more precisely according to behaviour'.[70] Having observed these systems in America and Germany, Stansfield worked with Hine to create at Bexley the first English pauper asylum to incorporate the 'villa system' into its original design.[71] Plans initially comprised three small, self-contained units. Constructed away from the main asylum building, they were placed under the charge of married couples and housed chronic, male working patients. Stansfield wrote that these patients had 'absolute freedom within the grounds. They go to and from their work without supervision, and the doors are open from the time they get up in the morning until they go to bed at night'. All Bexley villas were surrounded by a garden and lawns, with no 'retaining fence of any kind so that the prison element of asylum life is entirely absent'. As ever, moral management pervaded the ideology of the villas, too. Inhabitants were male working patients who were well aware of the consequences of not conforming to asylum rules or slacking in their duties. Stansfield wrote: 'The patients at these villas consider it almost the greatest calamity that could happen to them to be sent back to the main building, and they zealously guard their privileges among themselves'.[72]

Meanwhile, Bexley's North Villa was established for convalescing female patients and based on a similar ideology. Stansfield wrote

> The peculiar value of this villa is ... that it is in every detail an ordinary house; it is not in any way institutionalized: the outer doors are only locked at night, and the patients have free, homelike surroundings ... they do not come into contact with the patients in the main building ... and are consequently never subjected to the demoralising and degrading influences of the chronic institutionalized insane.[73]

It was in many respects not unlike the cottage homes for convalescent mental patients outside the asylum, which Stephen Soanes discusses in Chapter 7 of this volume.

In addition to the admission hospital, other general hospital practices were appropriated by Bexley and Claybury. These included more rigorous admission procedures, the training of attendants and nurses, greater patient observation and more detailed clinical note-taking. Another significant innovation was made by Stansfield in 1902 when he put female nurses in charge of male infirmary wards where the men were physically weak and debilitated, posing less of a physical threat. This action, he claimed, was prompted by the lack of suitable male attendants to provide intensive nursing care following the call for so many to fight in the Boer War.[74] Deploying women to work on male asylum wards, usually as servants subordinated to their husbands, was not an entirely new practice. Bexley was different because women were given authority to run male wards;[75] this practice was bolstered by hospital training and the growing professionalization of asylum nursing, which had become an appealing career alternative to domestic service for many single working-class women from the mid-century.[76] It addition to adding a distinctly clinical character to what had traditionally been male-only spaces, this new practice also smacked of moral management. Women were introduced to wards as moral and sanitary reformers where their 'mothering instincts' were believed to make them naturally suitable for nursing work,[77] as well as imposing a powerful civilizing effect on the patients. The eminent psychiatrist Henry Maudsley argued that when a female nurse was put on a male ward, the patient 'will not resist her violently as he would a man, and will perhaps yield to her persuasion more readily and with less feeling of humiliation'.[78]

How, then, might the arrival of nurses on Bexley's male wards have affected patients? This is an important question bearing in mind that these were homosocial spaces that had always been run by male attendants dressed in uniforms similar to those of prison officers and with a reputation for managing patients using strong-arm, disciplinarian tactics that were more in keeping with the old-style custodial role of the Victorian asylum. Psychologist Phyllis Chesler claimed in *Women and Madness* (1972) that there was a tendency for some groups of men to be framed within a criminal discourse, while women were treated within a medical discourse, both according to their behaviours that were also 'typed by race and class'.[79] It is conceivable that introducing female nurses to male wards changed the character of these spaces, making them more feminine and undermining the masculinity of some male patients, infantilizing and imbuing them with a sense of being 'sick' and powerless, thus making them easier to manage. For example, Bexley patient John L. complained that 'he could not put up any longer with the manner adopted by the nurses towards him' and that 'they treated him like a child'.[80] The same might be said of male patients who were admitted to the acute hospital, which was run along more clinical lines. Dr C. C. Easterbrook, superintendent of Ayr District Asylum, wrote:

> If ... a patient on admission is placed in bed amid hospital surroundings and treated as a sick man, as he really is, he from the outset comes to regard himself as a sick man and not as an injured man, as he is more apt to do if received straightway [*sic*] into the less familiar but readily recognised environment of the ordinary asylum dayroom or parlour ... for ... it is better that his mind should be occupied with the suggestion that he has been and is ill, than that it should become the seat of those more turbulent feelings of injured self-esteem, indignation, and the like, which effectually banish for the time all sense of peace and contentment.[81]

This suggests that new hospital-style practices were simply another form of moral management, drawing the Foucauldian 'clinical gaze' more intensely towards the male patient. Other changes on the ward, such as exchanging the urinals for lift-up pedestal closets, represented another step away from a traditional masculine environment. Indeed, during a period in which masculinity was more widely associated with financial independence, physical strength and technical skills, these wards may have diminished rather than bolstered masculine pride.

Conclusion

Throughout the nineteenth century, lunacy numbers rose at an alarming rate. This was particularly the case in large urban areas such as London where a massive asylum-building programme was implemented at the end of the century to accommodate this burgeoning population. Admission numbers continued to rise, while discharge rates declined, resulting in serious overcrowding. Little progress had been made in understanding the aetiology of mental disorders or in developing effective treatments, reflecting badly on the sub-discipline of early psychiatry. Alienists continued to draw on methods of moral management, which had been established a century earlier, and imbued the structures and practices of the institution with discourses based on class and gender norms to control patients' behaviour.

During the latter decades of the nineteenth century, a number of important shifts began to take place that influenced the character of some asylums and, consequently, the lived experiences of those living and working within them. First, smaller villa-style units offered certain categories of patient a less institutionalized living environment as part of their treatment or as a reward for their productive engagement with asylum life. Secondly, acute hospitals sought to prevent new patients from being absorbed into the asylum's chronic back wards. Other hospital practices were introduced which augmented technologies of surveillance and reconstituted the lunatic as a specific object of knowledge: the mental patient. Male patients, in particular, were encouraged into 'sick' and dependent roles. The third important shift took place in respect of the growing authority of women, albeit limited, brought about by new working opportunities for unmarried women and the professionalization of asylum nursing. Partially as a result of this, spatial boundaries became more porous as men and women began to access areas that had previously been restricted to one sex or another. Men as well as women began to move into new and different spaces. This suggests that the changes taking place in the asylum reflected those outside the institution.

Yet, despite these changes, we should be under no illusion that the movement of female patients continued to be anything other than highly circumscribed. Note that all three villas for the chronic and working patients at Bexley were for men, suggesting that their work was valued more highly. And, despite Stansfield's and Jones's glowing reports of the numbers of men and women who turned out to watch football matches, visit 'friends' on other wards or engage with interior decoration, it is unlikely that their accounts would have survived close scrutiny.[82] As Topp and Moran suggest, it is doubtful that many mentally disturbed patients were able to respond to visual stimulation in the manner that was intended; indeed, a number of authors contributing to their volume have argued that 'in all cases, users reinterpret and subvert the visual aspects of their surroundings', reinforcing an overall negative impression of their treatment.[83] It is a point that is well borne out by Thomas W., a patient at Bexley who, despite living in an environment ostensibly made cheerful by carpets, pictures and birds, complained in 1908 that 'he is like a canary and if not liberated will fall to the bottom of the cage'.[84]

Acknowledgements

My thanks to Jane Hamlett, Lesley Hoskins, Rebecca Preston, Leslie Topp and Hilary Marland for their extremely helpful comments and assistance with producing this chapter.

4 REFUGE OR PRISON? GIRLS' EXPERIENCES OF A HOME FOR THE 'MENTALLY DEFECTIVE' IN SCOTLAND, 1906–1948

Mary Clare Martin

Mental Deficiency and Institutional Care

The Mental Deficiency and Lunacy (England and Scotland) Acts of 1913 provided funding for the institutionalization of those considered to be 'on the borderland of imbecility' at a time of neither universal access to healthcare nor entitlement to education beyond elementary schooling.[1] One explanation historians have offered has been the influence of eugenics: contemporary fears that the 'feeble-minded' required permanent segregation or they would multiply and become a threat to society.[2] Another is that universal elementary education, which was compulsory in Scotland from 1872, and in England and Wales from 1880, drew attention to those who were considered incapable of being educated in ordinary schools.[3] For Mathew Thomson, a historian specializing in psychology and mental deficiency, the 'problem' also concerns the definition of citizenship within new forms of democracy, and new forms of disciplinary medico-legal power.[4]

Despite the potential impact of this legislation on children and adolescents as well as adults, only limited research exists on how these institutions were experienced.[5] Oral history accounts provide mixed responses, though Jane Read has shown how such sources might be problematic.[6] Steve Humphries highlights the opposition of working-class parents to attempts by the authorities to incarcerate disabled children, the grim realities of institutional life and inmates' resistance.[7] Anne Borsay argues that 'once inside, personal identity was systematically attacked'.[8] Pamela Cox claims that 'the transformation from delinquent to defective meant crossing a line of reformability' and that it was harder to exit from mental deficiency institutions than from the juvenile justice system.[9] Other scholars, however, have interpreted the institutional experiences of the mentally deficient and insane more positively. Eighteenth- and nineteenth-century lunatic asylums could be marketed as refuges and increasingly used moral therapy.[10] Hutchison concludes of Baldovan Asylum (founded in 1855) and Larbert National Institution (founded in 1862) that 'within the context of the times, both institutions probably did well in caring for the children in their trust'.[11] Pamela Dale emphazises the commitment to special education and training for employment of the Royal Western Counties Institution in Devon at Starcross, which was mixed sex and for all ages, from 1914 to 1948.[12] Although Kevin Myers has highlighted a case study of parental contestation to their child's certification in 1936, asylums and institutions for the mentally deficient could function as essential aspects of family strategies.[13]

This chapter analyses the experiences of inmates in Waverley Park Home, the third institution for the mentally deficient in Scotland to be established as a voluntary charity. It was founded in 1906 by the Glasgow Association for the Care of Defective and Feeble-Minded Children, with the aim of providing for the welfare, elementary education and training of 'higher-grade, educable, feeble-minded girls'.[14] The environment and social world of this institution are examined through its lived practices and through interactions between staff, inmates, the civic community and external professionals. The essay calls into question the frequent interpretation of inmate behaviour as 'resistance' to prison-like oppressive regimes and indicates that, for some, the home provided a place of refuge. Unlike previous studies, which have regarded such institutions as segregating the mentally deficient from the outside world, it argues that inmates also had a place in the body politic of Kirkintilloch and the city of Glasgow.

The Scottish Context

Matt Egan has characterized Glasgow as Scotland's 'flagship' authority where special education was concerned.[15] Poor relief in Scotland had been voluntary and kirk-based until 1845. While orphan children and lunatics had frequently been boarded out in the community (thus foreshadowing the 'colony' principle) large institutions certified for the mentally deficient were built in Scotland in the inter-war period and continued until the 1990s.[16] In Scotland, elementary education had been compulsory for five to thirteen-year-olds since 1872, compared to 1880 in England and Wales for five-to ten-year-olds.[17] In Glasgow, the school-leaving age was raised to fourteen in 1901 but only in 1918 in England, Wales and Scotland.[18] Special classes for the feeble-minded were established in Glasgow from the 1890s and, from 1901, school boards were required to pay special school fees if parents could not.[19] The Elementary Education (Scotland) (Defective and Epileptic Children) Act of 1906 allowed, but did not oblige, school boards to make provision, while the 1914 Act in England and Wales made this a requirement.[20] The Mental Deficiency and Lunacy Acts of 1913 (for England

and Scotland) instructed local authorities to make suitable arrangements for the 'care and control' of those unable to look after themselves, including adults. The Act identified four categories: idiots, imbeciles, the feeble-minded and moral imbeciles. The feeble-minded were defined as persons who

> from birth or an early age, from mental defectiveness, not imbecility ... require care,
> supervision and control for their own protection or the protection of others, or in the
> case of children, that they by reason of such defectiveness appear to be permanently
> incapable of receiving proper instruction in ordinary schools.[21]

Institutions for those certified under the Mental Deficiency Acts were supervised by a new central administrative body, the Board of Control for Scotland.[22] Whereas in 1903 there were only two Scottish institutions for mentally defective children – and none for adults – by 1925 there was a long list.[23] Indeed, Egan concluded that mental defectives were unnecessarily 'manufactured' in Glasgow, and that the assessment of eight per 1,000 of the school-age population in 1919–20 increased to fourteen per 1,000 in 1937–8.[24]

The Locus of Care

The objects of the Glasgow Association were 'providing and maintaining a home or homes for the protection, elementary education and industrial training' of defective and feeble-minded children and promoting their welfare and after-care.[25] Egan notes that, unlike some similar homes in England, the Association's reports 'avoided eugenics ideology'.[26] Waverley Park Home, near Kirkintilloch, Dunbartonshire, founded in 1906, was a voluntary charity, with a matron, visiting medical officer and a board of directors. The board included ministers, JPs, representatives of Glasgow school boards and parish councils, the local Medical Officer of Health and the chair of the School Board for Glasgow.[27] The first chairman (until 1918) was the psychiatrist, Dr David Yellowlees, consulting physician of Glasgow Royal Asylum at Gartnavel.[28] The House Committee met monthly.[29] There were only three matrons during the period 1906–48 and two doctors – a father and a daughter.[30] Kate Fraser, the Deputy Commissioner of the Board of Control, another doctor's daughter, had a long association with the home.[31] Nurses and assistants cared for the inmates.[32]

Although founded as a charity, and in receipt of endowments and voluntary contributions, most funding came from the state, through school boards, parish councils and, in particular, the Board of Control. This gave the institution a secure financial basis, while its structure gave the staff and managers flexibility and control over their affairs. In the early years, inmates might be certified under the Industrial Schools Act of 1866 or the Children Act of 1908.[33] Initially, the majority of its inmates were over sixteen years old, and 'after-care' was considered 'even more necessary than elementary training'.[34] From 1913, Waverley Park was certified under the Mental Deficiency Act for the reception of juvenile female 'defectives' of school age capable of benefiting by education, and this became the major source of funding.[35] Since the girls could be re-certified from sixteen until the age of twenty-one, the institution covered the period of transition to adulthood, which has been identified as an increased focus of public policy in this period.[36] In 1919 the Board decided to admit only feeble-minded girls under twenty-one.[37] However, attempts to accommodate all 'old girls', who brought no funding, elsewhere in order to focus on younger, educable, school-age girls, were unsuccessful.[38] In 1933 there were 110 inmates, 103 of them certified under the Mental Deficiency Act; by 1948 there were 152.[39] While the prescribed age range for admission was five to sixteen, by the 1940s the committee agreed to accommodate a number of younger children, with more disabling conditions, as a war-time measure.[40] The home was incorporated into the National Health Service in 1948 and closed in 1993.[41]

Between 1906 and 1948, 526 young females were admitted.[42] Most of the 484 entrants after 1914, when case notes began, were classified as 'feeble-minded'. Between 1914 and 1924, one third of admissions were classified as imbecile. Thirty-two of the 171 admissions from 1937 to 1948 were described as imbecile, and four, aged under five, from 1947 to 1948, as idiots. A number had attended day special schools or classes, which accommodated far more children than residential institutions.[43] Conditions included behavioural problems, mental or physical handicap, epilepsy and insanity.[44] Few admissions records mentioned sexual misdemeanours, though a small number had experienced abuse;[45] only two were classified as moral imbeciles.[46] As Egan found for Stoneyetts Certified Institution in Glasgow, concerns about consorting with boys or 'wandering about at night' were often reported by relatives, rather than professionals.[47] Indeed, basic socialization in terms of continence, ability to walk, talk and dress oneself and educational standards, were more significant concerns, especially by the 1940s.[48]

Sources and Methodology

The Waverley Park records demonstrate the challenges of interpreting the experiences of institutional life from differing archival sources.[49] Surviving annual reports from 1906 to 1912 and 1916 to 1923, produced for public view and to raise funds, present the home very positively.[50] So do the Commissioners' bi-annual reports, the Glasgow newspapers, and most written comments by official visitors, whether Commissioners of the Board of Control, managers or representatives of funding bodies such as school boards and parish councils and of voluntary organizations. Conversely, the manuscript committee minutes from

1930 to 1948 suggest that very few were released into the community and that complaints by relatives often led to more punitive treatment. Yet the case notes, kept by the matrons from 1914, could be very positive, describing one child as 'lovable' and another as 'bright' and 'happy'.[51] The 'Inquiry into Matters Arising out of the Methods of Discipline Used at Waverley Park Certified Institution' in 1938, conducted by two Commissioners of the Board of Control in response to allegations of abuse, included the testimonies of two teachers and six girls, and therefore presents a limited number of inmates' voices. However, as these girls were interviewed because they had been threatened with the 'sick needle' for misbehaviour, they were not necessarily representative.[52] Reports generated by external agencies, such as school boards and the Board of Lunacy provide contextualization. These varied sources highlight the hazards of overplaying the phenomenon of 'resistance' by relying on a few striking examples or one type of source. Although refracted through the viewpoints of adults, they nevertheless provide a corrective to the pitfalls of an uncritical reliance on oral history. Thus, the interviewees in Humphries's acclaimed *Out of Sight* justified destructive behaviour as a form of opposition to the regime but never admitted causing harm to other inmates.[53]

This chapter examines the ordering of space within Waverley Park, showing how the environment might be used for illicit purposes and the way that 'resistance' affected other inmates. While 'awkward' relatives might be excluded, the home was made a 'public' space, for local visitors, the general public and specially invited guests, where the inmates could be exhibited. For some girls, Waverley Park provided their only home. The discussion demonstrates that the institution also constituted a political space, a focus of civic pride and of contestation between professionals and voluntary workers as well as parents.

Organizing the Institutional Environment

Cox has argued that 'the ordering of space' was perceived as central to the process of reform in early twentieth-century reformatory institutions for girls, although most were not purpose-built.[54] Waverley Park Home began in an existing mansion and was frequently extended.[55] The initial annual reports for 1908–12, when there were between twelve and thirty-three inmates, commented on the freedom the children had to run about and play and how they were like members of a large family.[56] In 1931, the *Glasgow Herald* cited the chair, Alison McGregor, claiming that it was 'not a house of locked doors' and that the girls were put 'on their honour', so there were few cases of running away.[57] All could move freely within the grounds, and three had parole outside.[58] Nevertheless, by 1930, with about 110 inmates, it had apparently become more regimented. For example, in 1912 the absence of uniform was perceived as an indicator of freedom;[59] but in the 1930s the Commissioners reported on the pleasant aspect of the girls in 'fresh, clean print working frocks', which were in different colours for each activity.[60] One Commissioner noted a marked 'absence of discontent' given that they were a difficult group to deal with, having a 'high degree of intelligence but quite wanting in the powers of self-control'.[61] Just under half (about forty-five of them) were usually in school. Those who had left school (after sixteen) had specific household tasks, unless they were in bed, either through permanent disability or temporary illness. Usually there were about eight in the laundry, six in the kitchen and twenty-five assisting the nurses, doing general housework, or knitting and sewing.[62] Positions of responsibility, often held by the 'old girls', included being matron's maid, staff maid or taking care of the nurses' drawing room or dining room.[63] Others might be in charge of the ironing room, or work in the sewing room.[64] By the 1940s the older girls helped in the residential nursery with the younger children.[65] Inmates were started on simple tasks, given more responsibility if appropriate, and demoted or moved if necessary. Thus, Jessie McInnes, who in 1941 had been breaking dishes in the girls' dining room, was 'doing well' in the laundry in July 1942.[66] In 1937, however, she had been taken from the laundry because she had been difficult to manage.[67] Some girls could only manage limited tasks, such as 'a little dusting'.[68]

In mixed-sex institutions, girls usually did the domestic chores while boys worked outside or in crafts and trades;[69] but at Waverley Park, the children learned gardening and poultry keeping. In the First World War, an assistant taught gardening and the girls ploughed a field and planted potatoes, which were sold at a profit.[70] By the 1930s, eight usually worked in the garden.[71] In 1937, one girl was in charge of the poultry, assisted by two others.[72] Garden work was considered to have beneficial effects on the inmates' health; it was commended by the Commissioners and was reported as enjoyable. Thus in 1941, one inmate, aged forty, was 'devoted to livestock' and worked in the aviary.[73] Cox noted that many such institutions were remarkably successful financially and Waverley Park was no exception.[74] In 1912, all the sewing and laundry of the house was managed internally;[75] in 1939 no domestic servants were employed.[76] Garden produce and fancy work were sold, adding to the funds.[77] The home was considered cheaper to run per head than most Scottish institutions.[78]

Cox has suggested that, in Home Office certified schools, which included industrial and reformatory schools for the neglected and delinquent, education was neglected in favour of domestic skills; trained teachers were rarely employed as the girls left school at fourteen.[79] Schools for the mentally defective, however, catered for the age range up to sixteen, starting at age five in Scotland.[80] In 1909 Waverley Park claimed to be the first home in Scotland to be certified as an Industrial School for mentally deficient girls.[81] Its school was highly praised, the teachers being experts in special education;[82] this was also the case at the 'showpiece' school at Starcross in Devon.[83] There was one schoolroom in 1912 and three by 1920.[84] In 1916 the school was attended by day scholars sent by Kirkintilloch School Board.[85] The Commissioners' reports on the schooling provided were usually extremely positive. Exceptionally, in 1937, Dr Kate Fraser argued that children in the lower class were not sufficiently subdivided, since nine were ineducable, resulting in the others receiving less attention and education. In 1937, older girls who had left school attended an afternoon handwork class, continuing to develop their skills in fancy sewing and painting.[86] The inmates had recreation and no housework on Saturdays.[87] Leisure activities included a percussion band, Girl Guides, films, reading by the fire and listening to the gramophone.[88]

However, in 1938, the inquiry into methods of discipline revealed internal tensions between staff.[89] A teacher reported that the matron came over every day uninvited to see if the girls were behaving.[90] Conversely, the matron and managers claimed that the teacher could not control the children without the strap, which was forbidden, and had appealed for the matron's assistance.[91] A girl had refused to join in the dancing and been told to sit down. The matron took her away and later reported that she had been given the 'sick needle', to keep her quiet, been very sick and had diarrhoea. She had been given apomorphine, but the doctor, who later admitted that this was intended as a punishment rather than therapy, had only given consent over the telephone.[92] In the inquiry, the teachers reported that the girls were too regimented. It was also stated that the school-age children had been reading comics in class and complained that they had to crochet in their free time.[93] The managers responded that it was beneficial to the girls to have their time occupied.[94] However, it seems that 1938 was a moment of exceptional instability because of the arrival of new teachers. The matron felt that the teachers encouraged girls who needed to be 'kept under'.[95] Despite the criticisms of the matron made by the Commissioners in the report of 1938, she remained in post while both teachers left within a few months.[96]

Transgression, Resistance and Inmate Interactions

The counterpart to the organized surface of the home was misbehaviour and the illicit use of space. Such actions might be interpreted as demonstrating inmates' agency and their resistance to the institution. Certainly some of the acts were deliberately rebellious. Escape, consorting with men and attempted suicide constituted extreme forms of the subversion of the purposes of the institution. Tradesmen complained of being accosted or chased by girls working in the garden.[97] One inmate tried to hit a gardener with a spade.[98] In 1931, two girls were 'behaving indecently' behind bushes in the garden.[99] In 1938, others stole beetroot from the garden and boiled it in the laundry.[100] In 1947, Mary McDonald had been reinstated in the laundry but was found to be tearing up garments and selling them as rags to ragmen.[101] One girl attempted suicide by jumping into the canal.[102] Others found ways of meeting men, both inside and outside the institution.[103] Escapes mostly occurred through walking out of the grounds or climbing out of windows.[104] In 1937, Theresa Jamieson, who had already escaped and been locked up, stole a nurse's uniform and fled through a skylight.[105] However, the number of overnight escapes was small, less than one a year overall.[106]

Cox has acknowledged the disturbing implications of bullying within institutions, but most studies focus on celebrations of resistance.[107] However, to classify all acts of misbehaviour simply as resistant would be to overlook the complexity of their meaning, their actual effects and the context in which they arose. Routines might, for example, be disrupted through the physical or mental condition of the inmates, rather than through intentional resistance. The daily registers record the occurrence of girls' epileptic fits.[108] One inmate was taken from garden work for eating leaves instead of picking them up.[109] In the 1940s, some children were removed from school because they were ineducable. Thus, from 1944 to 1948, the matron recorded of Jane Baird: 'memory very poor and detached', 'absolutely devoid of powers of concentration' and 'little more than a baby mentally'.[110]

Further, violence, theft or quarrelling, which might be viewed as resistance to the institution, also affected the well-being of other inmates, as well as staff. In 1943, Mary McDonald, who was helping in the residential nursery, neglected the younger children and stole their food.[111] In February 1944 it was recorded of Anna Calder that 'hardly a day passes without a quarrel with some girl. Most difficult to manage and a menace to younger girls'.[112] In January 1931, Helen Mclaren, who had been in bed for two weeks 'got up and burned a good suitcase full of new clothing'.[113] In 1943, Margaret Grant threw a chair down the dormitory, striking a girl on the eyebrow.[114] The most able could be the most difficult to control. It was recorded of Lily Hunter: 'beautiful china painting, needlework ... good houseworker ... ungovernable temper and easily provoked'; in 1930, she 'struck a number of girls and nurses'.[115] In 1931, Helen McGregor threw slates around the classroom.[116] In 1942, Margaret Grant had stolen a number of items from a girl's bedroom, including a gold ring, which she put down the lavatory.[117] In 1941, one inmate frightened newly admitted girls by telling 'terrible tales of men coming in the verandah and fire escape during the night, armed with knives and going under patients' beds'.[118] One older girl allegedly compelled the younger girls to behave indecently.[119] Indeed, younger girls might be said to have exercised 'agency' by complaining about others' advances.[120] In 1940, when Anna Ferguson attacked a girl, other inmates restrained her while they waited for the nurse to arrive, indicating their role in mutual protection.[121] Thus, while rebellious behaviour may have been a response to institutionalization, it also appears to have made the environment less pleasant for other inmates. The concept of resistance is also complicated by the managerial situation within the Home. The 1938 inquiry, discussed above, reveals internal tensions between staff, notably the new teachers and the matron, and differing interpretations of the girls' behaviour or misbehaviour.[122]

Relationships with the Local Community

The organizers of the home, both paid officials and voluntary management, were able to exert considerable control over interactions with outsiders. They also managed external contacts so that visitors were encouraged when required, and could contribute to the reputation of the home through their glowing reports. Walsh argues that Scottish lunatic asylums were more deeply embedded in civic culture than their English equivalents, and the home would appear to exemplify this tradition.[123] As a charity, it attracted donations and gifts from 'kind local friends'.[124] The visitors' books commented on the happy appearance of the children, the exceptions being adverse comments on the state of the building.[125] Many Scottish and English institutions organized entertainments for the general public;[126] at Waverley Park, a concert was given by two Boy Scout troops in 1911.[127] In 1919, the school-age children gave a Christmas entertainment of choruses and recitations and, in September 1921, a display of musical drill, dancing and singing.[128] On that day 'the doors were thrown open to the public' and an exhibition of girls' work in crochet, embroidery, knitted garments, wool rugs and china painting 'attracted a large number of ladies'.[129] Such sales were held frequently; that in 1939 raised £98 12s 3d.[130]

Waverley Park inmates were also visible in Kirkintilloch and the city of Glasgow. They were given a free pass to the cinema every Saturday, visited the circus and were invited to concerts and entertainments in the Town Hall.[131] They attended church on alternate weeks and Roman Catholic girls were taken separately.[132] Indeed, attendance at public events was perceived as a mark of progress and a significant aspect of socialization.[133] Commissioners approved the policy of providing special clothes for trips outside, to foster individuality.[134] Some contacts with the opposite sex were approved, such as dances held with the boys from Lennox Castle from 1939.[135] Each year the *Glasgow Herald* reported the annual meeting of the Glasgow Association with approving comments.[136] The suggestion that inmates had a place in the body politic contrasts with Thomson's argument that the 'feeble-minded' were excluded from citizenship.[137] However, such participation was conditional on appropriate behaviour. One child was prevented from attending the cinema because she dirtied the seat.[138] In December 1940, Agnes Campbell behaved so badly at entertainments when men were present that she was also banned.[139]

The staff also controlled children's access to relatives, in part at least for their own convenience. In August 1930, visits were reduced from once a week to once a month for all children at the matron's recommendation.[140] Parents, grandparents or brothers whose behaviour was considered abusive were prevented from visiting.[141] Relatives of one girl were banned for a year, while another inmate was described as 'quieter – in better health' after visits were stopped.[142] However, it was sometimes recorded that children seemed much better after either a visit home, or a day-time visit from a relative.[143] Although requests for temporary leave of absence (for example to see sick parents) were usually refused, girls had regular scheduled visits to family or relatives.[144] The power of the Mental Deficiency Act could, however, extend into the parental home. Thus in 1918, when a child was allowed home for one day only, the mother 'kept child until brought back by Matron'.[145] In 1937, another girl, who had escaped and got married, but had then been charged with theft, was found under her parents' bed. As a result, her parents and husband were to be prosecuted.[146]

Between 1906 and 1920, fewer girls were discharged to other institutions than to parents or private guardianship. By 1921, this pattern had been reversed.[147] Initially, most of the 'feeble-minded' went to Woodilee Lunatic Asylum (founded 1875), which, from 1900, had a special unit for 'defectives', or to Stoneyetts (which had been built in 1913 as a colony for epileptics) or to Merryflatts (an asylum attached to Govan Poor House). From 1929, larger numbers went to the newly founded Caldwell House Certified Institution; the most (eighty-one) went to Lennox Castle Certified Institution – the largest mental deficiency institution in Britain, with 1,200 beds. Others went to lunatic asylums or hospitals such as Stobhill.[148] While this pattern contrasts with the home's original intention of training 'higher grade, educable' girls and returning them to the community, it reflects the attitudes of the doctor and matron and the increasing availability of certified institutions in Scotland. Thus, the response to requests from relatives for girls to leave, or to enquiries from the funding bodies once they reached the age of sixteen, was nearly always that they were not fit for outside life. Even when the Secretary of State for Scotland asked for a girl to be allowed home in 1939, the request was refused.[149] In 1938, the teachers commented that the matron seemed to be more concerned with 'suppressing what was bad than with fostering what is good, which is the basis for socialisation'.[150] The managers also defended the principle of 'permanent care', popularized by Mary Dendy, founder of Sandlebridge colony.[151] In England, indoor domestic service provided a 'way out' of certified institutions, but in Scotland, 'except where textile employment continued to dominate, by 1931, domestic service was the main occupation of Scottish women', so there was less demand for servants from institutions.[152] However, the doctor and matron were reluctant to agree to licensed discharge even when work opportunities did present themselves. In

1937, for example, when a local special-school teacher wished to employ Helen MacDougall as a domestic servant, this was refused.[153] However, by 1940 Mac-Dougall was 'doing well' in service with a minister's wife and was discharged in 1947.[154] When more girls were tried in domestic service in the 1940s, the Commissioners, who had pressed for this development, described it as 'progressive'.[155]

Haven in a Heartless World?

For some, the home functioned as a refuge or haven rather than as a prison or place of confinement. As at Starcross in Devon, a significant number of children were admitted due to family break up or their impact on other siblings.[156] A mother who took trouble reading picture books to her child was persuaded that the home would provide better care than she could.[157] Some elderly relatives and friends could no longer cope, as in the case of an eighty-year-old lodger who had cared for a child but could not manage her convulsions.[158] For some parents, even short visits home could be problematic. In 1937, for example, one epileptic girl who had gone home 'on licence' was 'brought back before her time ... as her mother could not manage her'.[159] Some relatives had internalized ideas about the need for supervision even before the passing of the Mental Deficiency Act of 1913. In 1911, Glasgow School Board reported that 'the parents are extremely anxious that the girl should be admitted to the Home, as they find it very difficult to give her the close supervision she requires'. As the child was over sixteen, her parents had to pay 7s 6d per week.[160] After 1913, in some cases, the Mental Deficiency Act would fund life-long residential care for all age groups.

Since a patient who did not attract government funding was unlikely to be placed elsewhere, Waverley Park was left with ten to fifteen 'old girls', who had no other home. Six died there, from 1969 to 1983, aged between seventy-eight and ninety-three.[161] Some were clearly attached to the institution. In 1942, twenty-six-year-old Helen Galloway, an inmate for twenty years, used to weep bitterly when out at service and plead to be taken back.[162] Others might choose to prolong their stay, against parental wishes, to further their education.[163]

Throughout the period, the practical organization of the home, including food and clothing was commended.[164] The general health of the inmates was considered good, with access to medical and dental care, and a significant improvement in the health of some.[165] The quality of the teaching was praised, as were arrangements for recreation.[166] Nevertheless, none of these factors may have compensated, from the girls' perspective, for the loss of freedom and the company of family members.

It is an open question whether the atmosphere was repressive. Although beating was consistently forbidden, in 1938 the teachers alleged that the children appeared to have an unhealthy preoccupation with punishment. One girl who was interviewed said 'You can't get peace to live here', though admitting she had been difficult. The teachers criticized the way some staff spoke to the girls.[167] Conversely, the managers claimed in 1938 that, according to the register, only twelve girls out of 144 resident had been punished in three years, two of them twice. A standard punishment was deprivation of privileges, especially entertainments, and Commissioners advised in 1938 that this should not be for long periods.[168] Spatial isolation was another punishment; in 1940, one girl was given bromide for 'indecent behaviour' and placed in the night observation dormitory.[169] Being put to bed was another penalty. One girl spent ten days in bed for speaking to a man in the adjacent housing scheme and receiving a parcel from him; another girl got six weeks in bed for running away and six weeks with no privileges.[170] One was admonished by the doctor and had always to be in the presence of a nurse, another was given castor oil and a bath for running away and spending the night with two men.[171] The final solution was to move the inmate elsewhere.[172] However, for many, confinement after leaving Waverley Park was not permanent. Few former inmates were named in the visitors' books for Lennox Castle (from 1930 to 1986) and some were discharged from Woodilee.[173] As occurred elsewhere, there were mass escapes when the system was breaking down in the Second World War, and those from Lennox Castle included many former Waverley Park inmates.[174] Thus, although the Waverley Park records might suggest many former inmates endured a lifetime of institutionalization, in practice the evidence for this is limited.

Conclusion

This chapter has attempted to reconstruct the social world of an enclosed institution, the interaction of inmates with their environment and the relationship of the organization with an urban setting and civic community nearby. Described as a home, it apparently constituted an orderly working community in which education was valued and skills training was provided, adapted to the capabilities of individuals. In contrast with mixed-sex institutions, the garden provided the girls with opportunities for outdoor work that were popular and beneficial. The care given to education resembles that in Starcross in Devon and contrasts with Cox's research on Home Office certified schools. In theory, attention was paid to the girls' self-esteem and concern for their appearance by providing good quality clothes for trips outside. However, by the 1930s, the doctor and matron were reluctant to release girls into the outside world, and were prepared to invoke the principle of 'permanent care' and even to challenge the Commissioners of the Board of Control or the Secretary of State. This is significant given that, as 'higher-grade' mental defectives, the girls at Waverley Park within the category of 'feeble-minded' most likely to be released and, in England and Wales, to go into domestic service. Yet, since some former inmates were released soon after their admittance to other institutions, other institutional staff clearly held more positive views of their capabilities. However, rather than this group being debarred from citizenship, the home acquired a particular status within Glasgow as a civic community. Displays of inmates outside the institution occurred on a weekly basis, while their craft work was admired and purchased. Such practices were common in Scotland. The home had a place within the civic fabric of Glasgow. Even when Commissioners of the Board of Control made trenchant criticisms of the regime in 1938, it was so well regarded that the matron continued in post for another ten years and retired with a pension and two inmates as domestic servants.[175]

This essay demonstrates the problems with defining behaviour which might be injurious to other inmates, as 'resistance'. Whereas previous studies have often celebrated acts which challenged the authorities, this investigation has shown how theft, violence and 'interfering with' other children might affect others negatively. Moreover, routines could be disrupted as much through inmates' physical or mental conditions as through deliberate opposition. Indeed, it is problematic to judge 'resistance' from a few high-profile cases rather than through systematic analysis of the available records. At Waverley Park the entertaining stories of escape and violent behaviour relate to a small minority of inmates.

Although the inquiry of 1938 at first appears to display a shocking level of abuse, this needs to be contextualized within the institution's temporary instability, as well as the relatively small number of punishments. For inmates who had no other home, or whose relatives and friends were unable or unwilling to support them, Waverley Park Home provided material care, work adapted to the capabilities of individuals, and the opportunity to develop skills in craft work which could foster employability. Judgement as to whether it fostered greater self-esteem than the 'community care' of the present awaits the oral historian.

Acknowledgements

I am indebted to Alistair Tough and his colleagues at the National Health Service Greater Glasgow and Clyde Health Board Archives (hereafter NHSGGCA HB) and also to staff at Glasgow City Archives (hereafter GCA) for their advice and assistance. I thank Marguerite Dupree, Colin Heywood, Mathew Thomson and Bernard Harris for discussions and Iain Hutchison for comments on the text. I am also grateful for Rebecca Preston, Lesley Hoskins and Jane Hamlett for their careful and patient editing.

5 PAUPERS AND THEIR EXPERIENCE OF A LONDON WORKHOUSE: ST MARTIN-IN-THE-FIELDS, 1725–1824

Jeremy Boulton and John Black

The Workhouse as an 'Institution'

Although workhouses had been constructed before the eighteenth century some 2,000 were built in England following the enabling legislation of what is often called the Workhouse Test Act of 1723. The workhouse movement in London was particularly vigorous and highly distinctive; most London parishes of any size were operating these establishments by the middle of the eighteenth century. As the geographer David Green emphasizes, the 1834 New Poor Law in London was not followed by a wave of new building, since almost all metropolitan parishes had already integrated indoor relief as part and parcel of their mixed welfare provision.[1] Such workhouses were designed to deter applications for relief, which could be refused if paupers would not enter them. In this sense the Workhouse Test Act anticipated the New Poor Law by over 100 years. The poor were to be subjected to the discipline of work and religious instruction. Lay religious societies, which aimed to reform the manners of the English people, were a further spur to the founding of workhouses in this period.[2]

Tim Hitchcock's doctoral thesis is still the starting point for those interested in the early history of London's workhouses. Green's recent magisterial *Pauper Capital* (2010) contains the first modern analysis of their role in London's welfare system from the end of the eighteenth century. Other recent work focuses on their contribution to the care of particular social groups, such as children, the elderly or the sick.[3] The experience of those living in London's workhouses is likely to have differed significantly, in some respects, from that of those inhabiting provincial institutions.[4] London establishments were often much bigger than their counterparts in the country; they contained an average of 201 inmates in 1776 compared to the national average of between twenty and fifty.[5] Large workhouses required more extensive regulation, were run on heavily bureaucratic lines and were usually governed and operated by experienced (if not always competent) professionals.[6]

Although towns and cities had long had hospitals, in the eighteenth century institutional life came to be experienced much more frequently. The wave of newly founded voluntary hospitals, asylums and especially workhouses transferred a significant amount of what had been essentially domestic, household-based activity to a non-familial, institutional setting. It was the London poor, more than any other social group, who were first to experience this sea-change in living arrangements. By the end of the eighteenth century, the care of the sick, elderly, lunatic, orphaned and foundlings, together with the relief of the destitute, had been transferred from household to institution in most parts of the capital city.

This chapter examines institutional life in the form of the parish workhouse of St Martin-in-the-Fields. St Martin's, a large (approximately 25,000 inhabitants for most of the eighteenth century), relatively wealthy, parish in the West End of London, was one of the first in London to erect a workhouse. It opened in 1725 and remained integral to the parish's poor relief system until about 1868. The building itself was demolished to make way for an extension to the National Gallery between 1871 and 1886.[7] This chapter considers in particular the built structure and spatial organization of the workhouse; its population; the making and breaking of rules; and inmate responses to their environment and to the intentions of the authorities.

St Martin's workhouse was relatively large – at its peak it contained 800–900 people – one of the biggest in London. Over the 100-year period of this study more than 50,000 individuals spent some time there. Experience of the institution was not confined solely to the inhabitants of the parish of St Martin-in-the-Fields. Thousands of inmates had been born in the provinces, and thousands more were removed from the workhouse under the settlement laws or as vagrants and sent back to towns and villages across England, Wales, Scotland and Ireland. There is no reason to think (other than its size) that the lived experiences of its inmates differed significantly from others in the London area.

The Built Structure and the Internal Organization of Space

The internal architecture of the institution was far from fixed. Throughout its history the workhouse was continually reconfigured, extended and once completely rebuilt (1770–2). Rather than referring to a unitary structure called 'the workhouse' it might be more accurately described as the 'workhouse complex' or 'workhouse site'. Over time buildings were purchased and redeveloped to expand the institution, or were purpose-built from scratch. The site also included Archbishop Tenison's Library and School (founded 1684 and 1697 respectively) and the offices of those running what was a professional and extensive parish bureau-cracy.[8] Throughout the period, as new needs were identified, or as new moral, medical or practical considerations arose, buildings on the site were erected, knocked down or redesigned, repaired and redecorated.[9]

There seem to be no surviving eighteenth- or early nineteenth-century plans or views of the workhouse. A ground plan and elevations exist for the institu-tion on the eve of its demolition in 1871, but this cannot be taken as a guide to its internal configuration in the eighteenth century.[10] Before the 1770–2 rebuilding, the 1746 Rocque Map depicts a smaller structure occupying only the western and northern sides of the churchyard of St Martin-in-the-Fields.[11] The original 1725 building was extended and altered over time. By 1769, how-ever, the workhouse was said to be in a 'very Ruinous Condition and some parts thereof in danger of Falling' which prompted the rebuilding in the following year.[12] The entire site was located on and around a large parochial graveyard. This ground was in heavy use between 1725 and 1778, and again in the early nineteenth century, but parts of it were used for building during the eighteenth century. The 1871 plan clearly shows structures, including a laundry, located on top of it. The workhouse, therefore, had an intimate relationship with the dead, which went beyond housing the parish morgue and providing the place where between 15 and 20 per cent of the parish's inhabitants would die.[13]

In 1871 the three principal blocks of the institution were portrayed by the architectural artist Charles J. Richardson.[14] The block that fronted Hemmings Row contained on the ground floor the women's dining hall, one of the women's wards, work rooms for men and women, the men's infirmary and the workhouse school. The block that fronted Duke's Court contained the men's dining room and a number of unnamed rooms. It is notable that the ground floor windows of the 1871 institution are barred, suggesting that the institution was concerned to keep inmates inside and interlopers out. Archbishop Tenison's School (and for-merly also Library) and adjoining workhouse structures (which contained two further women's wards and the workhouse kitchen in 1871) were also depicted.[15] There is no available elevation of the buildings that lay next to St Martin's Place, on the east. On the 1871 plan these included a men's ward and the parish morgue. Although there had clearly been significant changes between the 1772 rebuilding and the structure of 1871, it seems likely that much of the external appearance of the Victorian building dated from the late eighteenth century.

Paupers were placed in wards after entry. For much of the period individual ward numbers are given in the admission registers. Unfortunately it is not clear what particular function each ward had. Nor can it be assumed that the inmates remained in the wards in which they were initially placed, since it is obvious that they were moved as their status (age and health) changed. Some wards were allo-cated to the sick, with particularly distinctive diseases having their own spaces

– notably, after 1772, an 'itch' ward and a foul ward (for venereal patients). Adult wards were always segregated by gender, and thus married couples would have been separated at night. Only in 1820 were the sexes separated during the day.[16] There is little sign that the elderly were given any special treatment although they might be given more leave of absence and excused from working in the workhouse sheds. There were wards for nursing and expectant mothers. Very young children mostly stayed with their mothers. Each ward had its own nurse. Just as in most private houses at this time, beds were commonly shared.[17] Even relatively young children (aged between twelve and thirteen for example) shared a bed with an unrelated adult of the same sex. Jonas Hanway, philanthropist and writer, in remarks first published in 1775, condemned bed-sharing in London's workhouses, with anywhere up to eight children in the same bed and the sick sharing beds with the healthy.[18] In addition to the risks to health posed by bed-sharing, there were, as we shall see below, more sinister possibilities.

Most London workhouses in the eighteenth century served as local hospitals for the parish poor.[19] The erection of the St Martin's establishment, with its sick wards and in-house medical personnel, destroyed a local network of parish nurses who had hitherto looked after the sick poor in their own houses.[20] Increasingly the workhouse became the first port of call for the sick and dying, particularly as its medical facilities expanded. The 'hospital' function actually distorted patterns of workhouse residence as a large number of inmates died shortly after entry. Death rates declined with length of stay. So significant did its medical function become that even parishioners who were relatively well off were occasionally treated in its sick wards. The workhouse sent fewer inmates to public hospitals after the 1760s than before, preferring in-house medical treatment. In 1784 all parish lunatics were brought back from Harrison's private madhouse. But in 1805 the parish reconsidered this policy and began sending those considered dangerous to Warburton's private madhouse, retaining only the 'inoffensive'.[21]

The widespread nineteenth-century distinction between 'casual' and 'settled' inmates does not seem to have been reflected in any explicit spatial configuration throughout most of our period.[22] However, by 1817, the workhouse authorities distinguished between 'relieving wards' for the old and infirm, 'lock up' wards (only for women) and dormitories for men.[23] By the end of our period, too, greater sensitivity to the realities of downward social mobility meant that a few inmates thought to be of distinctively higher social status were allocated to a small 'quality ward'.[24]

Other structures in the workhouse included sheds where the able bodied worked at a variety of tasks, generating a fluctuating income. Workhouse-based industries almost invariably failed to make a net profit in this period.[25] There were also specialized rooms such as the bakery, a porter's lodge, the kitchen and a laundry. The multi-functional nature of the institution was reflected in its internal layout. When the emphasis on a particular function was changed, wards and rooms were unsurprisingly changed to accommodate this.

The Population of the Workhouse

The population fluctuated significantly in size, both over time and during the year. Applications for entry peaked in winter months and fell during the spring and summer. Levels of unemployment and therefore hardship were much higher during the colder weather. The workhouse must have been a very different, less crowded, place in summer than it was in winter.[26] It is not always straightforward to quantify workhouse populations before nineteenth-century censuses are available since, due to the often short stays that inmates made, there is a huge difference between numbers admitted every year and the number inhabiting the institution at any one point in time. Fortunately running totals of those living in the workhouse were recorded in surviving accounts and day books throughout the eighteenth century (see Figure 5.1).[27] The sharp dip in numbers in the graph relates to the period of rebuilding in the early 1770s, when the parish temporarily rented a house to accommodate the poor. Otherwise the graph shows how the rebuilding in 1770–2 dramatically increased the capacity of the institution. It also shows how use made of the workhouse could change over time. Although the institution was the third largest in London, as reported in a survey of 1803, it sank very considerably in the metropolitan rankings after 1834, partly because many of its young children were moved to Highwood House, a separate institution, from 1819.[28]

Its multi-functional nature also meant that it drew inmates from all age groups in the parish. Estimating the breakdown of ages living in the workhouse at any one time, as opposed to at admission, is again far from straightforward since older inmates tended to spend longer in the institution than younger ones and many inmates spent only a very short time there. For this reason the flow of admissions provides a highly unreliable guide to the age structure at any one point in time.

A reconstruction of the age structure of the workhouse at its maximum winter capacity has been carried out at selected dates. In addition to changing in size over time, the population experienced a change in age distribution. From the later eighteenth century there were proportionately fewer young children and more elderly people living in the institution. This finding may be partly explained by the fact that, in the eighteenth century, workhouse authorities increasingly sent children out to nurse or apprenticeship. It might also reflect elderly inmates tending to stay in the institution for longer in the later eighteenth and early nineteenth centuries.[29] Although the composition of its population changed, throughout the period our establishment contained, as was common in eighteenth-century urban workhouses, people of many different ages, from the newborn to the young, the adult and the very old – what was known in later centuries as a 'General Mixed Workhouse'.[30]

Figure 5.1: **Average number of inmates in St Martin-in-the-Fields Workhouse,
with maximum numbers, in each year, 1725–1817.**

The average length of stay of inmates in workhouses was relatively short. Figures calculated from admission and discharge registers demonstrate clearly that age was positively correlated to length of stay in St Martin's. An exception to this rule were those aged between five and nine at admission who remained for the comparatively lengthy period of around a year while attending the workhouse school.[31] Those entering in their late fifties and above stayed at least three times as long (well over a year on average) than did teenagers and young adults. Again, this reflects the greater health of those in younger age groups, and the greater likelihood of incapacity, unemployment, disability and chronic sickness as age increased. The figures on length of stay are similar to those found in a recent study of the Marylebone workhouse.[32] It should be noted again that the average figures conceal the distortions produced by the large numbers of inmates who were very sick or dying at the point of entry.

Calculations of length of stay in institutions usually refer only to discrete residential episodes. What is far more telling, and which reflects far better the use made of the institution by inmates, is the number of times *each individual pauper* entered the establishment. Of the approximately 50,000 individuals admitted to St Martin's in this 100-year period, the majority of inmates, nearly three quarters, experienced only one stay in the workhouse. Just under one in seven, 13.5 per cent, entered twice. Only a small proportion, 1.4 per cent, entered the workhouse ten times or more. It is essential to realize that the latter high-profile individuals were unrepresentative of the way in which most inmates experienced the institution. George Berwick, a farrier, seems to have entered no less than fifty-nine times (sometimes but not always with his wife) between 1744, when he was aged thirty-three, and 1779 when he died, in the workhouse, said to be aged seventy-three. Berwick was sent to Bridewell (a penal institution which typically punished petty offenders with short periods of hard labour) from the workhouse at least twice (in 1769 and 1775) for disciplinary offences, although he seems never to have absconded or run away.[33] Berwick fits the mould of the troublesome inmate of the sort described by Green in his recent article on pauper protests.[34]

Women formed a significant majority of those admitted, although this was beginning to change towards the end of our period. Some 68 per cent of all those admitted were female.[35] This is typical of workhouse populations in the eighteenth century, given that poverty was concentrated more heavily among women and girls, who earned less, were at risk of bastard bearing and who formed the majority of those in precarious domestic service.[36] The two sexes often had significantly different experiences of workhouse life. To take one very clear example, adult females (aged thirty and over) tended to stay longer than men of comparable ages. Women in their late forties or above spent on average 100 more days in the workhouse than men of similar ages. The explanation for such differences lies both with the relative health of those admitted and with local gender-specific employment chances. Beliefs about different training and schooling requirements, as well as differential employment prospects of boys and girls, may explain why boys aged between five and fourteen stayed significantly longer in the workhouse than did girls of comparable ages. The gender imbalance at admission in the second decade of the nineteenth century was significantly different from that pertaining for most of the preceding century. There are a number of reasons for this change. The most significant is probably a surge in male entrants following the large scale demobilizations following the end of the Napoleonic Wars.

Rules, Regulations and Pauper Disobedience

Green has argued that the nineteenth-century workhouse was often 'a deeply contested site of resistance'.[37] Almost all institutions, be they prisons, almshouses, hospitals or workhouses, attempted to regulate and control the daily life of inhabitants. Indeed, demands of efficiency, security and cleanliness mean that modern institutional living is still subject to extensive regulation and imposed routine. Workhouses were no exception and some in London, including several in parishes neighbouring St Martin's, published detailed rules and regulations in the eighteenth century. It is known that officials from St Martin's visited nearby establishments, so it is likely that they would have been familiar with rules then current.[38] It is clear from the parochial records that the inmates of St Martin's were subject to a list of largely coercive regulations, which were revised, reworded and supplemented throughout our period. A short series of rules and regulations survives for 1775, and another more comprehensive set was devised in the early nineteenth century and published in 1828.

The rules of 1775 mostly regulate the activities of the master, matron and ward nurses. Nurses were allowed out every day to go on errands for inmates but were not to bring in spirituous liquor or attempt to charge the inmates fees. Inmates were not allowed to leave the workhouse without permission from the churchwardens, overseers or the workhouse master (i.e. the steward). Inmates known to 'behave well' were allowed to attend services at church twice on Sundays. The porter and his wife, too, were forbidden to take bribes from inmates seeking to leave without permission or from visitors seeking access. Work was compulsory for those who were able; nurses were supposed to eject inmates who attempted to loiter in their wards instead. Paupers entering drunk after a leave of absence, or who behaved in a disorderly manner, were to be reported to the master.[39] The 1828 rules were longer (sixty-one in all) and far more prescriptive. They set out a visiting day (Tuesday), ordered that the porter search visitors and inmates for illicit drink and decreed that all able paupers were to attend 'the prayers and religious services of the House'. The rules also prescribed meal and working times and the form of diet; and 'that the liberty of the gate be granted on Sundays, after divine service, to the men and women alternately, and on Tuesdays to the men, and on Thursday to the women'.[40] Persons guilty of blasphemy or obscene conversations were to be reported to the Board. Those returning drunk would not be allowed to go out again for one month. Leave of absence was not to be longer than one day without permission. Those admitted would be scrutinized and cleaned, and foul clothes would be burnt. Smoking tobacco was allowed only in the halls and grounds.[41] It appears that there was a greater moral and religious tone prevailing in the third decade of the nineteenth century, and probably earlier. Rule sixty prescribed that 'when a boy or girl is apprenticed from the House, a Bible and Common Prayer book shall be presented to each child'. The fifty-fifth rule set out that 'the Rules, so far as they respect the Paupers, shall be hung up in the several wards, and pointed out by the Nurse to every new comer, in order that no one may plead ignorance respecting them'. Further regulations related to the Boys' School and to the separate infant poor-house at Highwood Hill (founded 1819).[42]

The 1828 regulations enshrined greater sensitivity to class differences and more care was taken to classify paupers by perceived social type. Rule twenty-five aimed to divide inmates into nine different classes 'as far as circumstances will admit'. These divisions were: 'Men and women who are of good disposition, regular in their behaviour, decent in their dress, or have been in better circumstances'; men and women 'of irregular behaviour, not clean in their persons, and of a vagrant disposition'; mothers and infants; boys capable of work; girls capable of work; children of both sexes not capable of work; lying-in women; sick women; and sick men. The last two were to be 'placed in wards where they may have free air, proper nurses, and classed according to their disorders'.[43]

Another marked difference between the early nineteenth-century environment and that of the eighteenth century was that large numbers of inmates were paid for tasks undertaken in the later period. The entire workhouse was monetarized at some point in the early nineteenth century, with small weekly payments for a range of tasks that included nursing, portering, gate-keeping and so on.[44] There is little evidence of such recompense in the eighteenth century, other than for manufacturing.

It is rarely clear that these rules were, in fact, followed or how they were interpreted or renegotiated in practice.[45] It would appear from the regulations that bribes sometimes changed hands and that inmates were occasionally drunk, or refused to work, or were abusive. To what extent did paupers resist or rebel against the pressures of institutional life? Many inmates stayed only short periods. And the establishment's 'carceral' regime was limited, since it allowed short trips outside and prescribed visiting times. The churchwardens and overseers also allowed further leeway, permitting many paupers longer leave of absence if they could show a good reason. As Green has noted, it must have been difficult to regulate the behaviour of those who came and went so frequently.[46] The ability of workhouse masters to inflict punishments on inmates was also limited by Parliament in 1814 and 1816.[47] The workhouse under the Old Poor Law might well have operated a more benign regime than that inflicted by the New Poor Law from 1834.

How Did Paupers React to Living in this Institution?

Every institution, of course, had its troublesome inmates. For this reason discipline sometimes required the use of external institutions. Between 1741 and 1824, 144 inmates of St Martin's workhouse were committed to Bridewell or other penal establishments for various petty offences, such as bringing in gin, refusing to work, stealing workhouse goods or provisions, disorderly behaviour, bastardy and vagrancy.[48] The workhouse in the closing years of the eighteenth century seems to have erected its own 'Refractory' or penitentiary where troublesome inmates might be confined. This was actually a 'shed at the bottom of the Ground'.[49] It may be significant that what might have been a harsher regime in the first decade of the nineteenth century corresponded with a few committals for abuse of workhouse officials and riotous behaviour. There also seems to be more evidence of assaults on other inmates in the post-Napoleonic period, when workhouse numbers, and the proportion of male inmates, were on the rise and perhaps internal tensions were at their highest. The numbers involved, however, are pretty small compared to the numbers found by Green in the later period. At least twenty-eight inmates were arrested by beadles, constables or police officers, usually for theft.[50] The problem of rowdy inmates might have been made worse, too, by the decision to bring back the parish lunatics from private madhouses in 1784.

Uncovering the everyday reality of life in an eighteenth-century workhouse is a problematic exercise since only those relationships that ended in conflict or abuse serious enough to be punished tended to be recorded.[51] Acts of kindness, friendships and positive relations went unremarked and unrecorded. Given that 50,000 or so individuals passed through the institution in this period (and their often short stays and frequent sickly or dying condition) it is striking how rarely disputes and acts of violence were recorded; most dated from the late eighteenth and early nineteenth centuries.[52] A few individuals were punished for attacks on fellow inmates and disorderly behaviour in the house. The assault 'upon Thomas Hawkins Superintendant of the Oakam Pickers', which earned one Thomas Newman a spell in the Tothill Fields Bridewell, is noteworthy because the latter was only fourteen years old. The effects of illness might explain why the fifty-six-year-old Mary Denham (after over five years in the workhouse) assaulted her nurse in 1790. It must have been difficult to prosecute those staffing the institution for petty acts of oppression and abuse but there were clearly boundaries. Jane Barrett, fifty-six, was sentenced to hard labour in 1821 'for Assaulting & striking Lawrence Rowen a Sick Patient in the Ward of which she was Nurse'.[53]

There is little evidence of sexual relations between inmates. However, the records do show at least one accusation of the sexual abuse of a child. An adult inmate, William Nicholls, was tried at the Old Bailey for sodomizing eleven-year-old Thomas Waldron while they shared a bed in St Martin's workhouse in October 1741. Despite the victim's account being corroborated by a fourteen year old, James Robinson, who also shared the bed with accused and accuser, Nicholls was acquitted of the sodomy but later tried for assault. He had, however, been accused of similar incidents previously. The parish overseers recorded payments 'On severall Indictments for Sodomy and several Assaults on diverse persons with Intent to commit Sodomy in the Workhouse'.[54]

These accusations of paedophilia tell us nothing about the intra-institutional incidence of relationships between consenting adults, about which no information has come to light. It must have been difficult to engage in heterosexual sexual relations within the workhouse given the single sex wards and lack of privacy, even before the sexes were segregated during the day in the early nineteenth century. It is striking that no bastard bearer, out of many hundreds of women examined by the parish under the bastardy laws, reported that impregnation had taken place inside a workhouse.[55]

Resistance to the workhouse regime is evidenced by the three and a half thousand paupers who absconded in some way. Such departures were more common after the 1770–2 rebuilding, when the workhouse itself might have been more secure. Most of these were merely stated to have 'absented' themselves, but others were described as running away or escaping over walls. The details are occasionally very revealing: 'Ran away from the Master of the Boy's School [*sic*] when going with him to his Mother'; 'Ran away, got out at the Gate leading to St. Martins Lane while Open for the Bearers to take a Corpse out'.[56] Occasionally there were quite elaborate break outs, such as the couple in 1817 who

> Ran away: Escaped over the Bakehouse having placed a ladder from the Drying Ground to the Roof of the Bakehouse and descended by a Rope which was fixed for that purpose. They have left their child Susannah in the House.[57]

Those who deliberately ran for it were not necessarily proto-rebels against a repressive regime. Quite often those who absconded left dependents or children behind. Occasionally escapees were returned by relatives. This suggests that workhouse security was far from perfect and that regulations about residence could be broken with relative ease by those who tired of their stay or who were keen to abandon dependents to the care of the parish. Workhouse porters who acted as 'door keepers' were sometimes charged with negligence and, on at least one occasion, in 1795, the workhouse porter delegated the all-important task of minding a main entrance to a boy, who was unable to prevent a number of inmates absconding.[58] It should be noted, of course, that many paupers were on the other hand seeking *entry* into the institution and that many of those who absented themselves may not have been doing much more than pre-empting an officially sanctioned departure by a few days. More to the point, there are plenty of examples of individuals who absconded only to return a few weeks or months later.[59]

Mention has already been made of those who visited workhouse inmates.[60] Regulations and parochial minutes, passed after the 1770–2 rebuilding, make clear the concern that visitors should not wander around unrestricted: 'no person as a visiter to any person in his house to be admitted further than the hatch in the passage except the pauper is ill' it was ordered in 1775, an order that was repeated thirty years later, at which time visits were limited to just fifteen minutes.[61] In 1811 visiting days were further restricted to Tuesdays and Fridays 'except in the sick wards'.[62] A recurrent fear of those running the workhouse was that visitors would bribe officials or be dunned for tips and perks. Samuel Hunt was dismissed as porter in 1775 for 'taking money of persons visiting poor in the workhouse contrary to the rules and orders thereof'.[63] Visitors might also attempt to smuggle goods in or out of the workhouse, which explains why in 1805 the porter and his assistant were ordered to search all those entering and leaving the workhouse and report any discovery of contraband to the workhouse master.[64]

The increasing concern to restrict visitors to the workhouse, which seems to coincide with more detailed regulations governing paupers obtaining leave of absence, suggests that the workhouse was becoming a less 'porous' institution by the early nineteenth century. That said, however, it is clear that for most of our period, inmates were far from being cut off from those on the outside.

Not all visitors were there to visit sick friends or family members. Some individuals, like Jonas Hanway (who visited the institution shortly after its re-building) were there to look around the workhouse out of curiosity and/or professional interest. A London guide book of 1802 reported that the St Martin's workhouse (one of only three singled out by the compiler) 'may be viewed on proper application to the master of the house, or to the church-wardens, who on every proper occasion readily gratify the curious'. Such visitors faced a restriction in 1817: 'No person be allowed to come into this House to view the same without a written order from one of the Officers or being introduced by one in person'.[65] It was clearly not just the lunatics at Bedlam who were on show in the eighteenth century.[66]

Conclusions

This chapter has some lessons for those studying institutions in almost any period. One needs to pay very close attention not just to the lay out, but also to the composition of the residential population. The question of typicality of resident is also significant; the most typical resident of this workhouse was an inmate who entered only once. Those who were in and out of workhouses were a troublesome minority. Workhouses in this period were multi-functional and catered for a wide range of individuals and families. Their internal configuration was repeatedly changed and altered. Perhaps of more significance is that the size and composition of the inmate body varied by the season, and over time.

Individual pauper perspectives on their experiences in these institutions were clearly likely to vary according to criteria such as length of stay, age and gender, health and status. The inmates lived under rules and regulations of varying degrees of complexity but these could be breached with some frequency. The extent to which paupers escaped, or left without permission, suggests that this institution and, one suspects, many others in the eighteenth century were less rigorous 'carceral' institutions than their forbidding reputations would suggest.

It seems likely that, even before the advent of 'less eligibility' (the notion that, in order to deter applications for poor relief, conditions inside workhouses must be harsher than those available outside) under the New Poor Law, the workhouse of St Martin-in-the-Fields was becoming an increasingly restricted place, with more elaborate rules and a more segregated classified environment. The rebuilding and expansion in 1770–2 seems to have increased restrictions on inmates and this may explain the ever more ingenious methods inmates resorted to in order to escape them. It is difficult to apply a strict chronology of 'incarceration' to these institutions. Inmates in the second decade of the nineteenth century were often paid for the tasks they undertook; they were allowed to smoke; and many returned time and again for temporary lodging and care. Moreover, for a period during the Napoleonic Wars numbers living in the institution sank to relatively low levels. There is an argument for seeing the early 1740s as a particularly difficult time, since the then relatively small workhouse may have been particularly overcrowded (see Figure 5.1). In sum, this new form of institutional living, in large mixed metropolitan workhouses, was rarely easy for the poor. And on occasion, as Thomas Waldron discovered, it brought unexpected danger.

Acknowledgements

This chapter is based on work from the ESRC/Wellcome-funded *Pauper Lives* Project (see http://research.ncl.ac.uk/pauperlives/esrcmain.htm) run by Jeremy Boulton and Leonard Schwarz. Thanks are also due to Drs Peter Jones and Rhiannon Thompson who collected some of the data used in this chapter, and to the helpful staffs of the City of Westminster Archives Centre and City of London, London Metropolitan Archives.

6 'A VERITABLE PALACE FOR THE HARD-WORKING LABOURER?' SPACE, MATERIAL CULTURE AND INMATE EXPERIENCE IN LONDON'S ROWTON HOUSES, 1892–1918

Jane Hamlett and Rebecca Preston

Space and Material Culture in a New London Institution for Working Men

In 1898 a journalist writing for *London Society* reported on a new institution that was attracting attention from the press. Impressed by the 'imposing structure' before him, he stepped off the street into Rowton House, King's Cross – where he found 'a veritable palace for the hard-working labourer'.[1] Rowton Houses were large-scale institutional spaces that housed hundreds of single men in turn-of-the-century London. Lord Rowton, a Tory peer and philanthropist, a nephew of the seventh Earl of Shaftesbury, and formerly Disraeli's private secretary, opened the first Rowton House at Vauxhall in 1892.[2] A lodging house for working men, this enterprise was not solely charitable but was designed to be self-supporting; it was one of a range of semi-philanthropic initiatives that emerged in response to the 1880s' housing crisis in London. The habitations of the urban poor caused a great deal of anxiety, especially common lodging houses, which were thought to harbour criminality and dirt. Rowton had surveyed conditions in common lodging houses in London's East End for the Guinness Trust in about 1890 and he intended Rowton House, Vauxhall, to be a model for accommodating the single working man.[3] Vauxhall's success led to the establishment of Rowton Houses as a limited company that built five, successively larger, Houses at King's Cross (1896), Newington Butts (1897), Hammersmith (1899), Whitechapel (1902) and Camden Town (1905), which alone contained over 1,000 beds. Despite their modest cost of 6*d* a night, the buildings offered suites of day rooms, separate laundry facilities and individual cubicles on the floors above; they were far in advance of comparable lodging houses. While the company architects were responsible for the buildings, Rowton and his co-director Richard Farrant oversaw the interior design. This chapter examines Rowton Houses through their material culture and considers the influence of ideas of home life, circulated and celebrated in nineteenth-century culture, on their design and representation. But it also explores the domestic life constructed and experienced by those who lived there.

It is widely accepted that the notion of home life played a central part in nineteenth-century middle-class culture. Leonore Davidoff and Catherine Hall's *Family Fortunes* demonstrated how a growth in evangelicalism helped create a culture of domestic virtue, with an emphasis on differentiated male and female roles.[4] For Davidoff and Hall, home was not just a physical space but also an imagined moral world. The importance of middle-class domestic objects as carriers of meaning has been emphasized by Deborah Cohen and Margaret Ponsonby.[5] Jane Hamlett shows how the use of rooms and goods in the home created a shared middle-class identity.[6] Working-class home life, and the significance of ideas about 'respectability' in creating different domestic practices, has been explored by Martin Daunton, Geoffrey Crossick and by Victoria Kelley.[7] What we know less about is domesticity – the shared material practices created in the home and the values that were attached to them – in an institutional context. Quintin Colville and Amy Milne-Smith suggest that elite men away from home could forge parallel domesticities in the club and officers' quarters;[8] but what of those lower down the social scale? This chapter explores the influence of powerful, middle- and upper-class ideas of domesticity on an institution designed for and (mostly) inhabited by working-class men.

The study of material culture – that is, the cultural and social meanings ascribed to the physical world and the practices associated with it – has recently gained currency with historians.[9] As Judy Attfield explains, people use goods 'as vehicles of meaning through which [they] negotiate their relations with each other and the world at large'.[10] Material culture can be helpful when exploring the lives of underprivileged groups in society. As the anthropologist Daniel Miller puts it, 'however oppressed and apparently culturally impoverished, most people nevertheless access the creative potential of the unpromising material goods around them'.[11] Work by Tim Hitchcock, Peter King and Pamela Sharpe on the eighteenth- and early nineteenth-century poor argues that historical research should turn to the voices of the poor and the material strategies they adopted in order to survive.[12] If, as is often the case, the words of the poor do not survive, sometimes we do have evidence of their possessions and can consider the spaces they inhabited, the objects they were provided with, and how these could be used.[13] Although recovering the voices of the poorer lodgers in Rowton Houses is highly problematic, one way forward is to look at the Houses' material culture. This lets us see the material restrictions imposed by rules and regulations but it also reveals the opportunities offered by the material world and the small spaces that lodgers could call their own.

Opening Rowton House doors also allows us to look closely at nineteenth-century class relationships. Recent work on social housing and philanthropy in London focuses on the narratives of middle- and upper-class men and women who made it their mission to enter the slums.[14] Seth Koven's *Slumming* (2004) examines this exercise in class-crossing from a range of perspectives.[15] Ruth Livesey demonstrates the tensions often inherent in spaces created by the middle and upper classes for the 'improvement' of others.[16] British social housing, including model lodging houses, has frequently been discussed as an institutional, philanthropic phenomenon;[17] but there have been few attempts to consider the use of space in these institutions.[18] Emily Gee examines large-scale lodging houses for women but since Rowton Houses Limited published its own history in 1956, establishments for men have largely escaped historical attention.[19] Rowton Houses in the late nineteenth and early twentieth centuries offer an interesting example of class-crossing. We consider how the transmission of a set of ideas was attempted through the material world – and the limitations and failings of that transmission. Rowton Houses' founders and many journalists represented the interiors as laden with domesticity, and they expected that their facilities would stimulate ideal behaviour. Yet Rowton House residents, rather than absorbing or resisting the domesticity apparently created by their surroundings, had their own ideas about how to achieve a sense of comfort and a feeling of security.

Rowton Houses in Words and Images

Rowton Houses were the subject of thousands of column inches of almost universal praise. Tory and Liberal London-based newspapers, provincial papers, the illustrated periodical press, and medical and architectural journals reported on every aspect of the Houses' design and management. They were also extensively photographed. The first part of this chapter explores how Rowton Houses were represented in the press, through words and images. As would be expected at this date, hygiene and fireproofing featured strongly in these accounts, most of which were heavily influenced by photographs and descriptions supplied by the company. But there was also an emphasis upon the domesticity and homelike qualities of the day rooms.

While it did not advertise directly, Rowton Houses Limited used photography to promote the aims of the company to potential lodgers, to allay public unease at cheap housing for large groups of poor men in comfortable surroundings and to satisfy shareholder concerns. The company carefully presented the light and airy interiors of Rowton Houses as the antithesis of the common lodging house of popular imagination, which was dirty, dark, crowded and criminal.[20] High quality photographic prints were used as internal company records but reached a wider audience through the press, where they appeared in seemingly independently authored magazine articles and newspaper reports. Archival evidence indicates that the company supplied these, with text written by the directors assisted by the architect. Not surprisingly, given his background, Rowton was on first name terms with London newspaper proprietors, and he corresponded with them about Rowton Houses, prior to the appearance of long articles in their publications.[21] In addition, photographs formed part of an article on the capital's model lodging houses in George R. Sims's influential work of popular photojournalism, *Living London*, which, for the first time, showed Rowton Houses populated with lodgers.

The discussion of the interiors in the press focused on their look and feel – summed up by the *Manchester Guardian*'s comment that 'comfort' as well 'health and cleanliness' were attended to and, moreover, that 'the internal decorations [were] artistic'.[22] Like other newspapers, the *Guardian* portrayed the institution as 'domestic', characterising the Vauxhall House as 'cheerful' and 'homely'.[23] *The Lancet*'s ostensibly sanitary reports stressed the 'homely' nature of the interiors. It claimed of Vauxhall, in 1893, that 'No one can enter without being gratified with the inviting appearance of homeliness, comfort and trust which are so pre-eminently the characteristics of everything in this [reading] room'.[24] In 1896 it published a mostly favourable report on the new House at King's Cross:

> To Lord Rowton belongs the honour of being the first to supply a real need in the lives of single men of the poorer working classes in London – a cheap and comfortable home. We say home advisedly, for if we eliminate the factor of mixed family life – not by any means an unimportant one – Rowton Houses, of which there are now two, really provide all that is implied by that word so dear to the heart of every true Englishman –'Home'.[25]

The report was dense with text but it was illustrated with five large photographs of the principal spaces of the interior, including the smoking room (see Figure 6.1).

This idea of home, presented by the *Lancet* and other publications, as a shared, English, identity that might transcend class boundaries was also present in the discussion of thematic decorative choices. These were seemingly endlessly mulled over both because these cultural reference points were expected to strike a chord with readers but also because middle- and upper-class reformers believed in the educative power of the visual and material world. Pictures at King's Cross included Landseer's 'Horse-Shoeing', Henry Wallis's 'Elaine' and a chromolithograph of Millais's 'Bubbles' in the dining room; Rosa Bonheur's 'Horses Coming from the Fair' and Stanley Berkeley's 'Prince Rupert: His Last Charge at Edge Hill' hung in the library. The *Economic Review* reported in 1893 that at Vaux-

Smoking Room.

Figure 6.1: The Smoking Room, Rowton House, King's Cross, from 'Private Action in Respect of Common Lodging-Houses, No. II', *Lancet*, 28 March 1896, p. 868. Reproduced with permission of the Wellcome Library, London.

hall 'the walls of the smoking-rooms and reading-rooms are hung with excellent prints of the frescoes which adorn the walls of the Houses of Parliament'.[26] Surrounding lodgers with the same images that hung in Parliament (and the relatively high cultural range of the other pictures displayed) can be seen as reinforcing the sense of shared Englishness that bound men together, transcending class boundaries. At Whitechapel, the decoration of the smoking room rendered this even more explicit. A painting hung above the fireplace in which 'a symbolical figure of England sits enthroned while the fruits of the land are brought to her by the cultivators'.[27] On the walls were 'a series of panels emblematic of THE SEASONS', depicting scenes of rural labour, which introduced striking images of the male labouring body into this feminized vision of England and Englishness. In a space designed for working men, this was a powerful political as well as social idea. Lodgers could see this daily but photography showed it to a wider audience.

Articles about Rowton Houses often made comparisons with hotels and clubs in the West End for upper- and middle-class men. This stressed continuity between domesticity as it might be experienced in privileged male spaces and what could be offered in Rowton Houses. Resident W. A. Somerville noted that Rowton Houses 'provided for him, in a humble way, comforts that are enjoyed by those who frequent the great club houses in Piccadilly and Pall Mall'.[28] Periodical writers were in no doubt that the care expended on the decoration and furnishings at Rowton Houses contributed to an atmosphere of warm domesticity. *All the Year Round* noted:

> At the other end of the corridor is a sitting-room, as pleasant and cosy a room as can be imagined, with a chequered dado of glazed tiles and walls of a soft, warm tint, hung with good engravings. Around each of the two blazing fires is gathered a sociable circle.[29]

Indeed, almost the only criticism of Rowton Houses came from politicians and clergymen, some of whom felt that the Houses made bachelor life too attractive to working men, and discouraged marriage.[30]

The creation of a domesticity that transcended class boundaries was also emphasized by playing up the similarities between the interiors at Rowton House and those of upper- and middle-class homes. The *Lancet* described an area in the reading room of the King's Cross House that Rowton had apparently christened the 'cosy corner'.[31] The 'cosy corner' was a common staple in domestic advice manuals aimed at the middle classes in this period, indicating how transferable some of the language of domesticity could be.[32] The smoking room and library at King's Cross were hung with stags' heads, which Rowton had stalked himself.[33] Accounts of the opening of the House in 1896 noted that this included a magnificent 'royal' that he shot last year 'never expecting that he [the stag] would end his days in a "doss-house"'.[34] Stags' heads – typically found in masculine spaces such as the library or billiard room in upper-middle-class and elite homes – are an interesting choice for this space. The use of these objects implies that the company sought to blur the distinction between spaces for upper- and middle-class men and those for the working classes.

Moreover, Rowton Houses were also particularly praised for extending privacy – a quality hitherto enshrined in middle-class domestic arrangements but widely assumed to be absent from working-class homes – to their inmates. The *Newcastle Weekly Courant* shared the London papers' view that Rowton Houses were hotels for working men rather than common lodging houses (and so exempt from municipal regulation and inspection), noting that such feeling was not only widespread but also transcended normal political and class divisions, as 'what are known as Radical papers were the stoutest fighters for upholding the status and privacy of the poor men's hotels'.[35] The press and lodgers applauded the notion that 'There is no suggestion of charity. Everybody is on an equality', as one resident put it in 1899.[36] The absence of 'any interference with the religious, political, or social relationships of those who seek and who pay for its hospitality' was also welcomed.[37] One early press account praised the cubicle sleeping arrangements because 'While the cubicle system insures each lodger privacy at night, the house is yet a democratic club'.[38] The cubicles were not presented as 'homely' in the same way as the communal dayrooms. But in allowing individual privacy, said the press, they brought accommodation for the working classes to a newly civilized level. The equation of access to the cubicle with the opportunity for self-civilizing chimes with Tom Crook's recent argument about the appearance of the cubicle in a range of different Victorian contexts (discussed further in Chapter 1 of this volume).[39]

Expectations about the kind of domesticity that these spaces would create were also informed by other, idealized, versions of sociability between working men, including the spit-and-sawdust comfort of the public house.[40] Articles often described lodger camaraderie and a general sense of their feeling 'at home', occasionally portraying this through engravings of lodgers leaning on fireplaces or relaxing in chairs. The same idea was developed in photographs of carefully orchestrated 'informal' groups of furniture – the semi-circle of armchairs arranged around a fireplace or unseen corner was a recurring motif – and, strikingly, in the *Lancet* images, the prominent positioning of spittoons (see Figure 6.1). The camera was also used to mitigate the institutional size of the Houses and to portray them as more intimate communal places for men. Meanwhile the shop, despite its looming aspect, emphasized that the men were paying guests rather than the recipients of charity. These images are quite different from most other contemporary press illustrations of institutional spaces for the poor, such as workhouses and prisons, where the rudimentary furniture tended to appear in rows – as did the inmates. Unlike workhouse photographs, shots of Rowton interiors did not show inmates before 1900; it seems likely that this was to avoid comparisons with institutional photography as well as to respect lodgers' privacy. Instead, contented lodgers were suggested through the arrangement of furniture and the placement of board games and newspapers in the dayrooms. Such compositions did not only conjure absent presences but were intended to be suggestive of comfort and 'home'. At King's Cross, for example, the *Lancet* reported 'a large number of easy and other wooden chairs, some of which, for the benefit of the rheumatic and feeble, are placed around a fire in a recess at one end of the room'.[41]

'Home' was not only to be created through the material fabric and spatial arrangements within the buildings, it was also to be shaped by less tangible notions of liberty. When the first House opened at Vauxhall, Rowton told the *Lancet* that 'one does not wish to have too much regulation at home, and, as I wish this to be a *home* for the working man, I want a minimum of regulation'.[42]

Eleven years after the first House was opened in 1892, lodgers made their first photographic appearance in three images of Rowton House, Hammersmith, published in George R. Sims's *Living London* (1902–3).[43] This serialization, through an innovative combination of text and image, introduced readers to life in the new twentieth-century metropolis, including its many charitable institutions (several of which are examined by Fiona Fisher in Chapter 1). In two of the Hammersmith photographs the superintendent is clearly identifiable by his clothes and manner but seems more akin to a hotel doorman than the chief authority figure and even appears to enjoy the lodgers' company on the roof garden or 'courtyard', seen in Figure 6.2. Like the interiors depicted in the company's photographs, this space was 'de-institutionalized' by portraying it as an ornamental garden for relaxation, with flower-pots and rockeries, thereby differentiating it from the more utilitarian exercise-yards of the workhouse and prison. Meanwhile in populating the living spaces with contented lodgers, reading or tending flowers, *Living London* succeeded where the institutional photographs failed, for it pictured the order without regulation that Rowton equated with 'home'.

'Shut up you Bloody Swine!': Life within Rowton House Walls

But did the Rowton men accept or resist the hopes of those who designed the spaces they lived in? Were they even aware of them? These questions are complicated by the nature of the surviving evidence. The second part of this chapter attempts to discover the thoughts and feelings of Rowton House residents by examining personal accounts and crime records. This is not to suggest that the stories presented here are about representation on one hand and experience on the other. Cultural imaginings of spaces often impinge on their occupants and, in the case of Rowton Houses, some of the writers who helped present the houses as a domestic haven also lived there. Many short personal accounts of Rowton life appeared in the press, some clearly written by 'slumming' journalists, donning the garb of the poor and spending a night at Rowton House for the sake of a story.[44] Others, however, were published by longer-term residents, jobbing writers who were able to turn their residential experiences to advantage. This chapter places these writings alongside other kinds of evidence, principally autobiographies and crime records. Published memoirs offer a picture of Rowton Houses that was not deliberately constructed for the periodical press. But these narratives were also shaped by the long processes of memory and editorial requirements and therefore are far from offering an uncomplicated version of experience. Autobiographies are reconstructed in relation to a later self, often as part of a life story in which great difficulties are overcome en route to personal success and so some experiences of Rowton life may have been exaggerated. Records of crime from the press, police accounts and the criminal courts carry

A ROWTON HOUSE : COURTYARD.

Figure 6.2: The Courtyard, Rowton House, Hammersmith, from T. W. Wilkinson, 'London's Model Lodging-Houses', in G. R. Sims (ed.), *Living London*, vol. 3, p. 172. Authors' collection.

their own interpretative issues: newspaper accounts are often salacious whilst excluding taboo subjects; police records, shaped by the needs of busy institutions, are often minimal; while witnesses often testified to what they thought a court wanted to hear. Brought together, however, they present a very different picture of life in Rowton Houses from the press accounts discussed above.

The class make-up of Rowton Houses was more complex than their creators intended. Although they were aimed at working men, in 1899 the *Review of Reviews* wrote that such was the extent of the middle-class occupancy of Rowton House, King's Cross, that working men 'are looked down upon, and made to feel themselves inferiors and interlopers'.[45] The 1901 census suggests that this was not quite the case at Vauxhall. Here 'general labourer' was the most frequent occupation listed, although there was also a significant number of more 'middle-class' inmates, including clerks and shopkeepers as well as an estate agent, a book keeper and an accountant.[46] A number of Rowton residents (including the lodging-house poets William Mackenzie and W. H. Davies) were working writers, who found the cheap accommodation and space to write useful; these lodgers were far more likely to leave a written record and are disproportionately represented in surviving accounts. For that reason, court and police records are valuable, as they are one of the few sources in which the voice of the more ordinary resident emerges.

Sources show that many men arrested for criminal offences gave their address as a Rowton House;[47] yet recorded crime *within* the houses seems to have been relatively low. A Booth investigator noted in 1899 that at Rowton House, Newington Butts, there was 'very seldom a row, only once in the police court in 18 months'.[48] Rowton Houses appeared infrequently in the reports of both the local police courts and the central criminal courts.[49] Nevertheless, a few cases of serious crime did come before the Old Bailey between 1892 and 1914, revealing that communal life in the Houses was sometimes a world away from the cosy domesticity imagined by their founders.

With the notable exception of writers who depended on the reading rooms and library to continue their professions, most personal accounts did not dwell on the quality of the interiors or their facilities and were mostly unconcerned with things visual. They concentrated on more pressing matters, such as food and the lack of it, the retention of possessions and the comfort or otherwise of the sleeping spaces. Above all they were concerned with the presence of other lodgers – physical, accoustic and olfactory.

The ability to feel 'at home' might be dependent on the possibility of semipermanent residence. From the early days lodgers were able to renew their cubicle tickets daily or weekly.[50] Early accounts of the Vauxhall House suggest that the majority of residents were booking rooms on a weekly, rather than a nightly, basis.[51] Long-term residents might expect to return to the same cubicle, but this could not be guaranteed. When a porter was accused, in 1898, of ejecting a lodger from bed too violently, it was stated in his defence that he was protecting another lodger, who 'lived permanently at Rowton' and who claimed that the bed belonged to him.[52] A distinction was made between residents who returned to the houses regularly and those who had arrived just for the night. However, as most cubicles had to be vacated during the day and could not be locked from the outside, inmates had little opportunity to establish continuity of possession through the display of personal objects or small decorative acts. The cubicles of weekly lodgers could also be searched for stolen goods.[53]

Weekly residents received a key to a locker where personal things could be stored. Each had only one key (although court records indicate these were often shared) but it is clear from Old Bailey cases that Rowton staff sometimes demanded that they be opened if suspicions arose as to their contents. Lockers were often the first port of call for the police if they suspected a Rowton resident of harbouring stolen or illicit goods. Several reports of trials in the police courts note that such items were found in them, including equipment used for breaking and entering, invisible ink, a stolen concertina, materials used for counterfeiting currency, a stash of 2,457 cancelled stamps and chemicals for removing postmarks and a 'quantity of tea'. But the lockers could also be secret, long-term repositories for personal items, prized by their owners but hidden from the world. In 1913, eighty-one-year-old Horace W. Burleigh died, having resided at Rowton House, Vauxhall for seven years. His locker, when opened, was found to contain 'hundreds of letters and photographs from different young girls'.[54]

For some early Rowton residents the ability to feel 'at home' was , then, created not so much by ownership of a particular space or belongings as by continuity of residence and exchange and interaction with those around them. It was relationships with others – and the position of other bodies in space – that informed how comfortable they felt in the Houses. For W. A. Somerville, a struggling journalist who made a semi-permanent home at King's Cross in the late 1890s, the homelike feeling of the House lay in the atmosphere and social interaction that it allowed; it was both 'More cheerful than the solitude of a private room' and 'a home where [the lodger] can pass his time in rational manner, where he may read books, write letters, and above all mix with what he pathetically calls "his mates"'.[55]

To a certain extent, the carefully designed interiors did allow Rowton residents to interact in a communal fashion, recreating some of the qualities of 'home' that we might expect to find in a shared family space. Colonel Lionel James, a war correspondent who spent a week at King's Cross in the early 1900s, was struck by the warmth of the dining room: 'It was heated by a monster coke brazier, rectangular in shape, that stood in the centre of things'. James himself, from a different class background to the majority of the inhabitants, felt rather put off by the circle around the fire: 'crossing-sweepers, pavement artists and other gutter-snipes who were combining the operation of drying their boots and socks with the toasting of kippers, bacon and bread'. He concluded that this reaction was, however, unfair as it was 'fulfilling the purpose of the institution'.[56] Others were more comfortable with communal cooking – this domestic practice, which would have taken place in the family home, was commonly reported amongst residents. Conrad Noel, a Christian Socialist and member of the Independent Labour Party, had spent some months living at Vauxhall soon after it opened. Looking back to his youth with some affection, he recalled how 'We cooked our meals in a common frying pan ... We either bought our food outside or at the counter – eggs and bacon or a rasher of ham'.[57]

While Rowton inmates could not decorate, the cubicle system did at least afford them a degree of separation from fellow residents at night. The cubicle storeys were designed to control the spread of fire and disease, but they also afforded some privacy. After experiments with shared rooms at Vauxhall, all the cubicles of subsequent Houses were for single lodgers and each had a window to the outside under their occupiers' control. At King's Cross the cubicles varied in size but the minimum measured 5 feet by 7 feet 6 inches.[58] Each cubicle contained a bed and bedding, a chair, a shelf, a clothes peg and a chamber pot.

In addition to affording individual privacy, the cubicles had an impact on the relationships between the men who slept at Rowton Houses. They probably facilitated rather than inhibited the illicit liaisons which Matt Houlbrook finds to be the case in Rowton Houses after 1918.[59] There is, however, very little evidence of sexual relationships between men in Rowton Houses before this date. Legal records of homosexual activity yield little and are rarely linked to a precise location.[60] Anecdotal accounts of Rowton life are unsurprisingly silent on this taboo subject although one inmate complained that sleep was impossible because of 'sundry grunts, and other indescribable noises'.[61]

This was, then, a partial privacy. Anyone who used a cubicle for an assignation might be spotted by an over-curious fellow lodger. The cubicles were open at the floor and ceiling, but with steel mesh on top, after early attempts at 'fishing' showed the cubicles to be insecure. As the opening between the partitions and the ceiling measured 18 inches, it was possible to see into neighbouring cubicles by standing on the bed. This is revealed by a case of suspected arson, brought before the Old Bailey in 1893. At Vauxhall, Frank Clark reported that he had spotted the flames in a fellow lodger's cubicle by jumping onto his bed and looking into the adjacent cubicle.[62]

The cubicle partitions were also completely ineffective as barriers against sound. Coughs and snoring were ubiquitous and figure in many accounts.[63] At Vauxhall in the 1890s, it was noted: 'The noise of snoring was loud, but louder still was the persistent banging on the wall, accompanied with cries of "Shut up, you bloody swine!" so that sleep was generally impossible'.[64]

Privacy was compromised further by the power of porters and superintendents to enter cubicles at any time and sometimes to lay violent hands on occupants. The Rowton authorities were criticized for this by some inmates.[65] Many staff had worked previously in the army and, despite the claims of some residents that the Houses were not adequately policed, were clearly capable of enforcing physical discipline.[66] This is demonstrated by two instances in which Rowton porters were brought before the courts. William Allen, head porter at King's Cross, was charged in 1900 with the manslaughter of John Neate, a forty-one-year-old former bank clerk and Rowton resident.[67] A verdict of 'death from apoplexy' was reached but the court was of the opinion that Allen had used more violence than necessary.[68] In 1898 the assistant porter at Vauxhall was charged with pulling a resident from bed and hitting and kicking him. But the court upheld the porter's actions on the grounds that he 'used no more violence than necessary in ejecting' the lodger.[69] It was therefore acceptable for staff to enter a man's cubicle and even to assault him. The thin cubicle walls offered only partial protection from the presence of other bodies and the threat of physical violence, sanctioned by the institution itself.

Fellow lodgers could also pose a material, and sometimes physical, danger. In 1906 the Parliamentary Committee on Vagrancy noted the presence of ex-convicts in Rowton Houses, stating that when 'men leave prisons [they] use one form of institution and another', often drifting between the casual ward, the common lodging house and Rowton Houses.[70] Yet serious crimes, including large-scale theft, were unusual. We have identified only one case where a Rowton resident was brought before the courts for stealing from other inmates.[71] But petty theft (perhaps not large enough to be reported to the police) appears to have been commonplace. As we have seen, the design of the cubicles was altered in the 1900s to prevent stealing from over cubicle tops. By 1904 it had also become necessary to lock library books behind glass doors. Nevertheless, according to a resident just after the First World War, there was far less threat of losing one's possessions here than in a common lodging house.[72]

Small, everyday thefts created a culture in which the inmates relied and preyed on each other simultaneously. Foodstuffs were a particular target. A 1910 article warned that 'should the unfortunate novice happen to turn his back a moment upon his supper, it is promptly "lifted" by "one of the old guard", as they are known, and he goes supperless to bed'.[73] Noel remembered that when cooking 'it was difficult to guard one's particular portion in the pan from some hungry tramp, who sometimes seized it if one was not on the look-out'.[74]

For one inmate who wrote anonymously for the *Charity Organisation Review*, the cosy domesticity that Rowton hoped to create had failed to materialize – instead, the house actually encouraged a culture of shabby shiftlessness and cadging.[75] Yet some viewed theft almost humorously. Mackenzie devoted a poem to 'My Friend – Mr Spunge', making light of a man who, feigning literary interests, cadged from the poet until Mackenzie stumbled on his Post Office book.[76] But the cadger's performance is celebrated, as much as denigrated.

Some inmates felt more threatened than others. For younger lodgers, cadging occasioned considerable anxiety. Sixteen-year-old Jack Smithers, a Rowton resident in 1907, recorded his dislike of, and unease in, a Rowton House in his autobiography; even keeping hold of soap whilst washing in the communal wash rooms required constant vigilance.[77] Smithers's account of his brief stay figures in a larger story of family breakdown. His father had been a successful publisher, but left Smithers and his mother destitute and homeless on his death. Deserted by his mother, Smithers was forced to take shelter at (probably) the King's Cross House. The inadequacies of the accommodation are thus compounded in the narrative by Smithers's loss of his familial home and his sense of class slippage. Nonetheless, we can read this as evidence of how more vulnerable inhabitants might have responded to their surroundings.

By the late nineteenth century large-scale residential institutions were a commonplace feature of the British landscape, both urban and rural. The idea of the institution had become a powerful metaphor and certain styles of building and architectural features were associated with it. A description of Rowton House, Hammersmith, in a Sheffield newspaper in 1900, took the architect (Harry Measures) to task for not moving away from institutional architecture: 'a vast pile of terraced windows and those flanking towers significant of exactly what Rowton House is not – a prison, a workhouse, or a lunatic asylum'.[78] Rowton Houses' directors resisted these references and sought to represent the interior spaces as 'domestic'. Nonetheless, residents were unable to break away from institutional associations. Comparisons with the prison were frequently made by slumming journalists and longer-term residents.[79] One short-term inmate in the early 1900s, although positive about some aspects of the Houses, remembered: 'I hated, however, the clanging bell in the morning and the raucous voice of unquestionable authority that informed us that we had half-an-hour in which to be clear of our accommodation ... It was something, I imagined, short of a prison routine'.[80] Even the journalists who praised the domesticity of the Houses were unable to escape completely from the idea of the institution. Throughout these texts the resident men are referred to as 'inmates' as well as lodgers, betraying an unspoken alignment with the prison, workhouse and asylum.

Conclusion

Rowton Houses were popular, successful and often full. They were a considerable improvement on common lodging houses and even on the other model lodging houses of the era. For many single men they were clearly the best available option. There was a marked contrast, however, in the way the press portrayed them and how inhabitants experienced them on a daily basis. Press representations of the interiors suggest that the company and journalists collaborated in portraying life in the Houses as essentially 'domestic' according to established middle- and upper-class ideas and expectations. The language of late nineteenth-century domesticity was used to describe spaces at Rowton that it was hoped would civilize and normalize working men. A careful reading of the company's photographs reveals deliberate attempts to de-institutionalize the space.

But there are clear limits to this reading. Available sources tell us that residents managed to feel at home, or at least achieve a sense of comfort and security within the Houses, not through identification with imagery or interior design but through continual residence and through familiarity with the buildings and their routines and with some of their fellow lodgers. Rowton inhabitants did not resist the version of the institution that was portrayed in the press or conveyed on the Houses' walls but they had other more pressing concerns. Security and comfort was produced, or removed, by the presence of other bodies in space – it was the other lodgers and the staff, and the rules that governed them, that were important in this equation. The cubicles offered a partial privacy at best. And, while these may have allowed some sexual assignations, they were also vulnerable to the gaze of neighbours and to the entry and potential violence of staff. Those who felt most uncomfortable pointed to the noise and disruption created by others and to the material threat of theft. When describing Rowton Houses, lodgers were often unable to break away from the now powerful metaphor of institutional life – ultimately they viewed themselves as inhabiting an institution rather than a home.

Acknowledgements

This work was supported by the Economic and Social Research Council (RES-061-25-0389). We would like to thank the archivists at City of London, London Metropolitan Archives and those at the borough archives of Hammersmith & Fulham, Southwark, and Tower Hamlets. Thanks too to the Brotherton Library, Leeds University, the Wellcome Library, LSE Booth Archive and the National Archives. We are also very grateful to Lesley Hoskins, Stella Moss and Susannah Ottaway for their careful reading and comments.

7 'THE PLACE WAS A HOME FROM HOME': IDENTITY AND BELONGING IN THE ENGLISH COTTAGE HOME FOR CONVALESCING PSYCHIATRIC PATIENTS, 1910–1939

Stephen Soanes

Psychiatric Aftercare and the Cottage Home

Cottage homes for convalescing psychiatric patients first appeared in England in the 1880s. Convalescent homes for the somatically sick had developed during the mid-nineteenth century, often located at the seaside or in the country, where they took patients for a time-limited interval after active treatment. Cottage homes provided similarly temporary residential care and recuperation for patients recently discharged from acute treatment within asylums. Although the homes discussed in this chapter were specifically reserved for the convalescent mentally ill, the term 'cottage home' had been applied to other institutions from the late nineteenth century. John Adams has described workhouse infirmary wards reserved for children as 'cottage homes'.[1] Similarly, Edward Shorter has found the term applied to turn-of-the-century sanatoria for nervous and mental disorders in North America.[2] Its usage is also associated with Barnardo's homes for 'rescued' girls (though not boys) in the 1870s.[3] The definition of 'cottage home' was, therefore, somewhat elastic. Nevertheless, in early twentieth-century British psychiatry it referred more specifically to a type of lay-managed institution for the temporary convalescence of psychiatric post-acute patients. This chapter explores how these homes influenced patients' experience of discharge, identity and belonging through residential psychiatric aftercare.[4]

Access to the cottage homes was regulated through the Mental After-Care Association (MACA). Established in 1879, the London-based organization initially restricted its support to 'poor and friendless female convalescents on leaving asylums for the insane'. From 1894, the MACA also began to provide convalescence and aftercare for male patients. The charity helped mental convalescents in a variety of ways that extended beyond referral for residential cottage-home placements. Some patients were simply offered gifts in kind, home visits or help finding work. For those considered for residential convalescence, referral typically came from asylum superintendents, with further interviews sometimes held with relatives, other institutional carers and the prospective convalescents themselves. If accepted, patients were then sent at the MACA's expense (sometimes reimbursed by patients or local authorities) to an approved private household for typically between a fortnight and three months.

Newspaper cuttings in the MACA's archive indicate that it regularly advertised for suitable homes in the local press.[5] These homes were not purpose-built, but their suitability was assessed prior to acceptance. The charity was selective over those it accepted, recording in its minutes for 1918 that a recent notice had yielded 'only one ... likely to be suitable'.[6] Minutes also indicate it regularly discontinued the use of homes where the standards or suitability fell short of the charity's requirements. Ideally they would combine spaciousness and homeliness, as well as a location that balanced accessibility from the charity's London offices with a relatively suburban environment. In 1928 the organization instructed Mrs Careless, for example, that it would consider sending more patients to her 'if she took a rather larger house not too far away'.[7] In return for taking convalescent mental patients into their own homes, usually for a few weeks, proprietors received payment from the MACA to cover board, lodgings and travel.

Unlike the majority of the other institutions explored in this volume, the cottage home was primarily a private residence and only secondarily an institution. Outwardly indistinguishable from any other middle-class suburban or seaside home, these dwellings became institutions through their selection, regulation and management. Their ordinariness was both planned and – among some patients at least – appreciated. In 1936, one ex-patient (case 31669) wrote to thank the MACA for the 'home from home' their funded convalescence had provided.[8] This case indicates how the use of private homes allowed some of their temporary residents to regard them as an extension of their own private milieu. Because the relevant extract from this letter subsequently appeared in the MACA's published annual report, it seems too that the charity positively promoted the perception that its homes offered an unremarkable domestic site for recuperation.[9] Caught between the unequivocally institutional asylum and their own abodes, this chapter suggests that cottage-home residents were encouraged to associate their stay with a return to their own domestic lives.

Nevertheless, the chapter further argues that despite its potentially welcome homeliness, the cultivated domesticity of the cottage home presented an artificial and essentially institutional environment for the management of psychiatric improvement. The idea of a 'home from home' itself conveys a sense of displacement: despite superficial familiarity, the resident quoted above felt one step removed from belonging. The MACA's frequent description of these homes as a 'bridge' between the asylum and the patient's home accurately, if perhaps unwittingly, betrays the artificiality of the support they offered to their short-term inhabitants. This metaphor of the 'bridge' figuratively constructed convalescence as a stable and sufficient route to recovery, which at the same time relied upon artificial third-party support. The allusion further hinted at the potential for alternative pathways to mental stability.[10] As this chapter illustrates, some patients did not always choose to take this 'bridge' to health, whilst others evaluated the convalescence they received on their own terms.

To date, historians have paid surprisingly little attention to the practices and places designed to promote continuity of psychiatric care, beyond the primary institution of the mental hospital. Scholars have widely portrayed a binary relationship between asylums and families and in the process have tended to marginalize the role of other forms of intermediate care-giving. John Walton and David Wright, for instance, have envisaged asylum admission and discharge as a process of 'casting out' and 'bringing back' negotiated principally between families and the asylum authorities.[11] So too, Akihito Suzuki has emphasized the choice families exerted in how far they 'enclosed' and 'disclosed' their insane relatives to the psychiatric authorities in the nineteenth century.[12] In turn, as John Welshman has observed, work on the historical roots of community care has remained largely preoccupied with the family home.[13] Consequently, the impact of halfway homes and other intermediate institutions on patient experiences of recovery, selfhood and community reintegration has remained substantially underexplored.[14] Welshman, however, has usefully begun work in this direction through his studies of the post-1940 hostel and rehabilitation centre. Extending this focus further back in time, the present chapter pays closer attention to their antecedents in the pre-eminent pre-war institution for mental convalescence: the cottage home.

Certainly, historians have begun to indicate how wider community contexts may have influenced patient pathways from institution to home. In particular, recent research has started to explore how correspondence with family members and asylum visitation potentially affected patients' institutional experiences.[15] Louise Hide's discussion of villa accommodation in this volume attests to turn-of-the-twentieth-century concerns over the achievability of domesticity within the asylum. Here I suggest that such debates continued in the twentieth century, as psychiatry itself extended into the community. Cottage homes melded the recognizable domesticity of the family dwelling with the planned and supervised care of the institution. Consequently, a study of these homes sheds further light on the contested meanings associated with 'institution' and 'community'. Several historians have traced the precursors of late twentieth-century community care to the After-Care Association's prototypical late nineteenth-century community-based aftercare services. In each case, however, these historians have only briefly offered a survey of the Association's activities.[16] Welshman has more specifically presented the cottage home as a precursor to the post-war hostel.[17] This chapter argues that cottage homes merit further examination in their own right, especially because they functioned to mediate patient pathways from sickness to health and self-sufficiency. These homes continued institutional care, inasmuch as they provided a structured environment for care-giving, but for some patients they may also have provided a welcome homely interlude prior to their return to independent lives.

This study focuses mainly upon the period between 1910 and 1939, when the survival of a run of patient case books coincides with a period of significant growth in the MACA's work. After several years of modest growth, the charity's aftercare activities multiplied twelve-fold, from 379 cases in 1910 to a pre-war peak of 4,269 cases in 1938. Cottage-home placements formed a significant part of this growth: more than twice as many went to cottage homes in 1937 (807) than the charity handled in total across all its aftercare activities in 1910.[18] The majority of the chapter concentrates upon the inherent tension between the professional and lay, and between the institutional and homely, in the MACA's own representations of its homes. Drawing primarily on annual reports, newspapers, journals and speeches, this analysis details the cottage home's planned domesticity and its implications for patients' temporary belonging as residents. The final part of the chapter then considers how some patients contested the functions that these halfway homes offered. Using the surviving case files and agenda registers, it indicates how residents independently assessed their place within (or without) the cottage home.

Institutionalism and Homeliness

From the outset, the MACA envisaged the cottage home as a pre-eminently homely environment, in contradistinction to the asylums from which convalescent patients would be referred. At a meeting held in June 1879 to discuss the principles for a mental aftercare charity, the organization's founder, Henry Hawkins, set out his vision for the ideal cottage home for convalescents. In terms of their form and staffing, he envisaged an unremarkable 'ordinary roomy, comfortable house, with garden ground ... preferably under the management of a sensible Christian-minded lady'. If perhaps unusually spacious compared with the domestic experience of its pauper inhabitants, Hawkins's institution promised to be a much smaller site in which to conclude psychiatric recovery than the late nineteenth-century asylum. Such homely dimensions, together with the moral authority he sought in the idealized matron, converged to create the image of the cottage home as a matriarchal middle-class family household.[19] In practice too, the respectable domestic household became the ideal to which the

MACA aspired. In their annual report for 1919 the organization set the maximum for cottage homes at four patients.[20] Although this figure was sometimes exceeded, numbers remained sufficiently low for the MACA to claim these houses represented essentially domestic spaces. Smaller numbers helped the charity differentiate its homes from asylums, as when it boasted in its annual report for 1930 that 'when patients go to our Homes, the atmosphere is that of a home rather than that of an institution'.[21]

It is evident from Hawkins's papers that he drew significant inspiration from 'existing Retreats for ordinary convalescents', suggesting that some of the same therapeutic principles found in these general homes might well apply '*a fortiori* ... in the case of mental convalescents'.[22] To this extent, it is possible to trace the antecedents of Hawkins's proposed cottage home further back, to the first purposely designated convalescent institution in Britain, which opened at Walton-on-Thames in 1840. From the mid-nineteenth century, such homes developed widely across southern England, often located in coastal and semi-rural locations. Similarly, the MACA's cottage homes were primarily concentrated in the south-east of England; provided a time-limited period of respite care; and rested on the therapeutic principle that patients would benefit from a change of air, scenery and associations. Indeed, the similarity of their cottage homes to other convalescent institutions is suggested in the charity's proposal in the 1880s to make places available to somatic convalescents, albeit with priority given to asylum patients.[23]

Even so, the cottage home quickly developed into a separate and increasingly specialized institution in its own right. From the 1880s, the MACA ultimately decided to reserve its homes exclusively for mental cases. In turn, it appears that general convalescent homes routinely excluded mental and neurological patients, although Gardiner's 1930–1 survey identified a handful (four of 431 homes) dedicated to mental and neurological disorder.[24] A mutual distinction between these institutions physically separated psychiatric and somatic convalescents, which partly reflected qualitative differences in the nature of the care they provided. Publicity on the MACA's work suggested that the mental convalescent faced particular needs that required a degree of specialization. In 1924, for instance, the organization claimed it offered lengthier placements compared with other convalescent institutions because mental convalescents often needed more protracted rest.[25] Although many cases stayed for a period similar to the one to six weeks that Jennifer Cronin has suggested was standard for general convalescent homes, MACA case registers indicate that the average stay was closer to four weeks, while some remained for as long as three months.[26] This perhaps afforded particular opportunities for its cottage-home residents to establish some sense of belonging. With mental convalescence often a longer process, it is also likely that it assumed greater significance within patients' personal narratives of sickness and health.

An article published in *Mental Welfare* during 1930 identified further qualitative differences between cottage homes and general convalescent homes, centred on the particular specialist supervision mental convalescents required. The anonymous author felt that for mental patients 'normal convalescent homes are, of course, out of the question, as ... they have no one with the specific knowledge and experience which is essential for the wise and sympathetic handling of this type of case'.[27] As this chapter explores, the MACA would increasingly emphasize the professional skill and experience of its cottage-home matrons. This identified mental convalescence as a specialist field of activity. The cover of the annual reports between 1890/1 and 1920 echoed this claim to distinctiveness in the assertion that it represented the 'only charity of the kind in the United Kingdom'.[28] At the same time, however, the MACA also strove to emphasize the domestic normality of its homes. Consequently, it represented its matrons as both specialists and laypeople who united 'specific knowledge' with the more personal qualities of sympathy and maternal care.

Initially, such support was exclusively restricted to female patients. For the first fifteen years after 1879, the Association offered convalescence exclusively to 'poor friendless females', because its founder believed that women often had fewer options for continued support after asylum discharge.[29] This policy, Henry Rayner (Treasurer, MACA; Physician, St Thomas's Hospital) argued in 1891, reflected the smaller number of recovered male patients, the intractability of male insanity associated with alcoholism, and the particularly onerous domestic responsibilities many women faced upon their return home. The last of these points is particularly notable, because it suggests that cottage-home convalescence may have functioned to withhold women from a return home that the charity believed held particular hazards to their recoveries.[30]

Despite the extension of convalescence to men in 1894, case books and minutes suggest women continued to outnumber men as recipients of placements into the inter-war period, perhaps accounting for around two-thirds of cottage-home intake. Registers further indicate that the MACA often helped men obtain access to Rowton Houses. It is possible, therefore, that many men who might have received convalescence were referred instead to lodging houses from the 1910s. Such gendered dimensions to discharge and psychiatric recovery merit further investigation, beyond the scope of this chapter. Nevertheless, it seems that, in its origins at least, convalescence became identifiable as a particularly feminized approach to post-acute psychiatric care.

The cottage homes themselves to some extent gendered the experience of psychiatric recovery. The charity's minutes through the 1930s recorded several homes reserved 'for men', while the annual report for 1931 indicates that the charity maintained separate homes for male and female early-care cases in the London area.[31] Such divisions rather undermined the Association's claims that these represented unremarkable family homes. Moreover, minutes show that several homes restricted admissions to a single sex, while case books suggest that male proprietors, in particular, tended to take male convalescents. Where married couples ran cottage homes, as was often the case, patients shared a more mixed environment.

An example of the artificiality inherent in the management of the otherwise outwardly ordinary domestic spaces can be seen in the imposition of a single-sex admissions policy at the Bard family's cottage home at Herne Bay, Kent. When Mr Bard died in 1931, his wife and daughter wrote to the Association asking whether his cottage home 'formerly for male patients could be used for female patients ... that they might then continue to run it'.[32] This case illustrates how cottage homes may have perpetuated the gender division that patients first experienced upon admission to asylums (as discussed by Hide in Chapter 3 of this volume). In turn, they perhaps represented an artificially segregated community space for convalescence which, for some patients at least, diverged from the homes they might expect to return to upon final discharge.

The MACA, however, did not draw attention to this relatively institutional and artificial separation between the sexes. Instead, it tended to accentuate the sociability found within its homes, which it closely associated with a familial ideal. In its annual reports, the organization emphasized the 'friendly feeling' and 'happy relations' between matrons and their convalescent residents in ways that support Chris Philo's speculation that cottage homes may have been 'less about places than people'.[33] These representations promoted the sense that the homes offered an environment of moral and interpersonal support, which hinged particularly on the quintessentially female figure of the matron. While some of the Association's cottage homes were registered to men, most were listed as belonging to married women.

The extent to which the supportive matron remained stereotypically a housewife is indicated in the annual report for 1931. This offered thanks to the charity's 'matrons, their husbands, staff, and other helpers' and, thereby, represented a chain of domestic support with the married female matron at its head. Patient letters quoted in the MACA's reports further reinforced her centrality. Two patients, for instance, referred to the 'motherly' care they had received, while many others specifically mentioned the 'kindness' and 'sympathy' matrons and sisters had shown.[34] In contrast, the male proprietor remained a shadowy figure in these reports. Instead, it appears the archetypical head of the cottage home 'family' was the married matronly housekeeper.

To a significant degree, the domestic environment provided was purposefully 'other' from patients' own homes. In common with other convalescent institutions, the MACA claimed its homes provided patients with a 'change' and 'rest'.[35] Despite their recognizable domesticity, they paradoxically primarily functioned to withhold patients from a premature return to their own households. In portentous language, a publicity sheet from about 1938 cautioned that 'the hurrying of a patient into a world of work and worry, to an unsatisfactory home, under unsympathetic conditions, is frequently to precipitate disaster'.[36] In contrast, the annual report from the previous year had presented its cottage homes as a 'haven of rest', which underlined the relative absence of any stresses that might imperil recovery.[37]

The MACA's representations of its residential convalescence suggest that it may have envisaged its homes as a temporary refuge from the pressures of wider community living, with the archetypically motherly figure of the matron providing relief from such anxieties – just as Diana Gittins has suggested the asylum functioned to shelter many women 'needing simply a chance to recover from extreme stress, often exhaustion, in their domestic lives'.[38] The MACA recognized its homes provided such a refuge, even as they regarded them as (favourably) distinct from the sorts of dwellings most ex-asylum patients might expect to inhabit after their final discharge. Indeed, the idea that a convalescent home might provide a respite from the demands of housework, parenting and employment extended beyond the MACA. In 1935 Gardiner observed the existence of other homes that provided neurotic patients with a change of scene, rather than a return to their dysfunctional lives in their own abodes.[39] 'Rest' and 'change' had likewise frequently appeared in the MACA's annual reports since the late nineteenth century. From the perspective of the organization, the points of divergence from ordinary domestic experience were solely positive, summed up in its claim that its cottage homes provided a shelter from a 'world of work and worry'.

Some within the Association even hinted that their homes could provide a better home environment than patients' own families. Its Chairman, Reginald Worth, claimed in a speech given to the Central Association for Mental Welfare Public Health Congress in 1934 that the main difference between the 'family' available to patients in cottage homes and their own blood relations was that 'the head of the "family" [in our homes] is a skilled individual and as such possesses the tact, understanding and sympathy so necessary' during convalescence.[40] Such representations established the cottage home as a potentially *more* homely domicile than the patients' own residence. As with the patient who described their stay as a 'home from home', Worth's speech identified a super-reality to the domesticity found in the cottage home. These extra-homely homes, Worth's speech implied, represented models of familial care. He went on to refer to a case where a patient from an 'undesirable home' had received convalescence and recovered. This case served to contrast the inadequacy of patients' own homes with the skilled, if artificial, 'family' environment that the MACA helped create through its residential convalescence. Nevertheless, the very detail Worth could provide on this case points to the distinctly institutional surveillance and staffing present in the charity's homes. The next section explores how claims for the cottage home's domestic ordinariness were to some extent contradicted by the artificiality of their planning, regulation and administration.

Professionalism and Supervision

The emphasis Worth placed on the skills of cottage-home matrons reflected the growing importance the MACA itself placed upon skilled training. In 1913, it expanded its convalescent work to include patients still officially certified, yet released into the community on probationary 'trial' periods to test the extent of their recoveries. Speaking at the annual meeting when the proposal was discussed, the Secretary, H. Thornhill Roxby, suggested that the charity's existing homes with 'trained mental nurses' might prove more suitable for certified trial cases than those without such specialist experience.[41] These comments indicate that by the 1910s, its homes were no longer managed solely under the lay supervision of the kind of 'Christian-minded' ladies that Henry Hawkins had first envisaged. At the end of the nineteenth century, the MACA's adverts for cottage-home matrons had asked simply for a place where patients might be 'boarded out'.[42] In contrast, articles published in the early twentieth century regularly referred to the experience and training in the management of psychiatric patients that the charity's matrons possessed, suggesting that the organization increasingly sought out skilled staff for its homes.[43] In Chapter 3 Hide argues that female asylum nursing was becoming more professionalized at the turn of the century; the MACA's comments suggest that experienced nurses found an additional outlet for their skills at a time (the 1920s) when Peter Nolan has suggested that within mental hospitals the profession had 'made little progress'.[44] The particularly liminal status of trial patients perhaps encouraged these increasing references to the training of its cottage-home staff.

To the extent that matrons often had a background in mental hospital nursing, however, the unremarkable domesticity of the cottage home was a stage-managed illusion. This tension between homely support and skilled institutional supervision is particularly evident in Reginald Worth's 1934 address. In this speech, Worth highlighted the recognizable domesticity of cottage homes yet further tacitly acknowledged the artificiality of the continued observation they permitted over their residents. He assigned matrons a dual role: at once matriarchal (or patriarchal) head of the cottage-home 'family' and 'skilled individual, almost invariably trained in a mental hospital'.[45] This attested to the split identity of the cottage homes, between ordinary household and site for the continued professional regulation of vulnerable ex-patients. Whilst Worth also claimed that these represented 'homes in the fullest sense of the word', the inverted commas he placed around the word 'family' betrayed its construction and contingency.

The background of many matrons in mental-hospital nursing served to identify the MACA's cottage homes ever more closely with institutional psychiatry. In evidence given to the Royal Commission on Lunacy and Mental Disorder (1924–6), the Association's Secretary, Ethel Vickers, laid particular emphasis on the psychiatric background of the charity's matrons. 'Each cottage home is run by a retired mental nurse', Vickers stated, 'so that they can understand the illness and not be afraid or nervous of anything that may happen'. By the 1920s, therefore, patients transferred to cottage homes remained under a form of trained psychiatric observation comparable to the nursing found within mental hospitals. Vickers further indicated that entry into these homes followed medical recommendation from asylum superintendents.[46] As such, both the referral procedure to cottage homes and the staff that managed them came from inside the public mental hospital system. Consequently, cottage homes occupied an ambiguous borderland between public medical institutions and private care homes. Although the retired status of matrons formally distanced them from the asylum, their training nevertheless associated their fitness to care for mental convalescents with their past employment within this system.

For at least some of those patients who failed to prosper as convalescents, contact between matrons and their asylums ensured that they never left psychiatric observation. Rules issued to matrons in about 1914 indicate that relapse amongst trial patients would inevitably lead to asylum readmission, with matrons instructed to telegram medical superintendents directly should these patients worsen.[47] For these convalescents, therefore, cottage homes served to extend asylum observation into the community. To the extent that matrons automatically returned trial patients to the mental hospital upon relapse, the cottage home may be regarded an outpost of these institutions.

There is less evidence that those already discharged from an asylum as 'recovered' would necessarily return there upon relapse. Once patients ended their period of certification, the MACA appears to have purposefully sought neutrality in recertification, even though it may have indirectly abetted the process. Edith V. E.'s case file indicates that she left a cottage home in 1916, only to relapse in her new employment, at which point her employer requested the Association's help in initiating asylum readmission. The summary of the MACA's reply suggests that it declined, on the basis that its rules precluded the charity from instigating recertification upon a patient's relapse. Instead, it recommended that the employer contact workhouse staff who, under lunacy legislation, provided the signature that accompanied the medical certificate for asylum readmission.[48]

While the MACA refused to initiate certification, Edith's case nonetheless suggests that convalescence retained patients within a wider web of referral procedures and psychiatric knowledge. The charity's central Westminster office collected reports from its matrons, whilst also keeping in touch with other social agencies, asylum superintendents and employers. Both within and beyond the cottage home, therefore, patients like Edith remained part of a bureaucratic network. This extended observation not only beyond the walls of the asylum but beyond the cottage home itself, into workplaces, workhouses and other public spaces.

It was the legal regulation of mental health that perhaps most clearly differentiated cottage homes from ordinary convalescent institutions, despite their superficial similarity in appearance and therapeutic function. Whereas patients within general convalescent homes ultimately retained control over the timing and nature of their discharge, cottage-home convalescents potentially faced an involuntary return to the asylum if they relapsed during their stay. As historians have widely noted, the judicial basis for the 1890 Lunacy Act vested significant control over psychiatric treatment in the courts. Consequently Roy Porter, Anne Rogers and David Pilgrim have suggested that, before the 1930 Mental Treatment Act introduced voluntary treatment, asylums remained essentially closed and segregative institutions.[49] Throughout this period, convalescence formed part of this asylum system that served to regulate pathways to health. While cottage-home matrons directly returned relapsed trial patients to the asylum, they formed one link in an ongoing chain of observation that determined where many other discharged patients would eventually return.

Some patients chose for themselves whether to accept the convalescence offered to them. To this extent, the cottage home represented one of the more 'open' parts of the Lunacy Act asylum system that Porter describes. Registers indicate that some patients refused places in cottage homes. In contrast, the MACA proudly recorded in its annual report for 1926 that many patients voluntarily paid return visits to their former matrons for advice and support after their placement, a claim borne out in some of the charity's few extant case files.[50] Such choices, however, could only be exercised by the few patients offered cottage-home breaks in the first instance. Published statistics suggest that only 5–10 per cent of discharged asylum patients received this convalescence in the 1910–20s.[51] Inhabiting the cottage home, therefore, depended upon initial referral and selection. Moreover, those patients subsequently offered places remained under some form of professional supervision, even though many patients appear to have formed genuine attachment to their matrons, carers and co-residents. It is to the patient's sense of identity and belonging within these homes that the chapter now turns.

Contested Convalescences

The three patients' responses to cottage-home referrals explored in this section are not assumed to represent the typical patient experience. Rather, they are intended to illustrate the potential importance of personal background and experience to patients' sense of belonging in cottage homes for convalescence. It has already been suggested that the MACA publicly accentuated the domestic normality of these homes. In contrast to the organization's representations, however, I have argued that the increasingly professionalized system of psychiatric surveillance employed within cottage homes marked them out as primarily institutional sites for the management of improved mental health. They combined aspects of both the domestic and the institutional. How did convalescents themselves regard these most homely of institutions?

At least some patients appear to have shared the MACA's perception that these temporary breaks provided a surrogate family environment in preparation for their return to busier, but comparably domesticated, lives in the community. The convalescent quoted in the title of this chapter exemplifies the comparability of the cottage home and life in the wider community. Their representation of their convalescent placement (about 1936) as a 'home from home' drew a parallel between cottage-home residency and life within a private household. '31669' appears to have identified the charity's home with their own, inasmuch as both places were defined by parental support and personal affection. As a former resident, this individual offered the MACA thanks for the 'kindness, good food and comfort' they had received. This representation conformed closely with the organization's image of its homes as a site of motherly matron-administered nurture, which perhaps explains why this particular extract was selected for inclusion in the published annual report. The principal contrast between cottage home and their own home in this case appears in caring duties. From having been the subject of care, '31669' now became the carer whose 'son and daughter were so pleased' to have them home. Restored to their own household, they made a particular point of stating that they were 'now having a good clean up', thereby emphasizing their renewed social role as both parent and housekeeper.[52]

For '31669' the cottage home appears to have afforded a quasi-parental environment for recovery, in ways that made it comparable to their own domestic experience as a mother or father. In contrast, Esther M.'s case record suggests how cottage-home referrals may, for some parents, have represented an unwelcome distraction from their own role as primary carers in the community. Referred for convalescence in 1918, the annotation beside Esther's entry tersely notes that she would not leave her child, so 'could not be convalesced'.[53] The MACA's refusal to take both mother and child reflects the institutional decision-making that regulated access to cottage homes. In turn, Esther's reticence at placing her own convalescence above the needs of her dependent hints powerfully that some patients at least may have regarded the temporary homeliness the MACA could provide as relatively less important than their own responsibilities and primary attachments in the wider community. While Gittins and Anne Shepherd have suggested that women resorted to asylum admission in times of stress, Esther's case suggests that other women and men may have sought to expedite their return to their own dependents.[54] The Association represented its homes as a haven from a 'world of work and worry', yet Esther's case indicates how such community-based anxieties might prove difficult in practice for some patients to forget or postpone.

Tracing Esther's case in the registers, however, suggests that patients may have reappraised their need for convalescence in the light of further difficulties encountered after discharge. A later entry indicates that Esther subsequently relapsed. After a brief stay in an asylum, she went on to accept a place in Mrs Fleming's cottage home at Hurstpierpoint, West Sussex, from where in December 1920 after a further relapse she was once more certified.[55] Sadly, despite the MACA's idealized representation of its homes as a stable and supportive 'bridge' to recovery, case records indicate that patients often relapsed. Most appear to have passed through homes just once, yet a substantial minority returned, sometimes several times. Such returns challenged the organization's claim that the familial domesticity within its cottage homes could reliably nurture convalescents to independence and health. Indeed, these records provide a glimpse into the pre-history of the 'revolving-door' patient of late twentieth-century community care. Far from being a relatively new phenomenon, Esther's case history suggests that some early twentieth-century patients also had experience of multiple readmissions across both mental hospitals and community-based intermediate institutions.

Where patients could look forward to the prospect of close friendship networks, supportive spouses, or simply a stable home and work life, the wider community itself might have presented a more attractive locus of care-giving. Not all patients, however, had a place to return to or kin to provide care. The final case considered in this chapter – that of Ernest S. – suggests that for the most vulnerable, cottage homes may indeed have provided a modicum of home-like belonging. Proprietor Mr Wood apparently gave a 'very good account' of Ernest after his referral in 1914. A fortnight later, Mr Wood wrote that he considered Ernest the 'best mannered and most sane man they had had' and, in an indication of esteem, took it upon himself to help him find work as a plumber. This comment perhaps reflects a degree of affection between cottage-home proprietor and patient. Because Ernest's observations are mediated through case workers, it is more difficult to evaluate how he viewed his time in the home. Nevertheless, it does appear that he showed some concern for his prospects for future self-sufficiency: the case worker recorded that after two weeks in the home Ernest was 'anxious to get work'. Like Esther M.'s decision to return home rather than take up convalescence, his concern to acquire employment suggests a mindfulness of belonging in the wider community.

Such belonging, however, was significantly dependent upon patients' health and ability to sustain independent lives once discharged. Like Esther, Ernest quite quickly relapsed. After a short and unsuccessful period working at Royal Victoria Military Hospital, Netley, where he found the work too arduous, he soon went back to Mr Wood's home for further care.[56] In this case, Ernest's voluntary return signals a sense of belonging, just as Mr Wood's favourable comments hint at a personal affinity between carer and convalescent. It further reflects the contingency of convalescence, as a period in which patients could plan for their future independence only insofar as they maintained adequate mental health. Such relapses indicate the failure of convalescence to reliably restore patients to health as the MACA intended. Nevertheless, Ernest's case does suggest that where patients established cordial relations with their carers, the homes provided a place to turn to in moments of need for at least some who experienced relapses in the community.

How far any of these patients regarded the cottage home as a place to which they belonged is difficult to determine, yet their responses suggest they may, each to different degrees, have considered it as a welcome source of support in times of personal crisis. Esther M. and Ernest S. both had to respond to medical and occupational challenges; in each case they ultimately came back to the cottage home. They exemplify what Allan Beveridge and Leonard Smith have individually proposed: that asylum patients have historically responded flexibly to dynamic changes in environment and personal circumstances while under psychiatric care.[57] Moreover, Ernest S.'s case indicates that it may not only have been women who, as Gittins and Shepherd have proposed, sought temporary respite from social pressures through recourse to psychiatric institutions.[58]

Conclusions

This chapter has expanded upon an existing call for historians to pay more attention to psychiatric institutions beyond the asylum.[59] It has built upon suggestions that the MACA offered prototypical community care through cottage homes, which Welshman has specifically suggested foreshadowed the post-1945 hostel. Perhaps due to a focus on nineteenth-century contexts, historians such as Walton, Wright and Suzuki have previously tended to depict the negotiation of institutional discharge as a binary process decided between asylums and families.[60] In contrast, the evidence of the MACA's archive suggests that cottage homes in the twentieth century may have served as clearing houses for the insane, within a more complex network of institutional care that in this period also included workhouses, Rowton Houses and outpatient clinics.

The Association itself to some extent utilized this binary distinction, in its identification of the cottage home as an unremarkable family environment in which patients could consolidate their recoveries. As existing homes and households, the MACA could legitimately claim that these offered a closer approximation to wider community contexts than mental hospitals. More than the fabric of the buildings, the charity particularly emphasized the quintessentially motherly care provided by its cottage-home matrons. To some extent, the MACA recognized differences between its homes and those the patients would return to, not least in the seclusion and rest it claimed cottage homes could offer. Beyond this, however, these homes formed part of a broader bureaucratic network of psychiatric surveillance. The gender segregation imposed between homes, the increasingly professionalized staffing, and the low-key surveillance of residents all constituted 'institutional' facets of cottage-home care.

How far patients found a sense of belonging in cottage homes and how far they defined their identities as convalescent patients within these spaces is likely to have depended significantly upon personal circumstance. Patient identity and belonging was contingent upon both their past experience and present contexts. The three case histories briefly explored suggest that medical relapse and (potentially associated) occupational difficulties may have predisposed patients to seek out placements. Ernest S.'s choice to return to his old cottage home in a time of difficulty, however, is also comprehensible in the light of the apparent affection and support his home proprietor had previously shown. In contrast, Esther M.'s initial refusal to take up convalescence and the emphasis '31669' placed on returning to her children raise questions over how far patients maintained primary filial and kin attachments in the community, which went beyond what cottage homes could offer. Situated ambiguously between institution and community-based residence, the cottage home contained aspects of both. It provided a temporary refuge and an early model of community care, albeit more closely linked to the mental hospital than the post-war hostel. How we interpret these antecedents of the late twentieth-century halfway house, arguably, depends upon closer attention to the shifting perspectives of those who organized and inhabited them.

8 'THE FATHER AND MOTHER OF THE PLACE': INHABITING LONDON'S PUBLIC LIBRARIES, 1885–1940

Michelle Johansen

It was resolved that Mr Henry J. Hewitt be appointed Librarian to the Chiswick Free Public Library at a salary of £90 per annum with rooms, gas and firing, such engagement being determined by a month's Notice [*sic*] on either side.[1]

'For the Free Use of the People': The New Public Libraries in Late-Victorian London

In 1885 there were two public libraries in London supported by rateable income; in 1890 there were twenty-one. By 1906 there were over 100 rate-assisted library buildings, affording ready access to novels, reference books, newspapers and journals for millions of men and women annually.[2] These were cultural institutions that also acted as unofficial information centres, labour exchanges and education hubs, with librarians arranging reading circles, evening classes and lectures for city dwellers wishing to undertake informal learning programmes in their leisure time. The new public libraries had links with the mutual improvement culture but they were aimed at a more numerous and heterogeneous readership. At a time when further education establishments for non-elite students were still not widespread (see William Whyte's chapter on the new civic universities in this volume), the quasi-scholarly ideals and open-doors policy of the so-called 'free' libraries meant that these institutions were frequently portrayed as the universities or polytechnics of the people.[3]

Prior to the establishment of the rate-assisted libraries, London had possessed a number of public reading rooms and newsrooms as well as numerous book lending and borrowing organizations, such as circulating and subscription libraries; but these were in effect closed to readers without a disposable income or established social connections, or both. For the majority of Londoners (working-class men and women earning low or irregular wages and unable to call upon respectable neighbours or colleagues to act as guarantors of good character by countersigning membership application forms), access to both light and serious reading matter was restricted. As most regions of the capital were slow to respond to the Public Libraries Act of 1850, this position remained unchanged until around 1890. Thus, some thirty years after the Act had allowed municipal authorities in Britain with a population numbering 10,000 or more to spend a proportion of their rateable income on accommodation and running costs for a free public library, only two rate-assisted libraries had opened in London. Modifications to the terms of the original Act, a shared belief in the need to educate and inform an expanding electorate, the increase in literacy levels following successive education acts, a growing awareness of the benefits of providing spaces of 'rational recreation' for working men and women, and the desire to commemorate Queen Victoria's Golden Jubilee in 1887 with impressive public architecture all played a part in accelerating the metropolitan library movement, leading to a boom in library building programmes in the 1890s.[4] By the early 1900s London possessed an accessible and remarkably well-used library service supported from the rates and established 'for the free use of the people ... no charge is made for admission, and no formal ticket of membership is necessary'.[5]

Strategic spending patterns indicate that the new libraries were civic buildings first and public learning and book-lending institutions second. Many rate-assisted libraries also served a third purpose – as homes for the chief or head librarian. At the turn of the twentieth century, more than forty metropolitan librarians lived over or alongside their libraries.[6] Each enjoyed a different residential experience but patterns and commonalities are discernible. These are described in the chapter which follows in order to analyse what it meant, in human or social terms, to live-in in the late-Victorian and Edwardian library. This analysis has much to add not only to our understanding of the occupational experience of the metropolitan public librarian during a critical period of emergence in the profession but also to scholarly debates around broader historical themes such as class, status, residency and domesticity in the city. It warrants emphasis that early municipal librarianship was dominated by men: the chief and branch librarians in charge of London's rate-assisted libraries during the period under scrutiny were all male. A narrative of gendered roles and expectations is thus embedded within the essay.

Evidence to support the arguments was collected from a range of contemporary sources including librarians' reports held in local studies libraries across London, the records of professional associations (most especially the archive of the Society of Public Librarians), cross-institutional correspondence and professional manuals, guides and journals. This 'public' evidence has been mapped onto 'private' data from public registers. Informed by the methodology of the genealogist, family histories for some thirty senior London librarians have been reconstructed from census data and birth, marriage and death records. Borrowing the concept of generational time pioneered by historians such as Raphael Samuel, Paul Thompson and Carolyn Steedman, the study pays particular attention to 'the idea of the lifecycle, of development and change within individual experiences and their intersection with historical time'.[7] The aim of the essay is to retrieve and describe the point at which work and the institution and home and the human met in the late-Victorian metropolitan public library. The chronology reflects certain key moments in the rate-assisted library story: the high tide of free library development and use in London; the consolidation of public librarianship as a profession; and the short-lived period (1885–1914) during which it was considered best practice to provide residential accommodation for the chief librarian on the library premises.[8] The extension of the date range to 1940 reflects the fact that most of the librarians examined in this study stayed in post until the inter-war period; where appropriate and practical they also resided in their library apartments until retirement.

The chapter is divided into three parts. The first outlines the formal power structures enshrined in the late-Victorian library before examining the themes of authority and intention on the premises, paying attention to the interactions between the inhabitant librarian and his off-site managers. It also seeks to locate the boundary separating the professional from the domestic areas of the premises. The second part explores the material world and the built environment of the live-in librarian and his non-resident colleagues (after all, they too spent long hours on the premises and made themselves very much at home in the library buildings). It describes the scale and splendour of the first rate-assisted libraries in London but, rather than viewing these spaces simply as products of design, the focus throughout is on how individual librarians responded to their surroundings and the extent to which they displayed and exercised personal control. The third and final part establishes a shared set of class origins for the early public librarian in London in order to comprehend the material and social significance of his residential occupational experience in human terms. The study begins, however, by posing the question: why did those in charge of library planning in the late nineteenth century provide accommodation for the librarian in charge?

'The Whole of his Time': Interactions, Authorities and Intentions

Because the sums raised from the rates alone were insufficient to fund new premises, library commissioners (as library committee members were then termed) typically turned to wealthy patrons such as John Passmore Edwards or Thomas Carnegie to provide one-off donations for ambitious building schemes. This convention gave rise to a curious anomaly. Many of the first rate-assisted libraries were magnificent structures operating on such restricted budgets that the chief librarian might be found organizing fund-raising bazaars to raise money to cover basic running costs, scrimping on heating and lighting costs, bartering over charges for cleaning and stationery supplies or drafting begging letters for books to stock half-empty shelves. Here was a climate in which every financial transaction mattered.[9] To cover the cost of renting accommodation in the private sector, a non-resident librarian received a housing allowance in addition to his salary. For library commissioners overseeing a building project funded by an external benefactor, insisting upon an apartment for the librarian on the premises secured a small but vital saving on his salary.

There were practical considerations, too, to bear in mind. Ideally set at a distance from other residential properties, libraries and their contents were vulnerable to theft and trespass. If a fire took hold, substantial damage might occur before the alarm was raised. Installing a librarian on site afforded protection outside library opening times. The library committee also gained a degree of flexibility from an inhabitant employee. When the East Ham Urban District Council advertised the post of chief librarian in 1898, the advertisement included the statement: 'The person appointed will be required to devote *the whole of his time* to the duties of the office'.[10] Whilst it is unlikely he would be expected to work literally around the clock, the typical chief librarian did face unusual pressures on his time. Local daily papers were delivered before dawn and someone was needed on site by 7 a.m. to remove the job advertisements for display in the library entrance areas. The typical London newsroom remained open until 10 p.m., including on Saturdays. A trusted member of staff was required to see junior assistants out and lock the building securely afterwards. Many libraries also experimented with Sunday opening: at Whitechapel, in the heart of Jewish east London, the rate-assisted library was open for eleven hours on a Sunday. Officially or unofficially, then, the live-in librarian was available after hours as fire warden, night watchman, caretaker and porter. He was also present to play the part of events co-ordinator (arranging and overseeing lectures) or master of ceremonies at debating society events or reading circles. The concept of residency was supported at senior management level because the live-in librarian might be better utilized, even exploited, than his non-resident counterpart. Equally, he might be more closely monitored and controlled.

Established for public use and financed with public money, these libraries were viewed as the responsibility of local vestry boards. By the late 1880s, most London vestries had adopted the Public Libraries Act and were establishing sub-committees to oversee library development in their region. Here were non-elected bodies, composed of local clergymen, businessmen and leisured gentlemen, who broadly shared a practical ignorance of public library procedures and organization. Notwithstanding this, the librarian was obliged to report back to his commissioners on a regular basis and all key decisions were authorized at committee level. One frame of historical reference, which remains submerged in the overall narrative of public library residency, is the domestic familial home. Library recruitment processes were seemingly weighted in favour of the married librarian: a candidate with a wife appeared reassuringly respectable and reliable. Moreover, the wife of an inhabitant librarian might usefully fulfil certain domestic obligations attached to the post. Anecdotal evidence suggests that such obligations included cleaning and dusting the library departments and acting the part of 'a kind of copper's nark' reporting on the late arrival of junior staff.[11] Apart from alerting us to the complex interplay between the public and the private in the late-Victorian public library, the fact that some applicants for top positions were expected to provide information on their marital status at the recruitment stage raises questions about dominion, authority and control. It also warrants remark that library commissioners did not tolerate staff transgressions of the conventions of Victorian domesticity. Married life was the ideal; quiet bachelorhood with a widowed mother or sister was accepted; but fractured households were not tolerated, and one librarian who separated from his wife without informing his off-site managers was forced to resign during the early part of the period.[12]

The language used by the chief in formal reports to his commissioners appears to confirm his relatively low positioning within a top-down hierarchical arrangement, the reports being punctuated by submissive words or phrases, or prefaced with hesitant preambles: 'I respectfully submit'; 'I should be glad to take your instructions'; 'I beg to report' and so on.[13] There is a distinction to be made, however, between formalistic written expressions of submission and the actuality of how power relationships were played out. We must likewise approach the occasional reference to leave being *granted* to a librarian to reside away from the library or to a librarian being *ordered* to reside at a specific address by his commissioners with caution: there is disparity between the levels of scrutiny and surveillance shown during the recruitment stage and thereafter.[14] Once a librarian had been appointed, library commissioners only took an active interest in what went on in the private areas of the library building if specific problems were directly brought to their attention. The resident librarian otherwise inhabited his living space and regulated his household arrangements with minimal interference from off-site managers. Over the years, his sense of ownership increased.

The first generation of London librarians approached their work with such whole-hearted commitment that they came both to define themselves and to be defined by their institutional affiliation and their occupational achievements: 'It has been truly said that the history of Willesden's library service is also [the librarian's] biography'; 'to praise their library service was to praise their librarian'.[15] So close was the connection between the librarian and the bricks-and-mortar structure he inhabited that when a long-serving chief died, 'his' library building might be closed on the day of the funeral as a mark of respect. This notion of identifi-cation was a two-way process, which developed incrementally and went largely undocumented in public records throughout the period under scrutiny; by the inter-war period, the chief librarian was openly acknowledged by readers, col-leagues and managers to be inextricably a part of his institution. Some librarians were ascribed a parental role in their library's development: 'I deeply regretted the [*sic*] hear that you are leaving the old haunt – I do not like that – why! You are the father and mother of the place!'[16] The complexly gendered aspect of this quotation reflected the close control the librarian assumed over every aspect of his library's administration; the sympathetic and enduring interest he took in the intellectual welfare and progress of his readers; and the unparalleled fact that this set of librarians had been on-the-spot to manage the development of their libraries from pre-professional infancy in the 1890s to institutional maturity in the 1920s and 1930s. That this quotation appeared in a letter written by a reader to a *non*-resident librarian underscores the ambiguity around borders, owner-ship and authority in the first rate-assisted libraries. Regardless of the official power structures, even those librarians who did not live on the premises expe-rienced a sustained, intimate and publicly acknowledged association with the built environment they occupied.

'A Commodious and Handsome Residence': Material Environments

Unless the librarian's accommodation was signposted as separate from the func-tional areas of the building, the whole institution might be punitively assessed for the rates as a house. To avoid this, the division between the domestic and the workspace was carefully delineated in structural design terms. Separate entrances and stairways were constructed to denote the frontier where 'home' ended and 'institution' began. However, a measure of ambiguity existed. Librar-ians were sufficiently at ease in both areas of the building to use communicating doors or back entrances to pass from the private to the public, and *vice versa*, as convenience or desire dictated. Officially, the librarian may only have occupied one small and self-contained part of the premises but the tendency was to appro-priate the whole building (this was no less true for the non-residential librarian than for the man living-in). To unpack the social-biographical significance of this statement, it is necessary to comprehend the material worlds inhabited by the late-Victorian public librarian.

Describing the new public library for Chelsea in 1889, an article in the *Library* journal pointed out that the architect's designs included 'a commodious and handsome residence for the librarian'.[17] Published in 1889, the floor plans of the Battersea Library indicated that the librarian's apartments were spread across three floors and included both a dining room and a drawing room. The provision of these two rooms was an important marker of middle-class status: the drawing room, in particular, was viewed as 'a polite space in which dress codes and certain rules of etiquette apply'.[18] The floor plans of Clapham Library show that the library was constructed upon an 8,000-square-foot site. Apart from a lecture room (45 feet by 24 feet), the second floor of the building was entirely given over to the librarian's residence. It appeared that the designers of London's first wave of public library buildings (many of which were prestige or flagship constructions, bearing the name of their benefactor in elaborately worked scrolls or tablets over the main entrance) had been generous in apportioning space to the residential librarian – perhaps too generous. By 1907, the author of an instruction manual aimed at library architects was advising a more economical approach: 'where ... the architect has to include accommodation for a librarian he should avoid making this unnecessarily commodious, and should not provide more than five or at most six rooms in addition to bathroom, closet, and the necessary offices'.[19] For the majority of London's live-in librarians, this exhortation came too late to disrupt their domestic arrangements. Appointed in the late 1880s or 1890s, they were very much at home in their 'unnecessarily commodious' accommodation by the time the manual was published.

The chief librarian and his wife lived-in at Ravenscourt Park Library in Hammersmith from 1889 until 1919. As part of large-scale library renovations in 1900, the librarian's apartments also were to be cleaned, repainted, repapered, washed and varnished. A new white enamelled sink would be installed in the apartment bathroom. This detail reminds us that, occupying one part of new and celebrated civic spaces, residential librarians and their families incidentally benefitted from relatively high standards of living in terms of upkeep, fixtures, fittings and design; bathrooms may have been standard in new middle-class housing at the time but were rarely provided in new working-class homes.[20] At the Spa Road Library in Bermondsey, the whole of the vast second floor was occupied by the librarian's apartments '*forming a complete residence*, with bath, larders, stores, coal lift and *every residential convenience*'.[21] The Bermondsey librarian and his wife and children lived-in at Spa Road from 1891 to 1923. As descriptions of the new library building confirm, it was not simply that the librarian occupied thoughtfully designed and well-maintained apartments; it was not only that both the public and private parts of the building were fitted out with up-to-date labour saving devices; it was also that his accommodation was self-contained.

Census data from 1901 and 1911 shows that a chief librarian typically lived-in with a wife and children as part of what we would today term a nuclear family unit; but more complex family groupings existed. At Chiswick, the librarian's widowed mother shared the library apartments with her son, daughter-in-law and two grandchildren, while at Kilburn the single librarian shared the library apartment with his widowed sister and her teenage son. Occasionally, the household might include a live-in domestic servant but more usually the librarian's wife or children were responsible for keeping the apartments clean. Across London, live-in librarians occupied their domestic spaces in different ways but, whether they were a nuclear family of nine (as at Newington in 1901), a nuclear family of five plus a domestic servant (as at Whitechapel in 1901), a nuclear family of four (as at Willesden in 1901) or an extended family of four (as at Poplar in 1911), they all shared one key aspect of residency in common. As a household, they existed apart from others. The significance of this should not be underestimated both in terms of comfort and status:

> The [middle-class] home was seen as a haven, a refuge affording privacy and comfort from the stresses of life in the world outside. The emphasis on the single family unit and the domestic ideal of protection and privacy was reflected in the preference for the detached or semi-detached house, screened off from neighbours and passers-by with gardens, hedges, walls and gates, blinds and lace curtains.[22]

Apart from placing the accent on private modes of living, this quotation also foregrounds the value of physical detachment. For the live-in librarian, an additional measure of domestic and social currency might be gained from the library's detached or semi-detached position: the best type of new library premises required a site of 10,000 square feet, set back from a main road, alongside open space or parkland. At the same time, the library should be located close to busy or bustling residential or shopping areas. These optimum building conditions indicate that in terms of situation (close to amenities but within reach of open spaces and cut off from surrounding buildings) the residential experience for the public librarian was a positive one.

Incidental proofs appear to support this suppositional statement. Large numbers of candidates competed for every new chief or head librarian post advertised; it was not uncommon for library commissioners to receive in the region of 200 applications for each vacancy. Appointed to top positions as relatively young men, this pioneering generation of London chief librarians remained on the premises until obliged to retire, afterwards describing their careers as 'the happiest years' of their lives in an explicit acknowledgement of enduring job satisfaction.[23] The quasi-literary character of the position contributed to the role's image. In *The Intellectual Life of the British Working Classes* Jonathan Rose builds up a portrait of an extended era of working-class self-education, an era which he believes peaked in the late nineteenth century. Rose's study places the new public libraries centre stage in a prevailing culture of reading and information-gathering, and it identifies a transformative quality embedded within the process of reading.[24] For 'bookish' young men, a career in a public library presented welcome opportunities for self-education, mutual improvement and daily close contact with literature.

And the material world and built structure of the new public libraries possessed strong and particular attractions of their own. The librarian appointed as chief of St Martin-in-the-Fields in Westminster in 1889, for instance, enjoyed expansive views of London's West End from a set of private apartments which occupied the whole of the top floor of the modern four-storey library. The Hammersmith librarian, based at Ravenscourt Park, enjoyed a semi-rural existence in a location the *Pall Mall Gazette* considered 'the pleasantest and prettiest piece of public ground to be found within an equal distance of Bow Bells'.[25] Librarians living-in at libraries situated in less conventionally picturesque surroundings might still enjoy comparatively large or luxurious gardens. At Shoreditch the librarian had access to around one-fifth of an acre of land with a fountain and summer house, while at Poplar the librarian and his young family used the walled library gardens as their own play and picnic area during the summer months.

London's new rate-assisted libraries were ambitiously conceived civic spaces – immense buildings decorated with a vanity of turrets, spires, gables and steeples. Every style was represented: Fantasy Gothic, Renaissance, Baroque, Arts and Crafts, Art Nouveau. Dozens of design flourishes were attempted, including drawbridge effects, porthole windows, ornate scrollwork and detailed pediments, panels and clocks. Inside the library, an atmosphere of weighty or serious intellectual endeavour was created in reference rooms equipped with highly polished oak reading tables and furnished with stone busts of great thinkers and writers. Interiors were fitted out to a high specification and included sweeping Jacobean-style staircases with gleaming brass handrails, elaborately worked mosaic floors, handsome mahogany counters and galleried reading rooms. Structural details were carefully thought out, with marble pillars and Corinthian columns introducing a note of grandeur. Lighting the library rooms was inevitably a priority. There were elegant light fittings, while stained glass skylights and decorated ceiling domes ensured sufficient natural light entered reading rooms.[26] Alistair Black has pointed out that the absence of consistency makes it difficult to position libraries within an architectural historical framework; at the same time, he acknowledges that it is possible to identify cross-institutional conventions in matters such as scale, impact and intent. In Black's view, many new library buildings were designed to be palatial – with an emphasis on 'lay notions of substance, solidity, taste, repose, worthiness, dignity, enduring impression, size, splendour, monumentality, prominence and simple beauty'.[27]

Inside the library, the chief librarian possessed a book-lined office from which he wrote letters on smartly headed notepaper, his name appearing in bold print beneath a borough crest. At a time when etiquette handbooks directed military men (lacking a stable home address) to use headed notepaper and calling cards provided by their London clubs to convey a sense of prestige, this was an important signifier of status.[28] The possession of relatively well-equipped offices provided a type of social currency, which was reinforced by residency. Operating out of comparatively grand cultural institutions, and building upon their growing reputations as local historians, antiquarians and minor literary men, chief librarians might by-pass conventional class barriers to establish and maintain relationships with a loose community of researchers, scholars and book-lovers from a range of social spheres, whether by correspondence or face to face. Residency helped cement the ties between library and librarian and blur the boundaries between the private and the public, or the domestic and the professional, spaces in the building. As the librarian became increasingly at home on the library premises we find evidence of informal gatherings taking place behind the scenes or out of business hours; for example, the librarian at Willesden Green hosted regular Saturday morning political discussions, the librarian at Plaistow in east London ran a Literary and Debating Society, and the librarian at Leyton organized language tuition lessons for junior staff after hours. The minute books recording the activities of the Society of Public Librarians (SPL) (1895–1930) provide examples of the ambiguity surrounding ownership and agency in the library building. From 1895 to 1897, the society operated as a peripatetic organization. Members convened in one another's libraries after hours for monthly get-togethers, with wives and daughters on hand to assist with refreshments or provide entertainment once official society business had been concluded. Given that many SPL librarians were literally at home in their library buildings, perhaps we should not be surprised to find the minutes of meetings peppered with words which gesture towards the familial domestic social occasion ('invitation', 'entertain', 'welcome', 'hospitality' and 'host'), notwithstanding the ostensibly professional setting.[29]

If we agree that the 'palatial interiors' of the first London department stores conferred gentility upon shoppers and that the 'distinguished' or 'grand' design styles of late-Victorian gentlemen's clubs bestowed a degree of prestige upon members, what might we infer from the bricks and mortar of the first public libraries?[30] What do these buildings tell us about the professional status and identity of the men inhabiting them? In this part of the essay, we have learnt that library accommodation offered a comparatively comfortable and spacious version of domesticity. We have gained an understanding of the sheer scale and relative magnificence of the workspaces occupied and managed by the first chief and sub-librarians. Finally, we have seen some of the ways in which the librarian might use his work premises as the setting for social or societal interests. The qualifications 'comparatively' and 'relative' above not only indicate that the buildings were magnificent in comparison with their immediate surroundings but they are also intended to convey a sense of the practical and material benefits that institutional residence might confer upon each individual librarian. To comprehend the significance of this statement, it is necessary to understand how and where the typical London chief librarian lived before moving into library accommodation and how and where he lived in the absence of residency.

'More True of Housing': Environments, Income and Inmates

'In general, to be a member of the working classes in Victorian Britain meant to lead either a poor or a precarious existence or both. This was more true of housing than of any other facet of life'.[31] As this quotation suggests, every aspect of life offered challenges for those without social connections, cultural capital or financial security, but it was finding a stable place to live which presented the greatest difficulty. In this part of the essay, the methods of the genealogist are used to access the early lives of the first public librarians in London. Information from birth and marriage registers, street directories and census data from the mid-nineteenth century indicates that these men broadly shared a class status as well as a set of domestic expectations or aspirations based upon their childhood experiences of environment and home. Additionally, an overview of the housing situation in 1890s London (when most chief librarians secured their residential posts) and a thumbnail sketch of an alternative living-in experience powerfully clarify the material, practical and personal significance of living-in for the chief librarian and his family.

In London in the early 1890s, the annual income of a chief librarian might be anything from £65 to £200 depending on the size of the library, his previous experience and whether or not the post came with accommodation as part of the remuneration package.[32] At this time, the average salary of a London clerk or school teacher was estimated at between £75 and £150; a skilled artisan might receive between £65 and £104 a year; and an unskilled labourer or factory worker around £39 to £52 a year.[33] An appreciation of these incomes allows us to position the public librarian within an expanding white-collar sector of late-Victorian lower-middle-class society while also confirming that the typical London chief or sub-librarian was only marginally better-off financially than the average skilled working man during the early part of the period studied here.[34] Equipped with this knowledge, it is possible to obtain a benchmark understanding of the expectations of the first London librarians in terms of accommodation. We might now ask: 'what size and type of accommodation would their salaries purchase *outside* their libraries'? Here the case of the Lewisham librarian is useful. As stated above, the new London libraries were frequently financed by donations from wealthy supporters of the free library movement. Without such donations, purpose-built premises were out of the question; instead existing properties were adapted as makeshift libraries and the librarian was either accommodated on site, or expected to live out. The former arrangement occasionally meant a librarian found himself occupying a property rich in local significance and redolent with decaying splendour, as happened at East Ham when both library and chief librarian were temporarily housed in The Limes in the 1890s. Although his rooms were damp and in some disrepair, the East Ham chief could be forgiven for imagining himself a grand gentleman for a short time; photographs from the period show that 'his' Georgian library residence dominated the landscape, eclipsing the surrounding terraced and semi-detached homes.

The story at Lewisham in south-east London was rather different. Unable to raise sufficient funds for a purpose-built library, the library committee requisitioned a lecture hall on the outer fringes of the region to serve as a temporary free library. A chief librarian was appointed in 1891 with a salary of £120 plus £30 in lieu of a house. This qualification confirms that it was generally accepted that accommodation would be provided for the librarian as part of his terms of employment. It also alerts us to the fact that this librarian would be renting in the private sector. Examining his domestic arrangements allows us to see how a chief librarian might live in 'the real world' and also to contrast the residential and non-residential experience. In 1891, the Lewisham librarian and his wife had part-share of a modest semi-detached house with a middle-aged solicitor's clerk and his wife and daughter in a suburban region of south-east London. By 1893, the librarian and his wife had moved to become sole occupants of a two-storey terraced house in a neighbouring street. Ribbons of tidy, terraced and semi-detached properties occupied by schoolteachers, clerks and commercial travellers stretched outwards from the main thoroughfares. Few of these homes employed a live-in domestic servant, a conventional indicator used by scholars to denote middle-class status or aspirations.[35] Not only does the Lewisham example reveal the marked difference between the type of property occupied by the residential librarian and that occupied by his non-residential colleague but it also introduces the question of social class or status. Using data from the 1911 census, it is clear that most living-out librarians occupied properties similar to that of the Lewisham librarian in the 1890s. If married, they rented two-storey terraced homes in outer suburban regions such as Ilford and Forest Gate in east London; if single, they lived at home with parents or as boarders in the family homes of artisans or clerks. Theirs were recognizably lower-middle-class existences of a type lampooned in the satirical *Diary of a Nobody* (1892) and more recently revisited and, to some extent, rehabilitated by historians such as Peter Bailey.[36]

By the close of their careers in the 1920s and 1930s, this generation of librarians (both resident and non-resident) had attained a degree of affluence and a social standing within their communities that located them more securely within the middle class. Their comfortable pre-eminence in 'their' library buildings, the status conferred upon them by their workspaces and the relatively superior quality of the material things surrounding them incidentally concealed the distance they had travelled in social, cultural and material terms as adults.[37] Partly for this reason, the relatively lowly origins of the majority of Victorian public librarians have been overlooked by library historians; if anything, the tendency has been to situate them at the heart of the middle class in a simplistic oppositional or binary relationship with working-class readers as part of a narrative of surveillance and control.[38] Perhaps this portrait was appropriate by the post-war period; arguably it might be applied during the inter-war period; but in the earlier part of the period examined it requires reconsideration. This is because in the 1880s and 1890s the vast majority of London chief librarians were precariously poised *en route* between the working and the lower-middle class. Census records and birth and marriage registers show that these men had grown up in skilled working-class homes, the sons of labourers, plasterers, miners, carpenters and bricklayers. They saw older brothers or sisters start their working lives in the 1870s or 1880s as labourers, pupil teachers, clerks or domestic servants. To help with the rent, lodgers sometimes shared the family home while mothers took on piecework alongside their household duties; nobody employed a live-in domestic servant. Neighbours' occupations reflected their own families' status: living across the road or up the street from our putative librarians we find labourers, cleaners, housepainters, laundresses, and so on.

Ambitious, and fond of books and learning, this cohort of men had followed a self-improvement or self-help path out of material hardship and insecurity via literature (broadly construed) – a path taken by thousands of bright young autodidacts of their class and generation. This is a complex statement which demands extended analysis elsewhere.[39] Here, emphasis is placed on the two points which relate directly to issues of residency. First, aware that they might be judged negatively on their humble origins, a number of public librarians later attempted to conceal aspects of their family backgrounds and early lives; moving into library accommodation had the unintended but welcome effect of highlighting the disjuncture between then and now. Conventional markers of individual status reflected through the size, character and location of house and home were disrupted at a stroke. Wishing to reinvent themselves socially and professionally, the benefits of this aspect of residency cannot be overstated. Secondly, attending to the working-class aspects embedded within the compound class construction of the first public librarians in London enables us to comprehend the true worth and meaning of the residential experience in material terms for a generation of men with first-hand and relatively recent childhood experiences of household overcrowding and financial insecurity. These men lacked social capital; they had only a basic formal education (none had been to university); and they had no private incomes to draw upon. In both their professional affairs and their domestic arrangements, everything depended upon their intellectual assets, sustained hard work and a degree of good fortune.

We have already seen that librarianship was a competitive profession in this period. Many of the first metropolitan librarians had moved to London specifically to secure a senior post in a rate-assisted library. If the post did not come with accommodation, as newcomers to the city they were dependent on the recommendations of managers or colleagues to find somewhere to live. This was not always a straightforward undertaking. Rents were high, and on the increase. Multi-occupation was growing more common in homes designed and built for single family use; such homes deteriorated in quality and comfort as a consequence.[40] In the fight to secure suitable accommodation in a competitive private rental sector, the public librarian was at a disadvantage. He had a relatively low income but his 'respectable' needs meant he could not compromise on quality in terms of living standards.[41] We know from his family background that he could neither anticipate nor expect financial support in securing accommodation appropriate to his rising occupational status. In this climate, it is reasonable to suppose that the live-in London librarian considered himself better off than his non-resident counterpart.

His inhabitant experience was also of a superior type when compared to other residential professions open to men of equivalent background. The shop-worker provides a useful point of comparison. The living-in system had been adopted during the nineteenth century by large department stores as well as by dozens of smaller grocers, drapers and so on, as a means of providing on-site or easily accessible accommodation for shop assistants. The type of accommodation varied from purpose-built shared dormitories to converted bedsitting rooms above small shops. Whether or not we fully accept contemporary claims of employer malpractice, or lurid descriptions of lodgings ('the ceilings were quite black, the walls ditto, the floors were repulsive, on one part the ceiling was all broken away, beds were crammed about wherever room could be found for them'), here was a cramped, communal inhabitant experience a world away from the comfortable single-family residency enjoyed by the live-in librarian.[42] One fundamental divergence surrounded the issues of surveillance, control and supervision. Christopher Hosgood has described an underclass of late-Victorian and Edwardian shop assistants intentionally kept in a condition of near-servitude in exchange for a modicum of 'gentility', a regular wage and a bed in staff quarters above or close by the shop.[43] This does not correspond with the residential experience of the public librarian; as we have seen, there were opportunities both for agency and self-realization on the rate-assisted library premises. The first London librarians were able to influence spatial provision and use the material benefits of living-in to accommodate and progress their own needs and desires, with class, gender, age and intellectual and social interests all playing a part in the inhabitant process.

Conclusion

This chapter has described the point at which the institution, the home and the human or social intersected in the late nineteenth- and early twentieth-century London public library. From the hierarchical structures formally established in the first libraries and the deferential language of the librarians' reports, we might suppose that the residential experience would bear witness to a straightforward power relationship between the librarian and his off-site managers, with the former subject to strict supervision and with boundaries clearly delineated and understood on both sides. In reality, once he had passed stringent recruitment processes and as long as his household remained compatible with Victorian conventions of domesticity, the private arrangements of the chief or head librarian were infrequently monitored and rarely disturbed; accordingly there existed scope for voluntary and meaningful personal development on the premises for the chief librarian. The inhabitant librarian enjoyed sufficient authority to utilize his institutional domicile in a range of ways. Not only was he able to provide a relatively secure, comfortable and spacious home for his family at a time when rented accommodation in London was scarce, expensive and frequently badly maintained, but he was also able to exploit his residency to consolidate his own marginal status, both within his own profession and in the wider world, with those who shared his hobbies and interests. In the absence of direct, personal testimony that library apartments were superior to the type of accommodation a chief or head librarian might rent for himself and his family in the private rental sector, this chapter described the type and size of accommodation a non-inhabitant librarian occupied and the relatively humble origins shared by the overwhelming majority of chief librarians in late-Victorian London to confirm that here was a comparatively deluxe residential experience. The benefits of living-in were appreciated and enjoyed by the man in charge and his family. At the point of retirement there appears to have been a reluctance to vacate the library accommodation. It was not simply that these spaces had represented 'home' to the librarian, in some cases, for upwards of thirty years; it was also that it was difficult to exchange an aesthetically-arresting, even beautiful, book-filled residence set in landscaped parkland or gardens for a modest, terraced or semi-detached home in an outwardly unremarkable suburban London street.

Acknowledgements

This chapter emerged out of a PhD research programme funded by the University of East London and Bishopsgate Institute. I also wish to acknowledge the financial assistance granted by the British Federation of Women Graduates and the Institute of Historical Research (in the form of a Scouloudi Fellowship). Thanks, too, to staff at local studies archives in Brent, Hackney, Hammersmith & Fulham, Hounslow, Lewisham, Newham, Southwark, Tower Hamlets and Waltham Forest for help with locating materials relating to the first generation of public librarians in London. Particular acknowledgement is due to Stefan Dickers of the Bishopsgate Institute Archives.

9 'DISCIPLINE WITH HOME-LIKE CONDITIONS': THE LIVING QUARTERS AND DAILY LIFE OF THE WOMEN'S ARMY AUXILIARY CORPS IN FIRST-WORLD-WAR BRITAIN AND FRANCE

Krisztina Robert

The Material Environments of Martial Femininity

In December 1918, the Women's Army Auxiliary Corps (WAAC) chose for its official Christmas card a drawing by a member of the lower ranks, which depicted a uniformed auxiliary worker with the hutted campsite of her unit in the background.[1] The selection of this image was not coincidental. Between 1917 and 1919 the living quarters of the WAAC became an iconic emblem of the organization, represented in a series of press reports, photographs and recruiting images, followed by several watercolours and oil paintings.[2] Such widespread and varied portrayal indicates the centrality of these lodgings in the public image and collective identity of the corps. In this respect the WAAC was unique among women's war organizations. Whether they worked for the munitions industry, public transport, the Land Army or the auxiliary services of the navy and the air force, women war workers were usually identified in visual representations by the places, tools and products of their labour, rather than their accommodation.[3]

This chapter explores the living quarters and conditions of the WAAC to explain how and why they became such a defining feature of the corps. It starts by investigating the ideological significance of women's military accommodation to uncover the role which WAAC housing played in integrating the first female corps into the masculine world of the army. The main section then discusses how the lodgings of the WAAC fulfilled this role. It examines the changing physical and discursive construction of these dwellings as well as their officially sanctioned furnishings and regulations. It also explores the gendered values that the main architects of WAAC housing sought to promote through this accommodation and how these ideals were embodied and reflected in the design, fittings and use of the lodgings. Regarding the creation of WAAC quarters, I distinguish four main groups whose distinct agendas shaped the building, portrayal and material culture of these sites. They consist of, firstly, the military authorities and the Whitehall bureaucracy, who controlled the corps, and, secondly, army officers in Britain and on the Western Front, whose practical considerations in employing the women often differed from the government's views. On the women's side, the main parties comprised the officers and other ranks of the WAAC. The former – 1,200 women – administered the corps on behalf of the authorities and acted as the resident staff in the quarters, while the latter – 56,000 auxiliary workers – constituted the inmates under their care.[4] The final part of the chapter discusses the experience of inhabiting these lodgings. It examines the main factors that enabled women to fashion their surroundings to suit their individual tastes and needs and the impact that the resulting environments had on their gender identity and consciousness.

The housing and institutional life of women war workers have been neglected subjects in historical literature. Although a handful of studies have briefly discussed them for auxiliary and munitions workers, scholars have not fully analysed their impact on women's individual and collective identities.[5] This gap stems from the overwhelming focus on wartime employment conditions. Since women spent the bulk of their time at work, it seemed obvious to assume that the material environments of their workplaces were the more crucial factor in shaping their sense of self. Recent scholarship, however, has demonstrated that institutional living conditions, especially in the military, were designed to mould the corporate values and identity of recruits.[6] Such conditions became even more important when women entered new fields of study or work. Since femininity was defined partly by women's material culture, the physical and discursive construction of their communal accommodation and life in formerly male institutions had a crucial impact on their integration into these establishments and on public acceptance of that process.[7] Exploring WAAC quarters with these questions in mind, can provide new perspectives on women's military war work. Previous studies have claimed that since the army treated the auxiliaries as subordinate civilians, traditional definitions of femininity remained dominant.[8] Scholarship on material culture, however, has shown that spatial and material arrangements both mirror and construct social identifications, value systems and hierarchies, including those of gender.[9] Drawing on this approach, I argue that the military quarters of the WAAC helped to integrate the corps into the army by contributing to the development of a new gender identity, martial femininity, among the women and by promoting more amicable relations with the men.

'The Army has no Place for Women': The Ideological Significance of
Women's Military Accommodation

The contemporary significance of the auxiliaries' housing can be summarized
by the oft-quoted saying that the army is no place or has no place for women. In
Victorian and Edwardian times, variations of this phrase were deployed to rebuff
women's efforts to play more active roles in the armed forces.[10] Metaphorically,
the expression conveyed the refusal of the authorities to create professional open-
ings for women in the military beyond a small number of nursing posts.[11] More
importantly, the phrase was used in a spatial and material sense as justification
for keeping women out of the forces. In this context, it expressed the widely held
belief that the harsh physical environments of military barracks or army camps
in war zones would erode women's femininity by coarsening their bodies, morals
and minds. Thus, during the second Boer War, army medical authorities limited
the number of female nurses serving in South Africa by arguing that 'there is no
place for women to live in a hospital camp ... [with] ... comfort and propriety'.[12]
Simultaneously, the phrase also articulated fears among military officers about
the impact of female presence on the army's fighting capacity. In 1894 critics
drawn from the army, the Volunteer Force and their medical services vetoed a
plan for a female medical corps acting in the war zone by arguing that soldiers'
anxiety for the women's safety would divert their attention from the enemy,
while the sexuality of female medics would compromise the men's discipline and
morale.[13] Thus, the saying that the army has no place for women implied that
martial environments and femininity were incompatible and mutually exclusive.

The establishment of the WAAC in February 1917 revived and magnified
this issue. Created to ease the army's manpower shortage, the corps supplied
female workers to release soldiers for frontline duty by replacing them in a series
of military support jobs first in France and then in Britain.[14] The unprecedented
scheme posed a major challenge to traditional gender norms. Although women
had already been working with the army overseas, they were either segregated
from able-bodied soldiers as nurses on closely regulated hospital wards, or were
shielded from controversy by their low numbers and elite background, as were,
for example, the female staff of Young Men's Christian Association (YMCA)
canteen huts.[15] The religious associations of these two groups and their semi-professional or volunteer status also ensured that their morals never became a public
issue.[16] In contrast, the WAAC recruited young women from a range of classes
for paid work on a mass scale. Recruiting notices did not specify the exact location of the auxiliaries' employment. Their captions, however, which called for
girls 'to help the men to fight' and 'work ... with the forces' suggested that they
might serve in close proximity with the troops.[17] Thus, the scheme provoked
considerable opposition.[18] As before, objections were expressed in terms of space

and materiality. Helen Gwynne-Vaughan, chief controller of the WAAC over-seas, recorded on her first visit to France that opposition to the corps was almost universal and that while army officers enthused about the scheme in general, they all insisted that their own station was the one place unsuitable for women.[19] Public anxieties focused on the auxiliaries' living conditions. Such fears were reflected in the early press campaign of the WAAC, which sought to reassure parents that their daughters would be properly housed and cared for.[20] To make substitution successful, it was vital to win over both the military and the public. Therefore, 'making place' for women in the army by constructing a new type of martial accommodation for them became a priority for the authorities.

From Holiday Villas to Nissen Huts: The Integration of the WAAC into the Army

When the WAAC was first established, the main concern of the Army Council was to convince public opinion about the safety of the scheme and thus facili-tate substitution. Therefore, the authorities emphasized that special efforts were being made to accommodate the auxiliaries in France. Press articles stressed that WAACs would not live under canvas or even in huts if possible, but would be lodged comfortably in hostels under the care of lady superintendents.[21] These promises were followed by the provision of higher-grade housing than was customary in the army. Depot hostels in Britain, which prepared recruits for posting, were converted from imposing residential clubs and hotels, such as the Connaught Club at Marble Arch and the Metropole in Folkstone. Likewise, in France, the first WAAC units were housed in elegant holiday villas and hotels in towns like Boulogne and Calais, parts of which were used as British military bases.[22] The choice of these buildings was, of course, also practical. They were large enough to accommodate several units and were near major transport links and army offices where the women would work. In addition, requisitioning existing buildings was the fastest way of housing military staff once the furnish-ings were replaced by army furniture.[23] Nevertheless, the first WAAC camps built during this period also reveal the intention to provide superior housing for the women. The Royal Engineers' regimental history notes that WAACs 'had to be accommodated in specially built camps', including huts with linoleum floors, electric light and curtained-off sleeping cubicles for two as well as ablu-tion blocks with basins and tubs partitioned individually for privacy. The first camps also featured covered pathways, used only in hospital camps, to protect the women from the rain by linking their sleeping huts to their mess, washing and latrine facilities.[24]

The superior quality of WAAC lodgings can be judged by comparing them with servicemen's quarters. Throughout the war soldiers' accommodation lagged

behind the rapid and massive expansion of the British armies and the resulting heavy and constant demand for housing for troops, offices and hospitals.[25]
In 1914 recruits to Kitchener's New Armies lived in severely overcrowded barracks, under canvas, or in the open air while training in Britain, causing hardship
and even deaths from pneumonia once bad weather arrived in October. Instead
of slowing down recruitment, however, the War Office resorted to billeting the
men with the civilian population.[26] Likewise, on the Western Front many troop
camps still relied on tents in 1918 and, even in hutted accommodation, servicemen's privacy, living space and ablution facilities remained limited. Soldiers slept
in dormitories the size of which was reduced if they had separate dining huts,
and their wash basins and tubs were provided for 12 and 1 per cent of their
strength, respectively.[27] This contrasted with washing facilities for 15 and 5 per
cent in WAAC lodgings; separate dining blocks that housed combined mess and
recreation rooms; and more spacious sleeping quarters partitioned into cubicles
for every two members of the other ranks and for every forewoman (the equivalent of a non-commissioned officer or NCO).[28] In addition, unlike in 1914,
recruitment for the WAAC, and therefore substitution, was held up in 1917
until suitable housing could be obtained for the women.[29]

Early portrayals of the auxiliaries' quarters and daily life exaggerated their
attractive features. The first press reports, generated by the Women's Section
of the National Service Department (WS), which ran WAAC recruitment
and publicity, represented living conditions in the corps through the discourse
of Edwardian middle-class domesticity. Articles about WAAC life in France
focused on the women's off-duty activities. They described 'charming' recreation
huts where the girls were having tea, writing letters at 'little tables' and resting in
deck chairs with 'gay cushions' after playing badminton and tennis in the garden.[30] Accounts of British hostels also portrayed conditions in terms of comfort,
pleasure and seclusion. They depicted spacious double bedrooms with chests of
drawers and soft pillows on 'little beds' and recreation rooms 'daintily-furnished'
with comfortable armchairs, luxurious couches, gramophones and pianos.[31] The
first official photographs published in magazines reinforced these portrayals.
The images pictured auxiliaries outside their quarters converted from an elegant
hotel in Paris Plage, having dinner in their frescoed dining room and reading
letters from home on their balcony.[32] These representations were produced with
a clear recruiting goal. Addressing parents and guardians directly, the corps'
publicists hoped to convince them, along with their daughters, that service in
the WAAC was both a safe and appealing option for war work, with no loss
of traditional femininity.[33] Such portrayals, however, and their reticence about
the corps' martial conditions, also reflected the background of the civilian lady
directors of the WS, who disapproved of militarism in women's war organizations.[34]

Army officers in the field, concerned that the women's presence would undermine the troops' discipline, insisted on segregated environments for the auxiliaries. At an early conference in France, discussing the association of soldiers and WAACs, one general protested that 'if these women are coming, we shall have to wire [fence] all the woods on the Lines of Communications'.[35] Likewise, the base commander in Rouen refused to sanction the joint use of YMCA club rooms, arguing that 'discipline must be maintained'.[36] One former WAAC also recalled that initially they were prevented from using soldiers' canteens, despite not yet having facilities of their own, and that they had to queue separately from the men once they received access.[37] Equal concern to protect the auxiliaries from soldiers' attentions was reflected in the design and regulations of the women's housing. Men were forbidden to enter WAAC quarters and all camps were surrounded by high fences of post and wire or corrugated iron and were guarded day and night by sentries with their own guard hut at the gate.[38] In large military camps in Britain, which were shared by soldiers and WAACs, similar arrangements were made to keep men and women apart. In Aldershot, A and D squares of the camp, where the auxiliaries were housed, were fenced around by iron posts and barbed wire with a large sign, 'Out of Bounds for Troops'; gates at both ends were locked at night. In addition, the lower halves of the women's sash windows were screwed down to prevent men from climbing in.[39]

This segregated domestic model could not integrate the auxiliaries into army areas and stations either as fellow workers or as comrades of the men. To start with, segregation between the two sides was impossible to maintain. Auxiliaries were forbidden to chat with soldiers at work or associate with army officers anywhere, but the women were neither willing nor able to abide by these rules.[40] Most of them had relatives and boyfriends in the army and resented having to apply for special passes to see their loved ones or make new acquaintances. In addition, they met numerous men both at and en route to work, and natural instincts and politeness compelled them to respond to the men's questions and banter.[41] Certain aspects of female domesticity also conflicted with military working practices. In many army stations where the auxiliaries were employed, the men were ordered to refrain from smoking and swearing out of respect for the women.[42] This added to soldiers' hostility to the WAACs, whose arrival meant the loss of their safe office jobs and redeployment to the front once the women were competent in their duties.[43] Seeing the auxiliaries as dangerous rivals, the men often resented what they saw as their co-workers' better conditions. At Calais base headquarters soldiers grumbled on pay days about the WAACs' seemingly higher wages, not realizing that while they were issued with full kit, the women only received one set of outer uniform and had to provide everything else for themselves.[44] Army officers' hostility also focused on the women's alleged domestic habits and their incompatibility with efficiency. Although both men and women took breaks from their duties to have tea, women were often criticized for wasting valuable working time through this custom.[45] One general, visiting a depot in Calais just when the auxiliaries were having their ten-minute tea break, was outraged that they were 'holding up the whole war' and demanded that the practice should cease.[46]

From late summer 1917, the short-lived model of segregated domesticity started to change, due partly to shifting military priorities and attitudes. A key factor in this process was the worsening manpower shortage. Seeking to speed up substitution and boost troop numbers in readiness for the large German offensives expected in the new year, the authorities expanded recruitment for the WAAC considerably in the autumn. In addition, dissatisfaction with the work of the WS led the War Office to replace the department with the Ministry of Labour supported by the WAAC leadership, which adopted more effective recruiting and propaganda methods.[47] The better recruiting returns produced by these changes altered the auxiliaries' housing. With more women joining up, especially from 1918, the need to accommodate them quickly and affordably outweighed considerations for protecting traditional femininity.[48] Therefore, building specifications were lowered, making the women's housing more similar to that of the soldiers'. This trend was reinforced by the changing environments where the auxiliaries were working. As substitution proceeded from base and garrison towns to rural army stations in both France and Britain, fewer large buildings suitable for hostels were available. Thus, new units were increasingly accommodated in hutted camps in the countryside. Military attitudes in the field were also shifting. Army officers responsible for the soldiers' welfare realized that the women were actually good for morale since they reminded the men of the families and homes for which they were urged to fight. Officers therefore initiated joint entertainment and athletic events for troops and the WAACs, which resulted in the shared use of recreation and sports facilities.[49]

Change was equally driven by the ambitions of the newly prominent WAAC leadership and officers. As politically active, professional women, corps leaders saw substitution as a chance to open up the army to women's permanent employment. Their carefully selected female officers, who had similar backgrounds, identified with this goal.[50] Leaders of the WAAC realized that their professional aspirations were contingent on two related conditions. Firstly, auxiliaries had to be accepted by the army on a relatively equal footing as comrades-in-arms. Since the non-combatant WAACs could not experience soldiers' danger levels, sharing the men's living conditions away from the fighting line was the main way in which they could demonstrate their military identity.[51] Corps leaders therefore willingly accepted the more spartan accommodation as the price of acceptance by the army. Thus, Gwynne-Vaughan, the overseas chief controller, agreed to the housing of the women in Nissen huts without knowing what they were, simply because she was told that this would be necessary.[52] Creating a new martial female identity was the other condition of inclusion into the army. By combining the positive attributes of military masculinity and modern womanhood, the female auxiliary made femininity and the armed forces compatible.[53] Contemporary definitions of womanliness were closely intertwined with women's material culture in the home. Therefore developing the identity of the servicewoman included the construction of new, martial female living quarters. Leaders and officers of the WAAC were ideally placed to create such locations both physically and discursively. Controllers' duties included the authorization of housing and publicity, while administrators in charge of the units were responsible for overseeing the equipment of quarters, inspecting them for order and cleanliness and supervising the auxiliaries' daily routine, catering, leisure activities and health.[54]

The new quarters of the WAAC produced military housing for women by combining the principles of army accommodation with the attributes of the 'artistic' country cottages that were popular before the war and which were characterized by economy, utility and hygiene as well as cheerful and cosy homeliness.[55] Comprising some of the values of martial femininity, they found expression in the corps' newly built hutted camps and their furnishings. Initially, campsites featured sturdy, traditional wooden huts. Due to labour and timber shortage, however, from mid-1917 these were used only for ablution and mess facilities, while sleeping quarters were provided by prefabricated, corrugated iron, semicircular Nissen huts.[56] Utilitarian fixtures, such as trenches for air-raid protection, also superseded other former luxuries like covered pathways.[57] These martial features, however, were softened by some of the attributes of rural country cottages. Most camps cultivated grassy patches between huts, grew vegetables for their kitchen in allotments and kept pets, including cats, dogs and canaries.[58] The interiors also merged austere militarism with cheery homeliness. Bedrooms had iron beds with square, straw-filled palliasses, three of which made up a mattress, complete with straw pillows and coarse army blankets. No sheets were provided to save labour in army laundries.[59] Corps leaders, however, encouraged the auxiliaries to feminize their lodgings with simple decorations. Suggested alterations included the painting or papering of walls and livening up rooms with pictures, photographs and colourful curtains and lampshades.[60] The most successful outcome of this design was the corps' recreation rooms created by Engineer officers, the auxiliaries and the Young Women's Christian Association. Furnished with wooden tables and wicker and deck chairs, they were brightened by magazine prints, tablecloths and cushions and boasted pianos, teapots and vases of flowers.[61]

The regulations of WAAC quarters and daily life were designed to inculcate the auxiliaries with the qualities of martial femininity. Cleanliness, order and health were the most crucial of these traits and were promoted primarily through high standards of hygiene in the sleeping quarters. Every morning women had to strip their beds and pile up their palliasses, pillows and neatly-folded blankets at the foot of their bedframes, placing their suitcases, which stored all their possessions, on the top.[62] Rooms were then swept by domestic workers and inspected by administrators to ensure that they were clean, tidy and free from food which might attract vermin.[63] Strict rules about personal hygiene completed this regime. Most units had weekly bath parades or bath books which women had to sign to show that they had taken at least one full wash a week. In addition, medical officers held periodic foot and hair inspections to prevent the outbreak of scabies and the spread of head lice. Those with symptoms of infection were isolated instantly in separate huts or in the sick bay under the care of a nurse.[64] A regular daily routine aimed to boost health further and instil punctuality and discipline. Between Reveille at 6 a.m. and Lights Out at 10 p.m., the auxiliaries' days were structured by three meals, two roll calls and route marches to and from their jobs at army stations. Curfew was at 8 p.m. during summer and 7.30 p.m. in winter after which time the gates were locked and women could stay out only with late passes.[65] Finally, exercise was designed to increase women's stamina and *esprit de corps*. Most units drilled at least once a week and also played hockey, cricket or rounders, while others held informal dances for the women in the evenings.[66]

The construction of martial female housing was completed by a new publicity campaign launched in the autumn of 1917. This aimed to boost recruitment by targeting leisured middle-class women and their servants for the clerical and domestic sections of the corps. Seeking to win over these groups, the campaign also tried to squash rumours about the WAACs' allegedly soft life and immoral conduct which arose in the wake of the early exaggerated press reports.[67] The portrayal of housing and daily routine remained central to achieving these goals. Within this broader context, however, publicists shifted both the subject matter and its representation, replacing stories about leisure activities depicted in the pre-war language of genteel domesticity with accounts of military training and work, which constructed the new discourse of martial femininity. A key theme of these articles was the transformation of traditional women into a new female army. Stressing the role that martial female environments played in the moulding of recruits, articles focused on the corps's training depots, exercise grounds and Orderly Rooms, which prepared women for their new army life.[68] Thus, the depot hostel in Edinburgh, where the removal of dressing mirrors, carpets and decorative curtains had made room for drill instruction, hygiene lectures and a disciplined daily routine, was described as 'utilitarian' but 'not unattractive'. Summing up the impression of the bright and spacious rooms, the writer stated that 'What they have lost in luxuriousness and seclusion, they have gained in a certain vitalising atmosphere of activity'.[69] Other articles compared WAAC life to a girls' boarding school to make it attractive to middle-class recruits for clerical posts and praised the sleeping cubicles, sewing machines and pianos in the quarters to appeal to prospective domestic workers.[70]

At Home in the Army: The Habitation and Impact of
WAAC Quarters

Notwithstanding the variety of WAAC lodgings, some experiences of their habitation were shared by most women. One such experience was the transitory nature of their residence. The majority of members spent less than two years on average in the corps before they were demobilized in 1919. In addition, they were frequently transferred to new army posts, and therefore new lodgings; most auxiliaries moved at least once during their service.[71] Officers led even more of 'a wandering life': Dorothy Pickford, for example, administered two hostels and a camp within a year.[72] Thus, settling down in new quarters was a familiar experience across the corps. Despite their temporary residence, women made considerable efforts to make themselves at home by domesticating their martial surroundings. This was due partly to the encouragement of the leadership. Former auxiliaries' recollections indicate, however, that many of them were equally keen to make their quarters 'as comfortable ... [and] homelike as possible' and 'take away a little of the stark bareness' of the rooms.[73] Equipping their lodgings with 'home comforts' also helped in overcoming homesickness, from which some women suffered. Through these efforts the auxiliaries developed strong bonds with members of their dormitory. Referring to themselves by their hut number, they shared treats and often competed with other dormitories in decorating.[74] Larger communities could also form in hostels and camps through the joint decoration of recreation rooms or the collective subscription of funds to buy pianos and other furnishings. In some cases even officers who participated in these projects or who took a personal interest in their unit could become part of such communities. One administrator described women in her hostel as 'a family of 80', while another referred to her old unit as her 'beloved children'.[75]

Other experiences of inhabiting WAAC quarters varied significantly, depending on the location and type of the lodgings and the auxiliaries' social backgrounds. Members serving in France, a minority, enjoyed the excitement of foreign travel and a closer view of the war, but suffered from air raids more frequently than their comrades in Britain.[76] British units, on the other hand, often benefited from better housing stock. Many of them were accommodated either in the married quarters of existing barracks, as in Aldershot, or in houses near urban garrisons requisitioned by the War Office.[77] Both types offered higher-quality structural features, such as insulation and washing facilities, than the hutted camps where most WAACs lived in France. The size of the quarters also influenced the auxiliaries' daily lives. Smaller units of twenty to forty women, comprising members of a single trade, were more cohesive and enjoyed better food, prepared in smaller quantities.[78] In contrast, larger units endured worse catering, as meals were cooked in bulk, and more tension ensued between the various occupational sections drawn from different classes.[79] Social background also shaped women's ability to alter their lodgings and control their routine. Officers and NCOs enjoyed greater freedom to furnish their quarters and, like the middle-class drivers, clerks and signallers, could afford more lavish decorations. They all benefited from a relative degree of autonomy – the former due to their rank and the latter because their jobs at army stations allowed them to spend less time under the supervision of WAAC officers. Working-class domestic staff were disadvantaged in both respects. Earning lower wages, they had less money to decorate their rooms and their duties in quarters or nearby cook-houses placed them more firmly under the control of administrators.

Female officers exercised considerable independence in ordering their living space. Regulations stipulated that they were housed separately from the other ranks to increase respect for their status. This afforded them more privacy and space, though the extent of the latter varied with the type and size of quarters and units. In camps, administrators each had half a hut for their bedroom but, in hostels, they often had to take the smallest rooms to accommodate the rest of their unit. In both types of quarters, however, they shared separate mess and sitting rooms with their colleagues, away from the other ranks.[80] The furnishing and decoration of these spaces depended on individual tastes and attitudes. Helen Gwynne-Vaughan slept with the same coarse blankets as soldiers and WAACs in order to follow army tradition by sharing the other ranks' conditions.[81] Many female officers, however, wrote home for sheets, bedding and ornaments for their sleeping quarters. May Gibson covered her bed with an eiderdown, while Dorothy Pickford decorated her bedroom with family photos, prints of Nevinson's war paintings and a pot of flowers.[82] Messes were furnished with even greater care, since they acquired a new diplomatic role. Realizing that they were missing female company, army officers started dropping in regularly on administrators for tea and dinner. This smoothed relations between the two sides and led to a more lavish fitting out of dining and living rooms. Gwynne-Vaughan equipped her mess with table silver and Malay silk, while Pickford and her deputy entertained army colleagues in their sitting room decorated in simple Arts and Crafts style.[83] In return for this hospitality, Engineer officers had shelves, notice boards and letter racks made for the administrators.[84]

Drawn from various sections of the middle class, signallers, clerks and drivers often found their material conditions uncomfortable and devoted money and energy to improving them. Most of these efforts focused on decorating their living quarters. Members of these sections bought cretonne fabric, wrote home for patterns and made curtains, lampshades and sometimes even matching bedspreads for their room. Bare walls were covered with popular magazine images, while shelves were adorned with photos and vases of flowers. Recreation facilities also benefited from the contributions of these women in terms of papered walls, settee covers and money for pianos.[85] Auxiliaries in these groups went to great lengths to supplement army food, which they regarded as appalling. They relied on their families for parcels, local cafes for cooked meals and YMCA huts for hot drinks and biscuits. They also kept small camp stoves and food hidden in their huts for night-time treats.[86] Evading annoying regulations was the other major goal of middle-class other ranks. Seeking to avoid humiliating medical procedures, they washed their hair regularly and sprinkled Keating's, a popular insecticide, on their blankets.[87] In addition, they beat evening curfew by persuading army clerks at work to make out their late passes for different hours or by asking friends to answer their names at Roll Call and climbing over the fence on their return.[88] Women in this group often found community life an irritation. Many escaped organized events by claiming work commitments, while others sought privacy by applying for promotion as NCOs.[89] Forewomen were entitled to individual sleeping cubicles or bedrooms, where sprung hospital mattresses and soft blankets could remain undetected, and had their own mess-sitting room shared with colleagues, where they could relax in relative seclusion.[90]

Working-class other ranks' efforts to control their daily life focused mainly on escaping the supervision of WAAC officers, which weighed heavily on them. This was due largely to the administrators' class prejudice. Regarding the morality and behaviour of working-class women to be suspect, many officers kept domestic and technical workers under close surveillance. At Pirbright, household workers were rarely allowed out in the evening while, at Denham, their periods were monitored to ensure they were not pregnant.[91] Members of these sections also suffered frequent punishment for minor offences. Resentful of such treatment, they often developed strong bonds of loyalty with roommates and defied regulations collectively in an organized manner. At Pirbright, domestic workers staged a protest march when fined for trying to get more coal for their stoves and covered for their hut-mates who were meeting boyfriends in the air raid trenches while administrators were checking numbers before Lights Out.[92] Recollections suggest that altering their living quarters was not a priority for these women. Coming from poorer and more crowded homes, they were less critical of their lodgings and appreciated the privacy of sleeping cubicles, the comfort of church services and the pleasure of pianos in the recreation rooms.[93] Lower wages also limited these women's ability to decorate their dormitories. Nevertheless, some recalled turning hard army biscuits into photo frames and making curtains and lampshades for their huts out of crepe paper.[94] Working-class auxiliaries used their own resources to increase food rations. Domestic workers in France made blackberry and apple pies out of wild fruit picked in forests, while their comrades in Bostall Heath cooked sausages in their hut over lighted candles when in isolation during a diphtheria epidemic.[95]

The martial quarters of the WAAC helped to shift attitudes both among the auxiliaries and soldiers. Corps members' letters and testimonies indicate that the use of army furnishings instilled many of them with some degree of military identity. One woman recalled how members of her unit felt they 'were [really] in the Army' when receiving their lunch on trestle tables in the open, while others described becoming fond of their rough and grimy army blankets which kept them warm on cold nights.[96] Women's use of army slang to describe their circumstances also points to the development of new, martial identities. Many former auxiliaries referred to their mattresses as 'biscuits', remembered being 'on the mat' when on charge for offences and characterized inferior provisions as 'duds'.[97] Finally, several stories reveal women's pride in sharing soldiers' conditions. Domestic workers in Pirbright refused the officer cadets' offer to give up their bread rations for the auxiliaries, and one unit in France decided to sleep on the floor so that their beds could be used by local hospitals overwhelmed by casualties.[98] Such gestures as well as joint programmes and the shared use of sports and recreation facilities also shifted attitudes among soldiers from hostility to friendly comradeship. This started with inviting the auxiliaries to mixed tennis, cricket and hockey matches. It was followed by a series of dances, concerts and whist drives which became regular events and were held alternately at army and WAAC quarters.[99] Recreation and mess facilities were transformed for these occasions. The auxiliaries decorated their rooms with flags, flowers and Japanese lanterns and spent hours preparing the floor for dances by treating the boards with tallow candles and chalk to make them more slippery. They also subscribed money for cakes, cigarettes and prizes for their guests.[100] Army units showed their gratitude by returning invitations, making WAAC Administrators honorary members of their officers' mess and including the auxiliaries in interservice sports competitions and victory celebrations in 1919.[101]

Conclusion

The living quarters of the WAAC did not survive long after the demobilization of the corps. The newly built camps in Britain and on the Western Front were demolished, while the converted hostels were returned to their original pre-war use. Despite their brief service, however, the quarters had achieved the objectives for which they were designed. Besides housing the membership of the corps, they also contributed to its integration into the British Army. They fulfilled this goal partly by creating a material environment which, through its combination of military and feminine attributes, fostered the development of martial female identities among the auxiliaries. In addition, the joint use of the corps' recreation and sports facilities by soldiers and WAACs helped dissolve the men's initial hostility towards the women and furthered amicable relations between the two sides.

The unique focus of WAAC propaganda on the housing of the corps underlines the key role of these quarters in the military integration of the auxiliaries. Images of rural campsites with huts overlooked by trees where cheerful and healthy women were drilling or tending their vegetable garden disproved at a glance the old saying that women had no place in the army. They provided visual proof that female auxiliary soldiers could fit harmoniously into the military without sacrificing their essential feminine qualities. The lack of similar portrayals in the imagery of other female war organizations confirms this ideological role of WAAC housing. Facing less opposition to women's industrial or agricultural work, munitions factories or the Land Army did not have to make place discursively for their workers at these sites. The female services of the navy and the air force, on the other hand, which used similar housing to the WAAC, had no need to publicize their quarters, since they could occupy the same niche carved out previously by the female army corps.

The evolution of WAAC quarters illuminates the material dimension of gender construction in wartime Britain. The shift from a segregated domestic model to a more integrated military one reveals one aspect of the process through which a new female identity, that of the servicewoman, was created. Exploring this shift also identifies the main participants in this process and the agendas that shaped its development. A key point in this respect is that change was driven by all parties concerned, whether consciously or unconsciously, making it impossible to maintain the segregation of men and women and the sharp differentiation of their material environments.

Examining the living quarters of the WAAC also throws new light on the position of the auxiliaries in the British Army. Focusing on the civilian status and different insignia of the women, previous studies have argued that their standing in the army was subordinate to that of soldiers in all respects. However, providing corps members with accommodation which was superior to soldiers' housing even in its reduced form indicates that military authorities applied positive discrimination in favour of the women in an area which not only cost considerable money and attention, but had a significant effect on the auxiliaries' daily life and health.

Acknowledgements

I would like to thank the Department of Humanities at the University of Roehampton for funding my research for this essay and Lucy Bland, Clare Midgley, Alison Oram, Katharina Rowold, Cornelie Usborne, Kelly Boyd, Simon Jones and Andy Simpson for their helpful comments on earlier drafts.

10 HALLS OF RESIDENCE AT BRITAIN'S CIVIC UNIVERSITIES, 1870–1970

William Whyte

'An Essential Part of the Best Kind of University Training'

In 1943, a pseudonymous author calling himself Bruce Truscot published a critique of modern higher education. Entitled *Red Brick University*, it had an explosive effect on its readers and still influences the terms of debate today.[1] Truscot wrote as an insider – he was actually Edgar Allison Peers, a distinguished professor of Spanish at Liverpool University – and he offered a devastating assessment of what he encountered in his day-to-day work there. He described the other Redbrick professors, exposing them as both underpaid and under-worked. He condemned the physical fabric of the modern university, outlining buildings of 'a hideously cheerful red-brick suggestive of something between a super council-school and a holiday home for children'. And he went on to con-trast the student experience at Redbrick with the undergraduate life of Oxford and Cambridge. For Bill Jones of Drabtown – Truscot's archetypical Redbrick student – he had only pity to offer:

> Poor Bill Jones! No Hall and Chapel and oak-sporting for him; no invitations to breakfast at the Master's Lodging; no hilarious bump suppers or moonlight strolls in romantic quadrangles; no all-night sittings with a congenial group round his own – his very own – fireplace. No: Bill goes off five mornings a week to Redbrick Uni-versity exactly as he went to Back Street Council School and Drabtown Municipal Secondary School for Boys – and he goes on his bicycle, to save the two-penny tram-fare.[2]

Truscot's picture was not a happy one – and it was reinforced by a series of other books in the 1940s, all of which spoke of a 'crisis' in the modern university, and each of which pointed to the stark difference between the gilded youth of Oxbridge and the Bill Joneses of Redbrick and Drabtown.[3]

By the time Truscot wrote, the institutions he described were a familiar part of British life.[4] Initially established in the great industrial towns, the civic universities were the product of local patriotism, middle-class ambition, and fear about the country's relative technological and economic decline.[5] From Owens College, Manchester, established in 1851, to its equivalent in Leicester, finally chartered as a university in 1957, the last half of the nineteenth and first half of the twentieth century witnessed a slew of similar foundations. Leeds gained a college in 1872; with Bristol in 1876, Sheffield and Birmingham in 1880, and Liverpool in 1882 all following suit.[6] Two decades later, each was transmuted into an independent university; Lord Rosebery observed in 1912 that 'every great city seems to consider it a matter of pride and a necessary appanage of its own position that it should hold a University within its walls'.[7] A second generation of institutions was granted university status in the years that followed, with Reading (chartered in 1926) and Nottingham (1948) leading the way, and Southampton (1954), Hull (1954), Exeter (1955) and Leicester (1955) following thereafter. Taken together, these were the civic – or as Truscot rechristened them, the Redbrick – universities.[8] Initially sustained by local support, they grew increasingly dependent on the financial aid of the state, drawing ever larger sums from the University Grants Committee (UGC), established in 1919.[9] Their students, too, were predominantly local, at least until the 1960s, when reforms of the funding system created the first genuinely national system of higher education.[10] The civic universities were consequently important institutions for their home city and region; in the words of the *Sheffield Daily Telegraph* the university was 'the Institution in which the city takes most pride, from which it is entitled to expect most, and which it will most gladly maintain at the highest point of efficiency'.[11]

The creation of the civic universities was celebrated as an epoch-making event by contemporaries; a moment, in the words of Stanley Baldwin, 'which historians of the future would regard as a Renaissance ... as genuine and as pregnant in its possibilities as the Renaissance of the fifteenth century'.[12] Subsequent writers, however, have been less enthusiastic. Although there are numerous excellent individual histories, each extolling the achievements of their own institution, there remains no single study of the movement as a whole.[13] Moreover, when historians have surveyed the civic universities more generally, they have tended to take Truscot's words at face value. They have looked at Redbrick and seen a story of failure. Although some, like Michael Sanderson, have argued that these modern, urban institutions created a genuinely distinctive new sort of higher education, most other writers have, by contrast, contended that the civics did not live up to expectations because they amounted to nothing more than a fruitless imitation of Oxbridge.[14] The 'provincial universities', Sarah Barnes has written, were 'defined – and redefined – first as pioneering alternatives to England's ancient institutions, then as second-class substitutes. The history of the civics ... thus represents a story of unrealised possibilities and the triumph of tradition'.[15] So too Elizabeth Morse has argued that 'the story of the civic universities ... is a sad one, for they never escaped the ancient idea of the university'.[16]

This assumption has been particularly pronounced for writers about the halls of residence at Redbrick universities.[17] For Truscot – and for the majority of other commentators in this period – these halls played a key role in transforming the student experience of university. Even in the minds of Victorian night-school students, who could not reasonably expect ever to attend one, a hall of residence was 'An essential part of the best kind of University training', allowing Redbrick undergraduates to create a true academic community.[18] Yet, with a few notable exceptions, very little historical research has been undertaken on them;[19] and, certainly, there has been nothing like the serious, sustained analysis to which colleges and fraternity houses in the United States have been subjected.[20] Moreover those very few writers who have explored the British experience have tended to see the hall of residence in rather negative terms, representing what Roy Lowe and Rex Knight have argued was nothing more than an 'unhesitating imitation of Oxbridge'.[21] Lowe, Knight, and other commentators, like the distinguished sociologist A. H. Halsey, have consequently seen growth in the number and importance of these halls as a regressive move, signalling the way in which Redbrick 'abandoned the modern urban conception of the university' in favour of 'the magic of Oxford', with its colleges, quads and sported oaks.[22]

This essay, by contrast, will argue that the history of the halls of residence at the civic universities in fact reveals quite the reverse. Looking at the debates which surrounded them, and the words of those who ran and inhabited them, it will show that the halls were the product of an almost entirely independent tradition, and thus actually expose more clearly the differences between Oxbridge and Redbrick. More importantly, from the perspective of this volume as a whole, the study of these halls also reveals the significance of architecture and design in the creation and development of the civic universities.[23] In a report written only a few years after Truscot took up his pen – and which quoted *Red Brick University* with evident enthusiasm – a committee set up by the vice chancellors and principals of the British universities concluded not only that halls were necessary but also that they needed to express their purpose in their form. They should possess public rooms of 'dignity, spaciousness, and beauty'. And they should do all this because these were believed to be vital to the university's core purpose: educating the young in the widest possible sense.[24] The halls were intended to take Bill Jones out of Drabtown, to expose him to a new life, and to transform him in the process. In that sense, too, these institutions illuminate another of the themes that this book addresses: here were places founded not just to supplement but to supplant the background from which its inhabitants came. Halls of residence thus provide an example of an alternative sort of institution, one intended to be better than the homes from which some of their inhabitants originated.

'A University Without Hostels is Not a University'

The halls of residence owed their existence to four inter-related factors. In the first place, some were the product of philanthropic and – especially – religious idealism. Places like Dalton Hall in Manchester (opened in 1881) were founded by particular denominational groups; in this case, the Quakers.[25] The same was true of nearby St Anselm's, established as an Anglican hall in 1907, the successor to a Church of England hostel for Manchester students set up as long before as 1872.[26] Indeed, from the foundation of what would become University College London in the 1820s onwards, different denominations sought to establish halls which would provide the religious atmosphere they found lacking in the secular civic universities.[27]

Secondly, some halls were founded specifically for the special needs of female undergraduates. Redbrick – unlike Oxbridge – was co-educational almost from the start, and this mixed-sex environment was believed, in the words of one hall principal, to present special 'difficulties' both to the university and its students.[28] How to teach men and women together; how to encourage healthy socialization while preventing undue fraternization: these issues prompted anxious debate and yielded such solutions as separate entrances to lecture rooms and the provision of screens shielding female diners from the male gaze in university refectories.[29] Residence was a particularly tricky problem in a mixed-sex institution. As the founders of University Hall in Liverpool unanswerably argued in 1900, 'The reasons against women students living in lodgings are so obvious that they need not be stated'.[30] In place of the lax landlady or the unchaperoned student in digs, halls were intended to reassure parents that their daughters would be properly cared for.[31]

Thirdly, and still more significantly, halls were established at a succession of institutions that wished to attract students from further afield. This was important for those places – like Reading, Exeter or Leicester – which simply did not have a large enough local population to sustain a university in an era before significant government funding.[32] But all civic universities came to see the provision of residential accommodation as a draw to potential students;[33] and colleges which aspired to university status acquired halls as a means of increasing numbers and establishing their claim to exemplify the 'University ideal'.[34]

Indeed, fourthly and, in many respects, most importantly of all, halls of residence were founded because they were increasingly believed to be a necessary – even a defining – part of university life.[35] As the National Union of Students put it in 1938, 'A University without hostels is not a University'.[36] Halls were needed, it was argued, because without them a university could not function as a community. It would develop no *esprit de corps* and descend into what became known as the 'nine to five university': a place that only existed for instrumental learning, for lectures and examinations; a university which had no social life and effectively shut up shop at the end of the working day.[37] This 'nine to five' attitude was believed to be a particular problem for the civic universities, situated as they were in the middle of big cities and drawing as they did on a predominantly local population. 'It seems that if the civic university is to be a true seat of learning and of culture it must be made comfortable – it must be a good club', wrote the young Cambridge clergyman H. C. G. Herklots in 1928. 'Only in attractive surroundings will Dental Jones be encouraged to discuss his own problems and the problems of metaphysics with Anthropological Robinson and Architectural Smith.' Halls of residence, he concluded, were a central part of providing this attractive academic environment and thereby creating a true university life.[38]

The halls, in other words, were intended to effect a process of enculturation: not just housing undergraduates, but transforming them by exposure to what one enthusiast described as 'the grace of living'.[39] For as the sociologist (and warden of a Leeds hall of residence) Bryan Wilson put it, the English universities believed themselves to be distinguished by their attempt 'to introduce students to the richness of our cultural inheritance, to provide access to the cumulative aesthetic, literary, philosophic and scientific resources of mankind'. In this widely-accepted programme, the halls were believed to play a central part; it was in the hall, as Wilson went on, that the student was 'introduced to the traditionally highly valued aspects of our civilization'.[40] And the hopes raised for the halls of residence went further still. 'Manners, conduct, and deportment are not merely frills on an education', observed the Committee of Vice Chancellors in its report on halls of residence, 'they are outward and visible signs of character and personality'.[41] Here, in the halls, what we might now call a properly academic *habitus* would be cultivated and inculcated in their inhabitants.[42] They would enter as raw adolescents and leave as mature bearers of university culture in its very widest sense, their transformation figured in their minds and even in their bodies, in how they thought, how they talked, and how they stood and moved.

'Thick Pile Carpets have a Remarkably Civilising Effect on Students'

The architectural idiom deployed by the halls reflected these assumptions and was consequently almost always highly traditional – collegiate, quadrangular, often based on the staircase system which had been pioneered in medieval Oxford.[43] Just as American universities – perhaps most notably Princeton and Yale – used the Gothic Revival to construct an ideal type of academic institution well into the twentieth century, so England's innovative institutes of higher education adopted old forms to build their new halls.[44] This was even true at colleges founded to teach science and engineering like Loughborough, where Rutland Hall (opened in 1932) was a self-consciously modern, '"all-electric" residence' which nonetheless embraced a conventional Tudor style, complete with 'heavy stone mullioned windows'.[45] Neo-Georgian also proved popular and, at places such as Nottingham, a broadly classical approach continued to be deployed for halls long after it had been abandoned for laboratories or lecture rooms.[46] Indeed, the impact of the modern movement in architecture after the Second World War was more muted when it came to residential accommodation than might at first be expected.[47] Older ideas, not least about gender, continued to shape design. At Liverpool in 1959, a report on halls was willing to consider all manner of reforms, but still argued that women needed the sense of 'luxury' that came from better bathrooms and a larger laundry – 'the ironing room is often the parish pump in a women's hostel'.[48] At Leicester, four years earlier, these assumptions were even more starkly expressed, with a committee first agreeing that it wanted new 'buildings ... in contemporary style', with 'plain, severe, clean lines', and then observing that such modernism 'might not be desirable for a women's hall'.[49]

The daily routine was also conventional, one might almost say conventual. At the turn of the twentieth century, many halls – even ostensibly non-denominational ones – required their residents to participate in daily prayers. Even in the 1940s, the women's hall at Exeter had time set aside for prayer at 8 a.m. and 9.30 p.m., with lights out an hour later at half past ten.[50] It was widely believed that 'A measure of formality' was a necessary part of hall life, so academic gowns were worn for dinner.[51] Latin graces were intoned. Archaic rituals grew up. And where traditions did not exist, they were deliberately invented. At Hull, the inhabitants of one hall drew up elaborate rules that prohibited freshmen from growing moustaches or beards and insisted that they should give up their chairs to senior students.[52] Other halls had rites of passage on entry and a complex code of behaviour at formal dinners. They evolved peculiar pranks and ways of dressing, with each hall cultivating its own idiosyncratic style.[53]

Hall furnishings were similarly shaped by the desire to create a distinctive, collegiate, academic atmosphere which would – almost imperceptibly – mould its inhabitants. Even the floor-coverings were considered important, for as the Committee of Vice Chancellors and Principals declared in 1948, 'it has been justly claimed that thick pile carpets have a remarkably civilising effect on students'.[54] Portraits of benefactors and past wardens lined the walls of the dining hall, providing a sense of history and a link to the great halls of ancient universities, London livery companies and the Inns of Court. Comfortable chairs, couches and Kidderminster carpets in common rooms all created a clubbable environment, fit for a civilized gathering of likeminded thinkers.[55] 'Furniture and furnishings should be of such a quality and quantity as to give dignity and graciousness to the hall', the Committee went on to observe – and the universities took note. As Richard Hoggart, who studied in Leeds in the 1930s recalled, the halls were 'carpeted and curtained at remarkable expense'.[56]

Naturally, there was often a gap between aspiration and reality. If good quality furnishing and decoration was believed to promote enculturation, then the reverse was also held to be true. In 1957 the UGC noted:

> A hall will not develop an urbane social life unless someone has taken the trouble that it should. A chilly and ill-kept building where the furniture has been knocked about by generations of students does not help to raise the level of social behaviour.[57]

Inventories kept by the halls suggest that, in many, the mismatched crockery and sparse furniture provided bore little comparison with the ideal set out in promotional literature or the luxury found in contemporary fraternity houses across the Atlantic.[58] A lack of money could also produce buildings that were considered less than optimal. At Exeter in the 1930s, 'reasons of economy' led to the undesirable position of students sharing rooms stretched out along long corridors, rather than inhabiting 'the ideal system' of single study-bedrooms, set off staircases which opened onto a quadrangle.[59] Still worse were the problems encountered at places like Keele and Hull as a consequence of university expansion after the Second World War. There, the halls were housed in abandoned army Nissen huts, something which encouraged close social integration, true enough, but which also permitted poor discipline, making it all but impossible to enforce curfews or effective supervision of any sort.[60] Oral histories suggest that this actually made the experience of hall – or, rather, hut – dwelling all the more enjoyable, but it was certainly not what the authorities intended.[61] As this suggests, different architecture produced different results, with halls sharply distinguished by their plan and their function.[62]

The halls also often operated in ways that diverged from the fine-sounding rhetoric of those who praised them. In theory, most were intended to be open to all. In practice, religious, social, sporting and academic considerations were taken into account when halls considered whom to admit. Students had to apply for membership; and not all were accepted. In some places, the interview for admission to a hall was more exacting than the application to the university itself. As a result individuals found themselves excluded – as in Manchester in the 1930s, where the warden of St Anselm's cheerfully admitted, 'I refuse all coloured gentlemen ... The tradition of the place is not strong enough to carry them along happily'.[63] More importantly for each university as a whole, this also meant that a hierarchy of different halls emerged, so that in Reading in the 1920s 'The smart hall', for women, 'was St Andrew's, just as among the men it was Wantage, with St Patrick's in the second place'; female undergraduates at St George's, by contrast, were regarded as the lowest of the low – at least among those who lived in official university accommodation.[64] Forty years later at Leicester a similar stratification was at work, with half a dozen halls, but only one – Digby – reserved for the 'social aristocracy' of the place.[65]

Within the halls, too, attempts to create a cohesive, unified community spirit, free from what the UGC described as 'exclusiveness, snobbery, a clannish spirit of the wrong type, narrowness of outlook, gossip', were often vitiated by the associational culture which they actually fostered.[66] Indeed, the physical structure of the place sometimes served not only to express but also to exacerbate divisions. Thus, the dining hall could become a theatre for the performance of social distinction: 'the "lads" congregated on a particular table; the "Christians" or "God Squad" occupied another; the sensitive sandals- and wrought-iron aesthetes avoided the "lads"; and the "nonentities" gravitated to their own table'.[67] So too, in larger halls, cliques were formed on the basis of propinquity, with different floors or blocks each cohering against the others.[68] This was, at least one contemporary sociologist argued, a 'licensed rejection of the "administration line"', an attempt to assert autonomy.[69]

If so, it was by no means the last time that the idealistic and totalizing programme of the halls of residence would be challenged. The 1960s, in particular, witnessed a growing dissatisfaction with them. Asserting the autonomy of student culture and rejecting the university's claim to mould and shape their lives, many undergraduates increasingly found hall life unappealing.[70] Their rules seemed irksome.[71] Their traditions became harder to maintain.[72] Their very existence was questioned. 'A university which does not aim to segregate its students from the ordinary business of life can have little or no use for halls of residence', declared a Liverpool academic in 1964.[73] By 1969 even the Federation of Conservative Students had come to believe that halls were now 'obsolete'.[74] In the years that followed, the traditional idea of student accommodation was irrevocably abandoned. So when Cardiff planned new accommodation in 1973, for example, it was keen to emphasize that it would not be a hall of residence in any sense of the word. 'Every effort is made to treat tenants as adults', asserted the Domestic Bursar. 'No restriction is placed on their way of life.'[75]

Yet this rejection of halls and all they stood for reveals in reality their importance – and, paradoxically, highlights their success. Student radicals were right to be especially exercised by the halls of residence. As they accurately observed, it was 'hall spirit', a 'hall mentality', which diverted many undergraduates from more overt political activity. They were 'hall marked' by their experience.[76] The perception that the halls achieved many of their goals appeared to be demonstrable. Research in the 1960s showed that the culture of many institutions did in fact foster the sense of academic community they were intended to imbue. As one sociologist observed, 'Hall students studied more, conversed more frequently with their fellow students on their subject, read more non-fiction books, attended more university societies and clubs, and entertained a member of the opposite sex in their room more frequently'.[77] When challenged by sub-optimal accommodation, students and staff were undaunted in adopting all the appurtenances of more formal halls – as at Keele, where gowns were worn in the Nissen huts.[78] And even when old customs like initiation rituals were abandoned, the previous patterns of behaviour lingered on.[79] Indeed, the 1980s would see some halls resurrect traditions – like grand, black-tie balls – that had been dropped as inappropriately elitist a generation before.[80]

'We Rather Looked Down on Oxford and Cambridge'

Was this hall life, though, just an imitation of still more elite education? Was it simply the perpetuation of public school tradition? Was it, as the critics suggested, nothing more than a misguided attempt to bring a sort of ersatz Oxbridge college to the great manufacturing towns? There were certainly those who thought so – and even those who welcomed such an effort.[81] But, as most of those with real experience of the halls recognized, these institutions were not, and were not intended to be, copies of colleges at the two ancient English universities.[82] For one thing, they served a different structural function. At Oxford and Cambridge the college was the primary institution for undergraduates: it admitted them and taught them as well as providing them with a bed. Students remained members of a college even when not accommodated by it – and by the early 1950s, Oxbridge colleges in fact housed fewer than half of their undergraduates at any one time.[83] At Redbrick, by contrast, the university was primary, admitting and educating students who then might – but need not – become inhabitants of a hall. Thus, even in Reading – the Redbrick institution which pioneered near-total undergraduate residence in the early 1900s, and which erected suspiciously collegiate-looking halls – the university was keen to emphasize from the very first that no imitation of Oxbridge was intended or desired.[84] Indeed, in 1912, the Principal publicly forbade teaching in the halls for fear of 'the growth in course of time of the Oxford or Cambridge collegiate system'.[85] At the same time, as a Reading student later recalled, 'We rather looked down on Oxford and Cambridge' as institutions where university unity had been comprised by collegiate autonomy.[86]

More importantly still, the halls were established precisely because these universities did not serve the social elite and were, by definition, not providing an elite education of the sort offered at Oxbridge. As the sensitive German observer, Wilhelm Dibelius, noted in 1922, Redbrick had no desire to compete with or imitate Oxford and Cambridge; it served 'a section of the population with other ideals'.[87] Indeed, that was exactly the point. It was precisely because Redbrick had been created to serve members of the local population who could not afford life in the ancient universities that the halls were established. As one warden put it as late as the late-1960s, the halls existed because 'Most of the students we get are from working-class or middle-class homes. There is no virtue in their being in lodgings'.[88] Similar assumptions led the UGC to defend the halls in comparable terms more than a decade earlier:

> when university students were largely drawn from the families in which higher edu-
> cation was normal ... it was assumed that the general education of the university
> student, as distinct from his formal course, could be left to take care of itself. It was
> assumed that he would come from a home in which he would have acquired cul-
> tural interests, so that the university could concentrate on turning him into an expert
> without risk to the general development of the whole man. If there was once some
> justification for this assumption, it is no longer tenable today, owing to the change in
> the social and economic background of students.[89]

But even this was not the first time such points had been made. In the mid-1930s, an Exeter academic had likewise noted the 'problem of the classes that are not used or trained to self discipline', seeing the halls as a solution;[90] whilst a genera-tion earlier still, in 1892, the head of the women's hall at Cardiff observed that her students were a 'class of girl ... accustomed to more freedom than girls of a higher class'.[91] For her, too, halls were a way of managing this difficulty. As this suggests, there was a consistent, not to say insistent, apologia for the hall of residence from the late nineteenth century onwards. It was defended and defined as a place which would provide a general education, self-discipline and proper boundaries for those students whose backgrounds had not prepared them for university life.

More than this, the halls of residence were intended to inculcate the children of working- and middle-class families with values it was believed they would otherwise not encounter. It was for that reason that one especially superior Exeter academic observed in the 1930s that 'few ... of the students in the modern Universities have had experience of living away from home, and therefore, their residential problems resemble those of the school boarding-house rather than those of an Oxford Col-lege'. But even this was not quite right, for, as he recognized, his students were not children. They would emerge from the university 'self-reliant citizens'.[92] The halls were therefore not the same as the public schools and could never resemble Oxbridge colleges. They were *sui generis*, providing access to a way of life and a sort of culture which their inhabitants had not experienced at school and would not have the opportunity of experiencing at a more elite university.[93]

'Growing Away from our Background'

But if the halls were not an uncomplicated imitation of Oxbridge or an attempt to reproduce the atmosphere of public schools, then nor were they meant to be a home away from home – a familiar, cosy simulacrum of the domesticity from which their inhabitants originated. It is here that Truscot's account of 'poor Bill Jones' – the Drabtown student whose education is impeded by his surroundings – becomes most pertinent. The easy reading of Truscot is one that contrasts Redbrick with Oxbridge, and therefore assumes that Truscot is urging Redbrick simply to imitate Oxbridge.[94] But, in reality, he recognized that this was not possible; and, indeed, he argued that it was not desirable either. Truscot did not want to create a Redbrick world of sported oaks or hilarious bumps suppers. He condemned much of what went on in the ancient universities as frivolous and superficial and questioned their seriousness as educational establishments too.[95] Rather, it is instructive to read on in *Red Brick University* and see what the real barrier to Bill Jones's progress was believed to be. It was his home; for, as Truscot put it:

> Between four and five o'clock he goes home to the same sort of high tea as he has had all his life and then attempts to settle down to an evening's work, either alone in an unused sitting-room, in his unheated bedroom or, more probably, in the living-room, where Lizzie, at the same table, is wrestling with her algebra, Bertie is continually appealing to him for help with his French, and at all too frequent intervals the wireless is turned on for the entertainment or edification of the rest of the family.[96]

This, Truscot concludes, is what really prevented Redbrick universities from helping Bill Jones: not the absence of Oxbridge, but the presence of his family; not the lack of sported oaks, but the suffocating effect of his domestic situation. The significant contrast Truscot draws is therefore not actually between the ancient universities and the modern, still less between Redbrick and the public schools, but between the idea of the university and actuality of the working-class home. The halls of residence, in this view, were never intended to be imitations of Oxbridge colleges, but alternatives to the working-class homes of Drabtown.

Truscot was far from alone in his assumption. Indeed, this argument long underwrote the provision of halls. In 1900, for example, it was maintained that a women's hall was required at Liverpool because 'the distractions of home life prove often an insuperable barrier to women studying for degrees'.[97] Nearly fifty years later, in 1949, the distinguished educationalist Eric Ashby argued that the same was true for all Redbrick students of either sex. The essential need in civic universities, he maintained, was for an alternative to the working-class home, a place imbued with academic values and university culture.[98] As late as the 1960s, hall wardens still conceived of their role in similar terms. 'Our job', one insisted, 'is to present [students] with counter-values; they won't get these in ordinary homes'.[99]

The students themselves also appear to have experienced their time as residents of the halls in this way. For the working-class Sheffield undergraduate, Alf Walker, for example, his time in university accommodation in the 1950s was a moment of revelation as he was exposed to high living as well as deep thinking:

> There was a library with wood panelled walls, a real coal fire and deep arm chairs in green leather; I'd never sat in a deep leather arm chair before ... There were tennis, squash and fives courts, table tennis, a darkroom and congenial company. Crewe Hall was perfect.[100]

Perhaps inevitably, not all students were equally impressed; and it is clear that some of the impetus for the growing rejection of hall life and hall culture in the 1960s arose from an irritation with this implicit – and sometimes explicit – criticism of working- and lower-middle-class life.[101] Yet, for nearly a century a consistent set of assumptions nonetheless informed policy throughout the Redbrick foundations. As Richard Hoggart recalled, 'The whole enterprise of hall provision was felt to be an integral part of the civilising mission of university education ... The assumption was that we were growing away from our background'.[102]

Conclusion

Halls of residence, then, fulfilled a particular educational and social function, a function that was specific to the students of the civic universities. Rather than being an alternative to – much less a poor copy of – the colleges of Oxford and Cambridge, they were a replacement for the working-class home. Hence the emphasis on fine furnishings; hence the deep-pile carpets and high-quality fabrics, even in accommodation intended for male undergraduates. For the hall of residence was intended to do more than just house students. It was meant to turn them into bearers of a social and intellectual culture that was defined against the working-class home much more than it was shaped by imitation of other, more upper-class, institutions. The hall – with its traditions, its materiality and its distinctive architectural form – was an all-encompassing institution designed to rescue its inhabitants from their own social situation and mould them in the image of their *alma mater*. Poor Bill Jones would probably not recognize that he lacked bumps suppers and breakfast at the Master's Lodgings, but he was intended to experience a sense of release and relief on entering his hall of residence. Once inside, he was finally free from what was presumed to be the constricting demands of his family and the cultural poverty of his background. He was meant to feel that, however strange it might seem at first, this institution was now where he really belonged.

Acknowledgements

I am grateful to the participants in the 'Inhabiting Institutions' conference and to the editors of this volume for their comments on my essay and to Dan Hicks and Zoë Waxman for their advice. The research for this chapter was supported by a Philip Leverhulme Prize from the Leverhulme Trust and forms part of a wider project on the Redbrick universities which is forthcoming.

NOTES

Hamlett with Hoskins and Preston, 'Introduction'

1. B. Lunn, *Switchback: An Autobiography* (London: Eyre & Spottiswoode, 1948), p. 77.
2. Ibid., p. 114.
3. Ibid., p. 117.
4. Ibid., p. 236.
5. S. McConville, 'The Victorian Prison: England, 1865–1965', in N. Morris and D. J. Rothman (eds), *The Oxford History of the Prison: The Practice of Punishment in Western Society* (Oxford: Oxford University Press, 1995), pp. 133–4.
6. Ibid., p. 133.
7. Ibid., p. 146.
8. C. Harding, B. Hines, R. Ireland and P. Rawlings, *Imprisonment in England and Wales: A Concise History* (London: Croom Helm, 1985), pp. 241–2.
9. D. Green, *Pauper Capital: London and the Poor Law, 1790–1870* (Farnham: Ashgate, 2010), p. 21.
10. M. Gorsky, J. Mohan and M. Powell, 'British Voluntary Hospitals, 1871–1938: The Geography of Provision and Utilization', *Journal of Historical Geography*, 25 (1999), pp. 463–82, on p. 465; M. Sheridan, *Rowton Houses 1892–1954* (Southampton: Rowton Houses Ltd, 1956); B. Trinder, 'The Model Lodging House: Window onto the Underworld', in F. Bosbach and J. R. Davis (eds), *The Great Exhibition and its Legacy* (Munich: K. G. Saur, 2002), pp. 223–42; J. N. Tarn, *Five Percent Philanthropy: An Account of Housing in Urban Areas, 1840–1914* (Cambridge: Cambridge University Press, 1972). For a discussion of university settlements see K. Bradley, *Poverty, Philanthropy and the State: Charities and the Working-Class in London* (Manchester: Manchester University Press, 2009), pp. 28–49.
11. C. P. Hosgood, 'Mercantile Monasteries: Shops, Shop Assistants and Shop Life in Late Victorian and Edwardian Britain', *Journal of British Studies*, 38 (1999), pp. 322–52; and Michelle Johansen's essay in Chapter 8 of this volume.
12. D. G. Chandler and I. Beckett (eds), *The Oxford History of the British Army* (Oxford: Oxford University Press, 1994), pp. 161–297.
13. P. Bartlett, *The Poor Law of Lunacy: The Administration of Pauper Lunatics in Mid-Nineteenth-Century England* (London and Washington, DC: Leicester University Press, 1999).
14. E. C. Casella, *The Archaeology of Institutional Confinement* (Florida, CA: University Press of Florida, 2007); S. M. Spencer-Wood and S. Baugher, 'Introduction and Histori-

cal Context for the Archaeology of Institutions of Reform. Part I: Asylums', *International Journal of Historical Archaeology*, 5 (2001), pp. 3–17.

15. Casella, *Archaeology of Institutional Confinement*, p. 2.

16. S. Cavallo and S. Evangelisti (eds), *Domestic Institutional Interiors in Early Modern Europe* (Farnham: Ashgate, 2009).

17. McConville, 'Victorian Prison', pp. 158–9.

18. E. Goffman, *Asylums: Essays on the Social Situation of Mental Patients and other Inmates* (1961; Middlesex: Penguin Books, 1968), p. 11.

19. Ibid., p. 22.

20. Ibid., p. 16.

21. M. Ignatieff, 'Total Institutions and Working Classes: A Review Essay', *History Workshop Journal*, 15 (1983), pp. 167–73, on p. 168.

22. D. Wright, 'Getting out of the Asylum: Understanding the Confinement of the Insane in the Nineteenth Century', *Social History of Medicine*, 10 (1997), pp. 137–55.

23. D. Green, 'Pauper Protests: Power and Resistance in Early Nineteenth-Century London Workhouses', *Social History*, 31 (2006), pp. 137–59, on pp. 146–7.

24. H. Rogers, 'Kindness and Reciprocity: Liberated Prisoners and Christian Charity in Early Nineteenth-Century England', *Journal of Social History* (forthcoming, spring 2014).

25. M. Foucault, *Surveiller et Punir: Naissance de la Prison* (Paris: Gallimard, 1975); translated from the French by A. Sheridan as *Discipline and Punish: The Birth of the Prison* (London: Allen Lane, 1977).

26. Foucault, *Discipline and Punish*, pp. 170–228.

27. J. Semple, *Bentham's Prison: A Study of the Panopticon Penitentiary* (Oxford: Clarendon Press, 1993).

28. See in particular Suzuki's reading of patient case notes that challenges Foucault's view that they were a vehicle for the objectification of the patient: A. Suzuki, 'Framing Psychiatric Subjectivity: Doctor, Patient and Record Keeping at Bethlem in the Nineteenth Century', in J. Melling and B. Forsythe (eds), *Insanity, Institutions and Society, 1800–1914: A Social History of Madness in Comparative Perspective* (London: Routledge, 1999), p. 117.

29. The British prison system seems particularly difficult to fit into a story of increasing centralization and uniformity. M. DeLacy, *Prison Reform in Lancashire, 1700–1850: A Study in Local Administration* (Manchester: Printed for the Chetham Society, 1986), pp. 225–8; R. W. Ireland, *'A Want of Order and Good Discipline': Rules, Discretion and the Victorian Prison* (Cardiff: University of Wales Press, 2007), p. 11.

30. Melling and Forsythe (eds), *Insanity, Institutions and Society, 1800–1914*, p. 2; J. Melling and B. Forsythe, *The Politics of Madness: The State, Insanity and Society in England, 1845–1914* (London: Routledge, 2006), p. 6; Ireland, *'A Want of Order and Good Discipline'*.

31. J. Haslam, *Fitting Sentences: Identity in Nineteenth- and Twentieth-Century Prison Narratives* (London and Toronto, ON: University of Toronto Press, 2005), p.10; J. Haslam and J. M. Wright, *Captivating Subjects: Writing Confinement, Citizenship and Nationhood in the Nineteenth Century* (London and Toronto, ON: University of Toronto Press, 2005), p. 6.

32. J. Alber and F. Lauterbach, *Stones of Law, Bricks of Shame: Narrating Imprisonment in the Victorian Age* (London and Toronto, ON: University of Toronto Press, 2009), p. 10. For its limited effect on asylum architecture see L. Smith, 'The Architecture of Confinement: Urban Public Asylums in England, 1750–1820', in L. Topp, J. E. Moran and J. Andrews

(eds), *Madness, Architecture and the Built Environment: Psychiatric Spaces in Historical Context* (London: Routledge, 2007), pp. 41–61, on p. 54. But for the view that Foucault uses panopticism to refer to the principle of supervision and control rather than architectural form, see C. Philo, '"Enough to Drive one Mad": The Organization of Space in 19th-Century Lunatic Asylums', in J. Wolch and M. Dear (eds), *The Power of Geography: How Territory Shapes Social Life* (Winchester, MA, London, Sydney and Wellington, ON: Unwin Hyman, 1989), pp. 258–90. For a sustained critique of panopticism as mode of viewing, see C. Otter, *The Victorian Eye: A Political History of Light and Vision in Britain, 1800–1910* (Chicago, IL: University of Chicago Press, 2008), p. 5.

33. Ignatieff, 'Total Institutions', p. 168.
34. For similar findings see Green, 'Pauper Protests'.
35. De Lacy, *Prisons*, pp. 225–8.
36. Ireland, *A Want of Order and Good Discipline*, p. 11.
37. H. Rogers, 'The Way to Jerusalem: Reading, Writing and Reform in an Early Victorian Gaol', *Past and Present*, 205 (2009), pp. 71–104.
38. H. Johnston, 'Moral Guardians? Prison Officers, Prison Practice and Ambiguity in the Nineteenth Century', in H. Johnston (ed.), *Punishment and Control in Historical Perspective* (Basingstoke: Palgrave Macmillan, 2008), pp. 77–94, on p. 78.
39. R. W. Ireland, 'Confinement with Hard Labour: Motherhood and Penal Practice in a Victorian Gaol', *Welsh History Review*, 18 (1997), pp. 621–38; H. Rogers, 'Singing at Yarmouth Gaol: Christian Instruction and Inmate Culture in the Nineteenth Century', *Prison Service Journal*, 1999 (2012), pp. 35–40.
40. A. Brown, *English Society and the Prison: Time, Culture and Politics in the Development of the Modern Prison, 1850–1920* (Suffolk: Boydell Press, 2003), p. 4.
41. Ibid., p. 8.
42. A. Wills, 'Resistance, Identity and Historical Change in Institutions for Juvenile Delinquents, 1950–1970', in Johnston (ed.), *Punishment and Control*, pp. 215–34, on p. 217.
43. A. Clark, 'Wild Workhouse Girls and the Liberal Imperial State in Mid-Nineteenth Century Ireland', *Journal of Social History*, 39 (2005), pp. 389–409.
44. Green, 'Pauper Protests'.
45. R. D. Laing, *The Divided Self: An Existential Study in Sanity and Madness* (Harmondsworth: Penguin, 1960).
46. L. D. Smith, *'Cure, Comfort and Safe Custody': Public Lunatic Asylums in Early Nineteenth Century England* (London and New York: Leicester University Press, 1999), p. 99.
47. L. Hide, 'Inside the Asylum: Gender and Class in English Mental Hospitals, 1890–1914' (PhD dissertation, University of London, 2011), p. 307.
48. Rogers, 'Jerusalem', p. 75.
49. J. Alexander and C. Anderson, 'Politics, Penality and (Post-) Colonialism: An Introduction', *Cultural and Social History*, 5 (2008), pp. 391–4, on p. 391.
50. L. Smith, '"Your Very Thankful Inmate": Discovering the Patients of an Early County Lunatic Asylum', *Social History of Medicine*, 21 (2008), pp. 237–52, on p. 237.
51. Haslam, *Fitting Sentences*, p. 3; Haslam and Wright, *Captivating Subjects*, p. 4; Alber and Lauterbach, *Stones of Law*; S. Grass, *The Self in the Cell: Narrating the Victorian Prisoner* (London: Routledge, 2003).
52. J. Z. Wilson, 'Pecking Orders: Power Relationships and Gender in Australian Prison Graffiti', *Ethnography*, 9:1 (March 2008), pp. 99–121; J. Z. Wilson, *Prison: Cultural Memory and Dark Tourism* (New York: Peter Lang Publishing, 2008), pp. 67–130.

53. J. Andrews, 'Case Notes, Case Histories, and the Patient's Experience of Insanity at Gartnavel Royal Asylum, Glasgow, in the Nineteenth Century', *Social History of Medicine*, 11 (1998), pp. 255–81; F. Driver, *Power and Pauperism: The Workhouse System, 1834–1884* (Cambridge: Cambridge University Press, 1993), p. 3.

54. H. Marland, *Dangerous Motherhood: Insanity and Childbirth in Victorian Britain* (Basingstoke: Palgrave Macmillan, 2004), p. 96.

55. Smith, '"Your Very Thankful Inmate"'; L. Wannell, 'Patients' Relatives and Psychiatric Doctors: Letter Writing in the York Retreat, 1875–1910', *Social History of Medicine*, 20 (2007), pp. 297–313.

56. L. Topp and J. Moran, 'Introduction', in Topp, Moran and Andrews (eds), *Madness, Architecture and the Built Environment*, p. 3.

57. Driver, *Power and Pauperism*, p. 13.

58. Ibid., and Philo, '"Enough to Drive one Mad"'.

59. J. Attfield, *Wild Things: The Material Culture of Everyday Life* (Oxford: Berg, 2000), p. 75.

60. M. Guyatt, 'A Semblance of Home: Mental Asylum Interiors, 1880–1914', in S. McKellar and P. Sparke (eds), *Interior Design and Identity* (Manchester: Manchester University Press, 2004), pp. 48–71; R. Wynter, '"Good in all Respects": Appearance and Dress at Staffordshire County Lunatic Asylum, 1818–1854', *History of Psychiatry*, 22 (2011), pp. 40–57; J. Hamlett and L. Hoskins, 'Comfort in Small Things: Clothing, Control and Agency in County Lunatic Asylums in Nineteenth- and Early Twentieth-Century England', *Journal of Victorian Culture* (2013); D. Mackinnon, 'Snatches of Music, Flickering Images and the Smell of Leather: The Material Culture of Recreational Pastimes in Psychiatric Collections in Scotland and Australia', in C. Coleborne and D. Mackinnon (eds), *Exhibiting Madness in Museums: Remembering Psychiatry through Collections and Display* (London: Routledge, 2011), pp. 84–100; K. D. B. Rawling, 'Visualising Mental Illness: Gender, Medicine and Visual Media *c.* 1850–1910' (PhD dissertation, University of London, 2011).

61. Their chapter draws on a wider project that investigates the material culture of nineteenth-century institutions, available online at http://www.rhul.ac.uk/history/research/researchprojects/athomeintheinstitution/athomeintheinstitution.aspx [accessed 21 March 2013].

62. B. Edginton, 'Moral Architecture: The Influence of the York Retreat on Asylum Design', *Health and Place*, 3:2 (1997), pp. 91–9; S. Cherry and R. Munting, '"Exercise is the Thing?" Sport and the Asylum, *c.* 1850–1950', *International Journal of the History of Sport*, 22:1 (2005), pp. 42–58; C. Hickman, 'The "Picturesque" at Brislington House: The Role of Landscape in Relation to the Treatment of Mental Illness in the Early-Nineteenth-Century Asylum', *Garden History*, 33:1 (Summer 2005), pp. 47–60; C. Hickman, 'Cheerful Prospects and Tranquil Restoration: The Visual Experience of Landscape as Part of the Therapeutic Regime of the British Asylum, 1800–1860', *History of Psychiatry*, 20:4 (December 2009), pp. 425–41; C. Hickman, *Therapeutic Landscapes: A History of English Hospital Gardens Since 1800* (forthcoming, Manchester University Press, 2013); C. Philo, *A Geographical History of Institutional Provision for the Insane from Medieval Times to the 1860s in England and Wales* (Lewiston, NY and Lampeter: Edwin Mellen Press, 2004); S. Rutherford, 'The Landscapes of Public Lunatic Asylums in England, 1808–1914' (PhD dissertation, De Montfort University, 2003), 3 vols; and S. Rutherford, *The Victorian Asylum* (Botley: Shire, 2008).

63. S. Cavallo and S. Evangelisti, 'Introduction', in Cavallo and Evangelisti (eds), *Domestic Institutional Interiors in Early Modern Europe*, pp. 2, 4.

64. J. Hamlett, "'Nicely Feminine, yet Learned": Student Rooms at Royal Holloway and the Oxbridge Colleges in Late Nineteenth-Century Britain', *Women's History Review*, 15 (2006), pp. 137–61.

65. A. Milne-Smith, 'A Flight to Domesticity?: Making a Home in the Gentlemen's Clubs of London, 1880–1914', *Journal of British Studies*, 45:4 (2006), pp. 796–818.

66. A. Scull, 'The Domestication of Madness', *Medical History*, 27 (1983), pp. 233–48; Guyatt, 'Semblance of Home'.

67. A cross-institutional study of the material culture of schools, asylums and lodging houses in nineteenth- and early twentieth-century Britain is currently underway: J. Hamlett, *At Home in the Institution: Inside Lunatic Asylums, Lodging Houses and Schools in Victorian and Edwardian England* (London: Palgrave Macmillan, forthcoming 2014).

68. For a recent restatement see D. Birch, *Our Victorian Education* (Oxford: Blackwell, 2008), p. 124. But see also Heather Ellis's discussion of the influence of public-school education on how working-class schools were set up: H. Ellis, 'Elite Education and the Development of Mass Elementary Schooling in England, 1870–1930', in L. Brockliss and N. Sheldon (eds), *Mass Education and the Limits of State Building, c. 1870–1930* (New York: Palgrave Macmillan, 2012), pp. 46–70.

69. For a recent reconsideration of this, see Rogers, 'Kindness and Reciprocity'.

70. Hosgood, 'Mercantile Monasteries'.

71. Q. Colville, 'The Role of the Interior in Constructing Notions of Class and Status: Case Study of Britannia Royal Naval College Dartmouth, 1905–39', in McKellar and Sparke (eds), *Interior Design and Identity*, pp. 114–32.

72. J. S. Pedersen, *The Reform of Girls' Secondary and Higher Education in Victorian England: A Study in Elites and Educational Change* (London: Garland, 1987).

73. C. de Bellaigue, *Educating Women: Schooling and Identity in England and France 1800–1867* (Oxford: Oxford University Press, 2007); S. Skedd, 'Women Teachers and the Expansion of Girls' Schooling in England, c. 1760–1820', in H. Barker and E. Chalus (eds), *Gender in Eighteenth-Century England: Roles, Representations and Responsibilities* (Harlow: Longman, 1997), pp. 101–25.

74. P. Summerfield, *Reconstructing Women's Wartime Lives* (Manchester and New York: Manchester University Press, 1998) and '"She Wants a Gun not a Dishcloth!" Gender, Service and Citizenship in Britain in the Second World War', in G. de Groot and C. M. Peniston-Bird (eds), *A Soldier and A Woman: Sexual Integration in the Military* (London: Pearson Education, 2000), p. 123; E. Crosthwait, '"The Girl Behind the Man Behind the Gun": The Women's Army Auxiliary Corps, 1914–18', in L. Davidoff and B. Westover (eds), *Our Work, Our Lives, Our Worlds: Women's History and Women's Work* (Basingstoke: Macmillan Education, 1986), pp. 161–81; L. Noakes, *Women in the British Army: War and the Gentle Sex, 1907–1948* (London and New York: Routledge, 2006).

75. N. Vance, 'The Ideal of Manliness', in B. Simon and I. Bradley (eds), *The Victorian Public School: Studies in the Development of an Educational Institution* (Dublin: Gill and Macmillan, 1975), pp. 115–28; F. Neddam, 'Constructing Masculinities under Thomas Arnold of Rugby (1828–1842): Gender, Educational Policy and School Life in an Early-Victorian Public School', *Gender and Education*, 16 (2004), pp. 303–26.

76. G. Best, 'Militarism and the Victorian Public School', in Simon and Bradley (eds), *Victorian Public School*, pp. 129–46; J. A. Mangan, *Athleticism in the Victorian and Edwardian Public School: The Emergence and Consolidation of an Educational Ideology* (Cambridge: Press Syndicate of the University of Cambridge, 1981; London: Frank Cass, 2000); E.

Showalter, 'Rivers and Sassoon: The Inscription of Male Gender Anxieties', in M. Higonnet et al. (eds), *Behind the Lines: Gender and the Two World Wars* (New Haven, CT and London: Yale University Press, 1987), pp. 61–9; T. Bogacz, 'War Neurosis and Cultural Change in England, 1914–22: The Work of the War Office Committee of Enquiry into Shell Shock', *Journal of Contemporary History*, 24 (1989), pp. 227–56.

77.   D. French, *Military Identities: The Regimental System, the British Army, and the British People, c. 1870–2000* (Oxford and New York: Oxford University Press, 2005); Q. Colville, 'Corporate Domesticity and Idealised Masculinity: Royal Naval Officers and their Shipboard Homes, 1918–39', *Gender & History*, 21 (2009), pp. 499–519; M. Roper, *The Secret Battle: Emotional Survival in the Great War* (Manchester and New York: Manchester University Press, 2009); S. Das, *Touch and Intimacy in First World War Literature* (Cambridge: Cambridge University Press, 2005).

1 Fisher, 'Viewing the Early Twentieth-Century Institutional Interior through the Pages of *Living London*'

1.   It is likely that the fortnightly editions and *Living London* volumes reached a wider working-class audience through, for example, libraries, clubs and other social and educational institutions.

2.   G. R. Sims (ed.), *Living London: Its Work and its Play, its Humour and its Pathos, its Sights and its Scenes*, 3 vols (London: Cassell & Company, 1902–3), vol. 1, p. 6.

3.   K. Wilson, 'Surveying Victorian and Edwardian Londoners: George R. Sims' "*Living London*"', in L. Phillips (ed.), *A Mighty Mass of Brick and Smoke: Victorian and Edwardian Representations of London*, DQR Studies in Literature, 41 (Amsterdam and New York: Rodopi, 2007), pp. 131–49, on p. 141.

4.   Booth's survey was conducted between 1886 and 1903 and published between 1889 and 1903. C. Booth, *Life and Labour of the People in London*, 17 vols (London: Macmillan, 1902–3).

5.   On the urban photographic survey see V. L. Pollock, 'Dislocated Narratives and Sites of Memory: Amateur Photographic Surveys in Britain 1889–1897', *Visual Culture in Britain*, 10:1 (March 2009), pp. 1–26.

6.   On nineteenth-century visual culture see J. Crary, *Techniques of the Observer: On Vision and Modernity in the Nineteenth Century* (Cambridge, MA, and London: MIT Press, 1992) and V. R. Schwartz and J. M. Przyblski (eds), *The Nineteenth-Century Visual Culture Reader* (London: Routledge, 2004).

7.   Sims (ed.), *Living London*, vol. 3, p. 361.

8.   D. MacDougall, *The Corporeal Image: Film, Ethnography, and the Senses* (Princeton, NJ: Princeton University Press, 2005), pp. 3–4.

9.   L. Davidoff and C. Hall, *Family Fortunes: Men and Women of the English Middle Class, 1780–1850* (London: Hutchinson, 1987); J. Hamlett, *Material Relations: Domestic Interiors and Middle-Class Families in England, 1850–1910* (Manchester: Manchester University Press, 2010); S. McKellar and P. Sparke (eds), *Interior Design and Identity* (Manchester and New York: Manchester University Press, 2004); P. Sparke, *As Long as it's Pink: The Sexual Politics of Taste* (London: Pandora, 1995).

10.   D. Cohen, *Household Gods: the British and their Possessions* (New Haven, CT and London: Yale University Press, 2006); K. C. Grier, *Culture and Comfort: Parlor Making and Middle-Class Identity 1850–1930* (1988; Washington, DC; London: Smithsonian Institution Press, 1997); T. Logan, *The Victorian Parlour: A Cultural Study* (Cambridge: Cambridge University Press, 2001).

11. L. Walker, 'Home Making: An Architectural Perspective', *Signs*, 27:3 (Spring 2002), pp. 823–35, on p. 824.
12. Recent studies of the design of the modern interior include: C. Grafe and F. Bollerey (eds), *Public Interiors: Cafés and Bars the Architecture of Sociability* (London: Routledge, 2007); P. Sparke, *The Modern Interior* (London: Reaktion Books, 2008); P. Sparke, A. Massey, T. Keeble and B. Martin (eds), *Designing the Modern Interior: From the Victorians to Today* (Oxford: Berg, 2009); A. Myzelev and J. Potvin (eds), *Fashion, Interior Design and the Contours of Modern Identity* (Farnham: Ashgate, London, 2010); F. Fisher, T. Keeble, P. Lara-Betancourt and B. Martin (eds), *Performance, Fashion and the Modern Interior: From the Victorians to Today* (Oxford: Berg, Oxford, 2011).
13. L. Stalder, 'Turning Architecture Inside Out: Revolving Doors and other Threshold Devices', *Journal of Design History*, 22:1 (2009), pp. 69–77, on p. 74.
14. As a result of his research into Victorian working-class housing, which charted a shift from communal to private residential models, Martin Daunton posited a parallel shift in public environments. Following Daunton, the turnstile can be situated within the context of a domestic ideal of residential segregation that informed the design of dwellings for all classes, as well as a wider shift towards more clearly defined, bounded and regulated municipal and commercial spaces. M. J. Daunton, 'Public Place and Private Space: The Victorian City and the Working-Class Household', in D. Fraser and A. Sutcliffe (eds), *The Pursuit of Urban History* (London: Edward Arnold, 1983), pp. 218–19.
15. See I. Altman, *The Environment and Social Behavior: Privacy. Personal Space. Territory. Crowding.* (Monterey, CA: Brooks/Cole Publishing Company, 1975); A. F. Westin, *Privacy and Freedom* (New York: Atheneum, 1967); S. T. Margulis, 'On the Status and Contribution of Westin's and Altman's Theories of Privacy', *Journal of Social Issues*, 59:2 (2003), pp. 411–29.
16. Altman, *The Environment and Social Behavior*, p. 41.
17. See, for example, *Living London*'s photographs of dining spaces at Ham Yard Hospice and at the Victoria Home in Whitechapel. Sims (ed.), *Living London*, vol. 1, p. 332 and vol. 3, p. 173.
18. See, for example, *Living London*'s photograph of the interior of the Alexandra Trust Restaurant. Sims (ed.), *Living London*, vol. 1, p. 298.
19. See Sims (ed.), *Living London*, vol. 1, p. 376 and vol. 1, p. 239.
20. See, for example, *Living London*'s photograph of an old women's ward at Nazareth House in Hammersmith. Sims (ed.), *Living London*, vol. 2, p. 253.
21. For the image of box beds at Medland Hall, see Sims (ed.), *Living London*, vol. 1, p. 334. See also 'The Aristocratic Sevenpence', *The Times*, 10 June 1914, p. 5.
22. T. Crook, 'Power, Privacy and Pleasure: Liberalism and the Modern Cubicle', *Cultural Studies*, 21:4 (2007), pp. 549–69, on p. 552.
23. A case of over-crowding brought against the Salvation Army under the Public Health Act in 1895 provoked significant debate about institutional interior design, the reform of charitable lodgings and the specific requirements of individuals for space, air and ventilation. See 'Police', *The Times*, 22 August 1895, p. 2; 'Salvation Army Shelters', *The Times*, 5 December 1895, p. 13; 'The Salvation Army Shelter Case', *The Times*, 9 December 1895, p. 7; 'The Question of Overcrowding in Salvation Army Shelters', *The Times*, 10 December 1895, p. 9.
24. In contrast to the cubicles at Parker Street, and in keeping with the model of the hotel, which informed its representation, London's Rowton House cubicles, also mentioned in

the article, are described as 'bedrooms'. See 'Rowton Houses', *The Times*, 29 May 1896, p. 11.

25. Sims (ed.), *Living London*, vol. 3, pp. 172–8, on p. 176.

26. Ibid., vol. 2, pp. 151–7, on p. 153.

27. See 'The Fossan (Keate and Tonge) Estate', *Survey of London, vol. 27: Spitalfields and Mile End New Town* (1957), pp. 245–51, online at http://www.british-history.ac.uk/report.aspx?compid=50176&strquery="flower and dean street" [accessed 3 October 2012].

28. A report on improvements in military barracks, for example, suggested that men of 'self-respect' would be unwilling to sleep in 'a common sleeping room in which the good characters of the regiment do not sleep'. See 'Improvements in Military Barracks', *The Times*, 20 January 1903, p. 10.

29. Sims (ed.), *Living London*, vol. 3, pp. 172–3.

30. Ibid., vol. 1, pp. 371–7, on p. 377.

31. Ibid., vol. 1, pp. 376–7.

32. Ibid.

33. Ibid.

34. For example, a children's ward at Great Ormond Street Hospital and an infirmary at Holloway Prison. See Sims (ed.), *Living London*, vol. 2, p. 169 and vol. 1, p. 239.

35. Sims (ed.), *Living London*, vol. 1, pp. 234–40, on p. 238.

36. Ibid., p. 238.

37. Ibid., p. 239.

38. Ibid., p. 240.

39. On the relationship between the design of public and private spaces of modernity and the influence of the domestic within the public sphere, see Sparke, *The Modern Interior*.

40. Sims (ed.), *Living London*, vol. 3, pp. 279–85. The image can be seen on the Museum of London website. See http://www.museumoflondon.org.uk/Collections-Research/Research/Your-Research/RWWC/objects/record.htm?type=object&id=718335 [accessed 2 October 2012].

41. The three *Living London* volumes include articles on German, French, American, Italian, Jewish, Indian and Oriental London, among others.

42. On wrapper writers see Sims (ed.), *Living London*, vol. 3, p. 176. On lodging-house kitchens see Sims (ed.), *Living London*, vol. 2, p. 153.

43. H. Mayhew, *London Labour and the London Poor; A Cyclopædia of the Condition and Earnings of Those that Will Work, Those that Cannot Work, and Those that Will Not Work* (London: George Woodfall & Son, 1851), vol. 1, p. 1.

44. A. Davin, *Growing Up Poor: Home, School and Street in London: 1870–1914* (London: Rivers Oram Press, 1996), p. 31.

45. A. Blunt and R. Dowling, *Home* (London and New York: Routledge, 2006), p. 22.

46. Sims (ed.), *Living London*, vol. 2, p. 100–6, on p. 105.

47. L. H. Lees, *The Solidarities of Strangers: the English Poor Laws and the People, 1700–1948* (Cambridge: Cambridge University Press, 1998), p. 258.

48. Sims (ed.), *Living London*, vol. 2, p. 156.

49. Ibid.

50. Ibid., vol. 2, pp. 151, 154.

51. Ibid., vol. 2, p. 154.

52. M. Csikszentmihalyi, 'Why We Need Things', in S. Lubar and W. D. Kingery (eds), *History from Things: Essays on Material Culture* (Washington, DC and London: Smithsonian Institution Press, 1993), pp. 20–9, on p. 25.

53. M. Douglas, 'The Idea of a Home: A Kind of Space', *Social Research*, 58:1 (1991), pp. 287–307, on p. 289.

54. P. Overy, *Light, Air and Openness: Modern Architecture between the Wars* (London: Thames & Hudson, 2007).

2 Newsom Kerr, '"French Beef was Better than Hampstead Beef": Taste, Treatment and Pauperism in a London Smallpox Hospital, 1871'

1. 'Christmas under the Poor Laws', *Morning Post*, 26 December 1872, p. 7.

2. *Morning Chronicle*, 27 December 1851, p. 4.

3. G. R. Sims, 'Christmas in the Workhouse', in *The Dagonet Ballads* (London: Francis & Co., 1879), pp. 8–15.

4. The contentious place of pauperism in state medicine is also seen in the troubled history of smallpox vaccination. N. Durbach, *Bodily Matters: The Anti-Vaccination Movement in England, 1853–1907* (London: Duke University Press, 2005).

5. P. Bourdieu, *Distinction: A Social Critique of the Judgment of Taste* (Cambridge, MA: Harvard University Press, 1984), p. 6. See also W. Schivelbusch, *Tastes of Paradise* (New York: Pantheon Books, 1992), pp. 6–8.

6. Quoted in F. Driver, *Power and Pauperism: The Workhouse System, 1834–1884* (New York: Cambridge University Press, 1993), p. 59.

7. Quoted in I. Anstruther, *The Scandal of the Andover Workhouse* (London: Geoffrey Bles, 1973), p. 16.

8. A. Digby, *Pauper Palaces* (Boston, MA: Routledge, 1978); D. Englander, 'From the Abyss: Pauper Petitions and Correspondence in Victorian London', *London Journal*, 25:1 (2000), pp. 71–83; D. Green, 'Pauper Protests: Power and Resistance in Nineteenth-Century London Workhouses', *Social History*, 31:2 (2006), pp. 137–59.

9. [F. B. Head], *English Charity* (London: John Murray, 1835), pp. 30 and 10–11.

10. B. Rogers, *Beef and Liberty* (London: Chatto & Windus, 2003), p. 9.

11. J. Pereira, *A Treatise on Food and Diet* (London, 1843), p. 490.

12. E. Ross, *Love and Toil: Motherhood in Outcast London* (New York: Oxford University Press, 1993), p. 32.

13. P. Gurney, '"Rejoicing in Potatoes": The Politics of Consumption in England during the "Hungry Forties"', *Past and Present*, 203 (2009), pp. 99–136.

14. N. Edsall, *The Anti-Poor Law Movement, 1834–44* (Manchester: Manchester University Press, 1971), pp. 21–3.

15. R. Oastler, *Damnation! Eternal Damnation to the Fiend-Begotten, 'Coarser Food' New Poor Law* (London: H. Hetherington, 1837), p. 19.

16. Anstruther, *Scandal of the Andover Workhouse*.

17. 'A New Chamber of Horrors', *All the Year Round*, 2 March 1861, pp. 500–1; *Morning Post*, 16 January 1867, p. 7.

18. L. Twining, *Workhouses and Women's Work* (London, 1858).

19. L. Twining, *A Letter to the President of the Poor Law Board on Workhouse Infirmaries* (London: William Hunt, 1866), p. 13; F. P. Cobbe, 'Workhouse Sketches', *Macmillan's Magazine* (April 1861), pp. 448–61.

20. *Lancet*, 18 November 1865, p. 576.
21. S. North, 'What Means Ought to be Adopted for Improving the Management of Workhouses?', in *Transactions of the National Association for the Promotion of Social Science, 1866* (London, 1867), p. 644.
22. J. Rogers, *Reminiscences of a Workhouse Medical Officer* (London: Fisher Unwin, 1889), pp. 59–60; C. Hamlin, *Public Health and Social Justice in the Age of Chadwick* (New York: Cambridge University Press, 1998), pp. 90–102.
23. D. Green, *From Artisans to Paupers: Economic Change and Poverty in London, 1790–1870* (Brookfield, VT: Scolar Press, 1995), pp. 233–6.
24. *Lancet*, 1 July 1865, p. 16. See also E. Hart, 'Metropolitan Infirmaries for the Pauper Sick', *Fortnightly Review*, 4 (1866), pp. 459–63.
25. M. W. Flinn, 'Medical Services under the New Poor Law', in D. Fraser (ed.), *The New Poor Law in the Nineteenth Century* (New York: St Martin's, 1976), p. 66.
26. D. Green, 'Medical Relief and the New Poor Law in London', in O. Grell, A. Cunningham and R. Jütte (eds), *Health Care and Poor Relief in 18th and 19th Century Northern Europe* (Burlington, VT: Ashgate, 2002), pp. 220–45.
27. Quoted in G. Ayers, *England's First State Hospitals and the Metropolitan Asylums Board* (Berkeley, CA: University of California Press, 1971), p. 9.
28. J. Greenwood, 'A Night in a Workhouse', *Pall Mall Gazette*, 12–16 January 1866; J. C. Parkinson, 'A Real Casual on Casual Wards', *Temple Bar* (March 1866), vol. 16, p. 498; S. Koven, *Slumming: Sexual and Social Politics in Victorian London* (Princeton, NJ; Princeton University Press, 2004), especially pp. 25–87.
29. *Daily News*, 19 January 1866, p. 4.
30. Quoted in R. C. Austin, *The Metropolitan Poor Act, 1867* (London: Knight & Co., 1867), pp. xx–xxi.
31. [R.] Grieve, 'An Analysis of 800 Cases of Smallpox Observed during the Present Epidemic in the Hampstead Small-Pox Hospital', *Lancet*, 18 March 1871, p. 372.
32. Ayers, *England's First State Hospitals*, p. 62.
33. A. Collie, *Report of the Commissioners Appointed to Inquire Respecting Small-Pox and Fever Hospitals, Minutes of Evidence* (London, 1882), p. 139.
34. Originally intended for 120 patients, the hospital was repeatedly expanded to eventually accommodate over 500 at once. *The Times*, 12 October 1871, p. 11.
35. 'The Hampstead Fever Hospital', *Lancet*, 29 January 1870, pp. 173–4.
36. *Pall Mall Gazette*, 19 June 1871, p. 4; *North Londoner*, 9 September 1871, p. 2; *Camden and Kentish Town Gazette*, 10 June 1871, p. 2; *Morning Post*, 15 September 1871, p. 7; *The Times*, 27 September 1871, p. 11.
37. *The Times*, 29 August 1871, p. 8; *The Times*, 30 August 1871, p. 8; *The Times*, 1 September 1871, p. 8; *The Times*, 5 September 1871, p. 8; *The Times*, 12 September 1871, p. 3; *The Times*, 15 September 1871, p. 3.
38. *The Times*, the *Lancet*, the *Medical Times and Gazette* (hereafter *MTG*), the *Echo*, *The Standard*, *Lloyd's Weekly Newspaper*, the *Daily News*, the *Morning Post*, the *Illustrated Police News* (hereafter *IPN*), and undoubtedly many more.
39. 'The Hampstead Hospital Enquiry', *Medical Press and Circular*, 8 November 1871, p. 413. On melodrama and the New Poor Law, see E. Hadley, *Melodramatic Tactics: Theatricalized Dissent in the English Marketplace, 1800–1885* (Standford, CA: Stanford University Press, 1995), pp. 77–132.
40. *The Times*, 5 October 1871, p. 11.
41. *MTG*, 30 September 1871, pp. 421–2; *MTG*, 14 October 1871, p. 477.

42. *The Times*, 13 October 1871, p. 9.
43. *The Times*, 5 October 1871, p. 11.
44. *The Times*, 27 September 1871, p. 11; *The Times*, 5 October 1871, p. 11.
45. *IPN*, 30 September 1871, p. 2.
46. *MTG*, 30 September 1871, p. 421; *The Times*, 4 October 1871, p. 11.
47. *The Times*, 22 September 1871, p. 9.
48. *The Times*, 26 September 1871, p. 9.
49. *The Times*, 22 September 1871, p. 9. See also *IPN*, 30 September 1871, p. 2.
50. *The Times*, 5 October 1871, p. 11.
51. *MTG*, 30 September 1871, p. 419.
52. *The Times*, 23 September 1871, p. 11; *MTG*, 30 September 1871, p. 420.
53. *The Times*, 5 October 1871, p. 11.
54. *MTG*, 30 September 1871, p. 422; *The Times*, 27 September 1871, p. 11.
55. *MTG*, 7 October 1871, p. 452; *The Times*, 4 October 1871, p. 11.
56. *Borough of Marylebone Mercury*, 30 September 1871, p. 2.
57. *The Times*, 27 September 1871, p. 11.
58. *The Times*, 5 October 1871, p. 11.
59. *The Times*, 26 September 1871, p. 9.
60. *The Times*, 22 September 1871, p. 9; *MTG*, 30 September 1871, p. 419.
61. *The Times*, 4 October 1871, p. 11.
62. *The Times*, 27 September 1871, p. 11.
63. *The Times*, 4 October 1871, p. 11.
64. *The Times*, 26 September 1871, p. 9.
65. *MTG*, 30 September 1871, p. 419; *The Times*, 27 September 1871, p. 11.
66. *The Times*, 4 October 1871, p. 11.
67. *The Times*, 5 October 1871, p. 11.
68. *The Times*, 22 September 1871, p. 9; *The Times*, 23 September 1871, p. 11; *The Times*, 3 October 1871, p. 9.
69. C. Forth, *Masculinity in the Modern West: Gender, Civilization and the Body* (New York: Palgrave Macmillan, 2008), pp. 92–113.
70. *The Times*, 27 September 1871, p. 11.
71. *The Times*, 4 October 1871, p. 11; *MTG*, 7 October 1871, p. 453.
72. *The Times*, 26 September 1871, p. 9.
73. *The Times*, 22 September 1871, p. 9.
74. Ibid.
75. *The Times*, 26 September 1871, p. 9.
76. *The Times*, 27 September 1871, p. 11.
77. Ibid.
78. *The Times*, 6 October 1871, p. 9.
79. *The Times*, 11 October 1871, p. 11; *IPN*, 14 October 1871, p. 2.
80. *The Times*, 28 September 1871, p. 9.
81. *The Times*, 17 October 1871, p. 12.
82. *The Times*, 11 October 1871, p. 11; *The Times*, 27 September 1871, p. 11; *MTG*, 30 September 1871, p. 423; *IPN*, 14 October 1871, p. 2; *MTG*, 21 October 1871, p. 506.
83. *MTG*, 30 September 1871, p. 424; *MTG*, 14 October 1871, p. 479.
84. *The Times*, 7 October 1871, p. 11; *MTG*, 14 October 1871, p. 478; *The Times*, 27 September 1871, p. 11.
85. *MTG*, 30 September 1871, p. 420. See also *The Times*, 22 September 1871, p. 9.

86. *The Times*, 3 October 1871, p. 11.
87. Ibid.
88. *The Times*, 5 October 1871, p. 11; *The Times*, 6 October 1871, p. 9.
89. *The Times*, 4 November 1871, p. 6.
90. *The Times*, 22 September 1871, p. 9.
91. Ibid.
92. *The Times*, 4 October 1871, p. 11.
93. *The Times*, 24 October 1871, p. 11.
94. Ibid.
95. *The Times*, 21 October 1871, p. 9.
96. *The Times*, 25 October 1871, p. 11.
97. Metropolitan Asylums Board Minutes, 6 January 1872, City of London, London Metropolitan Archives, MAB/5, p. 551.
98. *Morning Post*, 5 January 1872, p. 4.
99. *MTG*, 11 November 1871, p. 590.
100. *Lancet*, 16 December 1876, p. 864.
101. *Morning Post*, 5 January 1872, p. 4.
102. *Borough of Marylebone Mercury*, 30 September 1871, p. 2.
103. *Borough of Marylebone Mercury*, 2 September 1871, p. 2.
104. These developments are explored in detail in my forthcoming monograph on London isolation hospitals, of which this chapter forms a part.

3 Hide, 'From Asylum to Mental Hospital: Gender, Space and the Patient Experience in London County Council Asylums, 1890–1910'

1. The Twentieth Annual Report of the Asylums Committee as to the London County Asylums; Banstead, Bexley, Cane Hill, Claybury, Colney Hatch, Hanwell, Horton, Long Grove, The Manor and Epileptic Colony, For the Year ended 31st March 1909, City of London, London Metropolitan Archives (hereafter LMA), 26.21, p. 79. All reports, minute books and case notes are held at LMA. Dates quoted refer to the publication date of the LCC Annual Report.
2. G. T. Hine, 'Asylums and Asylum Planning', *Journal of the Royal Institute of British Architects*, 23 February 1901, pp. 161–84, on p. 161.
3. Ibid., pp. 175–6.
4. Ibid., p. 171.
5. M. Foucault, *Madness and Civilisation: A History of Insanity in the Age of Reason* (London: Tavistock, 1985); *The Birth of the Clinic: An Archaeology of Medical Perception* (London: Routledge, 2008); *Discipline and Punish: The Birth of the Prison* (London: Penguin Books, 1991).
6. A. T. Scull, *Museums of Madness: The Social Organization of Insanity in Nineteenth-Century England* (London: Allen Lane, 1979), revised and republished as *The Most Solitary of Afflictions: Madness and Society in Britain, 1700–1900* (New Haven, CT and London: Yale University Press, 1993).
7. R. Porter, 'The Patient's View: Doing Medical History from Below', *Theory and Society*, 14 (1985), pp. 175–98; R. Porter, *Mind-Forg'd Manacles: A History of Madness in England from the Restoration to the Regency* (London: Athlone Press, 1987); 'Madness

and its Institutions', in A. Wear (ed.), *Medicine in Society: Historical Essays* (Cambridge: Cambridge University Press, 1992), pp. 277–302.

8. E. Showalter, *The Female Malady: Women, Madness and English Culture 1830–1980* (1985; London: Virago, 1998).

9. J. Melling and B. Forsythe (eds), *Insanity, Institutions and Society, 1800–1914: A Social History of Madness in Comparative Perspective* (London: Routledge, 1999); J. Melling and B. Forsythe (eds), *The Politics of Madness: The State, Insanity and Society in England, 1845–1914* (London: Routledge, 2006); D. Wright, *Mental Disability in Victorian England. The Earlswood Asylum, 1847–1901* (Oxford: Clarendon Press, 2001), J. Andrews and A. Digby (eds), *Sex and Seclusion, Class and Custody: Perspectives on Gender and Class in the History of British and Irish Psychiatry* (Amsterdam: Rodopi, 2004); C. Coleborne and D. MacKinnon (eds), *'Madness' in Australia: Histories, Heritage and the Asylum* (Queensland: University of Queensland Press, 2003), see in particular essays by Susan Piddock, Catharine Coleborne and Lee-Ann Monk.

10. L. Prior, 'The Architecture of the Hospital: A Study of Spatial Organization and Medical Knowledge', *British Journal of Sociology*, 39 (1988), pp. 86–113; B. Edginton, 'Moral Architecture: The Influence of the York Retreat on Asylum Design', *Health & Place*, 3 (1997), pp. 91–9; B. Edginton, 'The Well-Ordered Body: The Quest for Sanity through Nineteenth-Century Asylum Architecture', *Canadian Bulletin of Medicine*, 11 (1994), pp. 375–86; J. Taylor, *Hospital and Asylum Architecture in England 1840–1914: Building for Health Care* (London: Mansell, 1991).

11. C. Yanni, *The Architecture of Madness: Insane Asylums in the United States* (Minneapolis, London: University of Minnesota Press, 2007).

12. L. Topp, J. E. Moran and J. Andrews (eds), *Madness, Architecture and the Built Environment: Psychiatric Spaces in Historical Context* (New York, London: Routledge, 2007). This volume contains essays by Topp, Edginton and Taylor that are particularly relevant to this chapter.

13. J. E. Moran and L. Topp, 'Introduction: Interpreting Psychiatric Spaces', in Topp, Moran and Andrews (eds), *Madness, Architecture and the Built Environment*, pp. 1–16, on p. 3.

14. K. Jones, *Asylums and After, A Revised History of the Mental Health Services: From the Early 18th Century to the 1990s* (London: Athlone Press, 1993), p. 116.

15. Ibid.

16. Vast 'idiot' asylums, workhouses with lunacy wards and privately run establishments also housed the insane.

17. The LCC Asylums Committee was formed in 1889 and was the largest of its kind in England and Wales. D. Cochrane, '"Humane, Economical, and Medically Wise": The LCC as Administrators of Victorian Lunacy Policy', in W. F. Bynum, R. Porter and M. Shepherd (eds), *The Anatomy of Madness: Essays in the History of Psychiatry*, 3 vols (London and New York: Routledge, 1988), vol. 3, pp. 247–72, on p. 248.

18. The Committee inherited four asylums from Surrey and Middlesex counties: Hanwell (opened 1831), Colney Hatch (opened 1851), Banstead (opened 1877) and Cane Hill (opened 1883). The new asylums built by the LCC were Claybury (opened 1893), Bexley (opened 1898), The Manor (opened 1899), Horton (opened 1902), the Ewell Epileptic Colony (opened 1903) and Long Grove (opened 1907).

19. R. Jones, 'The London County Council and the Care of the Mentally Afflicted', *Westminster Review*, 163:4 (1905), pp. 409–21, on p. 409. These do not include asylums run by the Metropolitan Asylums Board, such as Caterham and Leavesden, for 'chronic and imbecile cases'.

20. LCC Seventeenth Annual Report, 1906, LMA, 26.21, p. 10.
21. Cochrane, '"Humane, Economical, and Medically Wise"', p. 250.
22. R. Jones, 'The London County Council Asylum at Claybury, and a Sketch of its First Working Year', *Journal of Mental Science* (hereafter *JMS*), 43 (1897), pp. 47–58, on p. 47.
23. *London*, 23 August 1894, pp. 535–8.
24. Cited by Scull, *Solitary Afflictions*, p. 330.
25. Hine, 'Asylums and Asylum Planning', p. 169.
26. Numbers quickly exceeded the estimated 2,000 patients, rising to 2,500 by 1897. Jones, 'Sketch', p. 49.
27. Ibid., p. 50.
28. LCC Ninth Annual Report, 1898, LMA, 26.21, p. 64.
29. Jones, 'Sketch', p. 52. Private male patients were from Claybury Hall, described by Jones as 'a small private asylum under public control ... for a class of patients above the pauper class, but who can ill afford to bear the cost of a private asylum, and who may find comparative quiet and comfort; perhaps even a touch of "home" in such an institution'. Jones, 'Sketch', p. 48.
30. B. Von Zweigbergk and M. Armstrong, *The Village on the Heath: A History of Bexley Hospital* (Brentwood: Doppler Press, 2004), p. 36.
31. Commissioners were responsible for ensuring asylums met standards and regulations.
32. LCC Twelfth Annual Report, 1901, LMA, 26.21, p. 97.
33. J. K. Walton, 'Casting Out and Bringing Back in Victorian England: Pauper Lunatics, 1840–1870', in Bynum, Porter and Shepherd (eds), *The Anatomy of Madness*, vol. 2, pp. 132–46, on p. 135.
34. Scull, *The Most Solitary of Afflictions*.
35. A. Digby, 'Moral Treatment at the Retreat, 1796–1846', in Bynum, Porter and Shepherd (eds), *The Anatomy of Madness*, vol. 2, pp. 52–72, on pp. 68–9.
36. LCC Seventh Annual Report, 1896, LMA, 26.21, p. 47.
37. R. Jones, 'Attendants Taking all their Meals in the Mess Room', in Claybury Asylum, Sub-Committee Minute Book 23, entry 19 November 1908, LMA, LCC/MIN/00829, pp. 1–2.
38. See Edginton's 'The Well-Ordered Body' for his discussion of design and architecture as treatment.
39. H. C. Burdett, *Hospitals and Asylums of the World: Their Origin, History, Construction, Administration, Management, and Legislation; With Plans of the Chief Medical Institutions Accurately Drawn to a Uniform Scale, in Addition to those of all the Hospitals of London in the Jubilee Year of Queen Victoria's Reign*, 4 vols (London: Churchill, 1891), vol. 2, p. vii.
40. Bexley Minute Book 4 (March–December 1900) LMA, LCC/MIN/00810, p. 140; Bexley Minute Book 2 (June 1898–May 1899) LMA, LCC/MIN/00808, p. 321.
41. Claybury Minute Book No. 3 (January 1891–March 1893) LMA, LCC/MIN/00917, p. 246.
42. Jones, 'Attendants Taking All their Meals', pp. 5–6.
43. LCC Sixth Annual Report, 1895, LMA, 26.21, p. 54.
44. LCC Ninth Annual Report, 1898, LMA, 26.21, pp. 56–7.
45. LCC Eleventh Annual Report, 1900, LMA, 26.21, p. 85.
46. M. Pugh, *State and Society: A Social and Political History of Britain since 1870*, 3rd edn (London: Hodder, 2008), pp. 77–8.
47. LCC Annual Report of the Council 1913, Vol. 2, ASYLUMS, LMA, 18.7, p. 29.

48. Bexley Minute Book 17 (December 1910–September 1911) LMA, LCC/MIN/00823, p. 230. This claim is hard to believe considering the number of patients who were infirm or simply disengaged with asylum activities.

49. D. Thomson, cited in C. C. Easterbrook, 'The Sanatorium Treatment of Active Insanity by Rest in Bed in the Open Air', *JMS*, 53 (1907), pp. 723–50, on p. 747.

50. LCC Fourteenth Annual Report, 1903, LMA, 26.21, p. 69.

51. Showalter, *The Female Malady*, p. 83.

52. LCC Eleventh Annual Report, 1900, LMA, 26.21, p. 57.

53. LCC Fifteenth Annual Report, 1904, LMA, 26.21, p. 89.

54. LCC Eighteenth Annual Report, 1907, LMA, 26.21, p. 63.

55. LCC Nineteenth Annual Report, 1908, LMA, 26.21, p. 69.

56. LCC Sixth Annual Report, 1895, LMA, 26.21, pp. 53–4.

57. Jones, 'Sketch', p. 52.

58. *Handbook for Instruction of the Attendants on the Insane* (Boston, MA: Cupples, Upham & Co., 1886), p. 123.

59. LCC Fifth Annual Report, 1894, LMA, 26.21, p. 53.

60. LCC Eighth Annual Report, 1897, LMA, 26.21, p. 54.

61. LCC Tenth Annual Report, 1899, LMA, 26.21, p. 65.

62. LCC Eleventh Annual Report, 1900, LMA, 26.21, p. 54.

63. Scull, *The Most Solitary of Afflictions*, p. 325.

64. Fresh air, exercise, electric baths, massage and baths were all valued for their therapeutic effect on the mind through the agency of the physical body. The notion that the mind and body strongly affected each other was one of the key principles underpinning moral treatment at the York Retreat in the early nineteenth century; the Retreat was very influential on subsequent thinking about asylum practice. See B. Edginton, 'A Space for Moral Management: The York Retreat's Influence on Asylum Design', in Topp, Moran and Andrews (eds), *Madness, Architecture and the Built Environment*, p. 92.

65. LCC Twentieth Annual Report, 1909, LMA, 26.21, p. 79.

66. Hine, 'Asylums and Asylum Planning', p. 171.

67. LCC Thirteenth Annual Report, 1902, LMA, 26.21, p. 88.

68. LCC Fourteen Annual Report, 1903, LMA, 26.21, p. 97.

69. J. Taylor, 'The Architect and the Pauper Asylum in Late Nineteenth-Century England. G. T. Hine's 1901 Review of Asylum Space and Planning', in Topp, Moran and Andrews (eds), *Madness, Architecture and the Built Environment*, pp. 275–6.

70. Moran and Topp, 'Introduction: Interpreting Psychiatric Spaces', in Topp, Moran and Andrews (eds), *Madness, Architecture and the Built Environment*, p. 6; see also in the same volume L. Topp, 'The Modern Mental Hospital in Late Nineteenth-Century Germany and Austria: Psychiatric Space and Images of Freedom and Control'.

71. LCC Thirteenth Annual Report, 1902, LMA, 26.21, p. 88; see Topp, ch. 12 in Topp, Moran and Andrews (eds), *Madness, Architecture and the Built Environment*, for more about this system in Germany and Austria. See Taylor, 'The Architect and the Pauper Asylum', p. 275–6 and Hine, 'Asylums and Asylum Planning', p. 169. A similar design was applied to Horton. Strictly speaking, Bexley was an adaptation of the villa system model developed in the German-speaking world, which did not include a main asylum building (my thanks to Leslie Topp for pointing this out).

72. LCC Thirteenth Annual Report, 1902, LMA, 26.21, p. 88.

73. Ibid.

74. LCC Fourteenth Annual Report, 1903, LMA, 26.21, p. 97; LCC Thirteenth Annual Report, 1902, LMA, 26.21, p. 91.

75. A practice that was already taking place in Scotland, see G. M. Robertson, 'The Employment of Female Nurses in the Male Wards of Mental Hospitals in Scotland', *JMS*, 62 (1916), pp. 351–62, on p. 355.

76. D. Wright, 'Asylum Nursing and Institutional Services: A Case Study of the South of England, 1861–1881', *Nursing History Review*, 7 (1999), pp. 153–69, on pp. 165–6.

77. Robertson, 'The Employment of Female Nurses', p. 360.

78. H. Maudsley, *The Pathology of Mind*, 3rd edn (New York: Appleton & Co., 1880), p. 540.

79. P. Chesler, *Women and Madness*, 3rd edn (1972; New York: Four Walls Eight Windows, 1997), p. 94.

80. Bexley Asylum Male Case Book 16, LMA, H65/B/10/012, F114.

81. Easterbrook, 'The Sanatorium Treatment of Active Insanity', pp. 730–1.

82. It would be incorrect to suggest superintendents always put a positive 'spin' on aspects of asylum life. They could be critical, although this might have been to draw attention to lack of funding.

83. Moran and Topp, 'Introduction: Interpreting Psychiatric Spaces', p. 9.

84. Bexley Male Case Book 10, LMA, H65/B/10/006, F156.

4 Martin, 'Refuge or Prison? Girls' Experiences of a Home for the "Mentally Defective" in Scotland, 1906–1948'

1. J. Lane, *A Social History of Medicine: Health, Healing and Disease in England, 1750–1950* (London: Routledge, 2001), pp. 187–8; M. Jackson, *The Borderland of Imbecility: Medicine, Society and the Fabrication of the Feeble Mind in Late Victorian and Edwardian Britain* (New York: Manchester University Press, 2000); W. B. Stephens, *Education in Britain, 1750–1914* (Basingstoke: Macmillan, 1998), pp. 94–6.

2. See M. Thomson, *The Problem of Mental Deficiency: Eugenics, Democracy and Social Policy in Britain, c. 1879–1959* (Oxford: Clarendon Press, 1998), pp. 297–304; M. Jackson, '"Grown-Up Children": Understandings of Health and Mental Deficiency in Edwardian England', in M. Hofstra and H. Marland (eds), *Cultures of Child Health in Britain and the Netherlands* (Amsterdam and New York: Rodopi, 2003), pp. 149–168; A. Brown, 'Ellen Pinsent: Including the "Feeble Mind" in Birmingham, 1900–1913', *History of Education*, 34:5 (2006), pp. 535–46.

3. Thomson, *The Problem of Mental Deficiency*, pp. 13–16; G. Sutherland, *Ability, Merit and Measurement: Mental Testing and English Education, 1880–1940* (Oxford: Clarendon Press, 1984), pp. 15–50.

4. Thomson, *The Problem of Mental Deficiency*, pp. 170–4, 302–4.

5. Thomson examined fifty-five London County Council case files; ibid., pp. 248–62.

6. See discussion in J. Read, 'Fit for What? Special Education in London, 1890–1914', *History of Education*, 33:3 (May 2004), pp. 283–98, nn. 21–5 on p. 287. For varied responses, see D. Atkinson and F. Williams (eds), *'Know Me As I Am'* (London: Hodder & Stoughton, 1990), pp. 157–8, 171–2, 189, 190–1, 197, 213–4.

7. S. Humphries, *Hooligans or Rebels? An Oral History of Working-Class Childhood and Youth* (Oxford: Basil Blackwell, 1981), pp. 209–39; S. Humphries and P. Gordon, *Out*

of Sight: The Experience of Disability, 1900–1950 (Plymouth: Northcote House, 1992), pp. 92–6.

8. A. Borsay, *Disability and Social Policy in Britain since 1750* (Basingstoke: Palgrave Macmillan, 2005), p. 115.

9. P. Cox, *Gender, Justice and Welfare: Bad Girls in Britain, 1900–1950* (Basingstoke: Palgrave, 2003), p. 201.

10. See J. Andrews and I. Smith (eds), *Let There Be Light Again: A History of Gartnavel Royal Hospital from its Beginnings to the Present Day. Essays Written to Mark the 150th Anniversary in 1993 of Gartnavel Royal Hospital's Existence on its Present Site* (Glasgow: Greater Glasgow Health Board, 1993), p. 112; J. Melling, 'Accommodating Madness: New Research in the Social History of Insanity and Institutions', in J. Melling and B. Forsythe (eds), *Insanity, Institutions and Society, 1800–1914: A Social History of Madness in Comparative Perspective* (London: Routledge, 1999), pp. 1–30; Lane, *A Social History of Medicine*, pp. 100–13.

11. See I. Hutchison, 'Institutionalisation of Mentally Impaired Children in Scotland, 1855–1914', *History of Psychiatry*, 22:4 (December 2011), pp. 416–33, which discusses the successive name changes of this institution; I. Hutchison, *A History of Disability in Nineteenth-Century Scotland* (Lampeter: Edwin Mellen Press, 2007), p. 217.

12. P. Dale, 'The Mental Deficiency Acts, 1913–1948' (PhD dissertation, University of Exeter, 2001); P. Dale, 'Special Education at Starcross before 1948', *History of Education*, 36:1 (January, 2007), pp. 22–45.

13. K. Myers, 'Contesting Certification: Mental Deficiency, Families and the State in Interwar England', *Paedagogica Historica*, 47:6 (December 2011), pp. 749–66; D. Wright, *Mental Disability in Victorian England: the Earlswood Asylum, 1847–1901* (Oxford: Clarendon Press, 2001), pp. 194–203; Melling, 'Accommodating Madness', p. 21; J. Melling and B. Forsythe, *The Politics of Madness: The State, Insanity and Society in England, 1845–1914* (London: Routledge, 2006), p. 208.

14. Glasgow Parish Records, *Glasgow Association for the Care of Defective and Feeble-Minded Children* (hereafter *GACDFMC*), *Report for 1908, GCA*, T-PAR 1.10, 'Rules and Constitution', pp. 53–6.

15. M. Egan, 'The "Manufacture" of Mental Defectives in Late Nineteenth and Early Twentieth Century Scotland' (PhD dissertation, Glasgow, 2001), pp. 72, 210.

16. L. Abrams, *The Orphan Country: Children of Scotland's Broken Homes from 1845 to the Present Day* (Edinburgh: John Donald Publishers, 1998), pp. 77–121; http://www.archives.gla.ac.uk/gghb/collects/hb20.html [accessed 23 November 2012].

17. Egan, 'The "Manufacture" of Mental Defectives', pp. 71, 93, 219–20; Stephens, *Education*, pp. 94–6.

18. J. M. Roxburgh, *The School Board of Glasgow* (London: University of London, 1971), pp. 52, 185–8.

19. Egan, 'The "Manufacture" of Mental Defectives', pp. 95, 105, 233.

20. Ibid., pp. 71, 93, 219–20; Borsay, *Disability*, pp. 104–7; Thomson, *The Problem of Mental Deficiency*, p. 218.

21. R. W. Roxburgh, *The Law of Education in Scotland, with a Commentary* (Edinburgh and Glasgow: W. Hodges & Co, 1928), p. 224.

22. Thomson, *The Problem of Mental Deficiency*, pp. 6, 86–8.

23. *Twelfth Annual Report for the General Board of Control for Scotland for the Year 1925* (Edinburgh, 1926), NHSGGCA, HB 13B 14/68, p. lxiv.

24. Egan, 'The "Manufacture" of Mental Defectives', pp. 151–7, 206–9; M. Egan, 'The "Manufacture" of Mental Deficiency: Why the Number of Mental Defectives Increased in Scotland, 1857–1939', in P. Dale and J. Melling (eds), *Mental Illness and Learning Disability since 1850: Finding a Place for Mental Disorder in the United Kingdom* (London: Routledge, 2006), pp. 131–53, on pp. 145–7.

25. *GACDFMC Report for 1910*, GCA, T-PAR, 1.10, p. 53.

26. Egan, 'The "Manufacture" of Mental Defectives', p. 103; M. Jackson, 'Institutional Provision for the Feeble-Minded in Edwardian Britain: Sandlebridge and the Scientific Morality of Permanent Care', in D. Wright and A. Digby (eds), *From Idiocy to Mental Deficiency: Historical Perspectives on People with Learning Difficulties* (London and New York: Routledge, 1989), pp. 161–83, on pp. 164–8.

27. *GACDFMC Report for 1912*, GCA, T-PAR 1.20, p. 95 and *Report for 1921*, GCA, T-PAR 1.34, p. 882.

28. *GACDFMC Report for 1918*, GCA, T-PAR 1.31, p. 1571; Egan, 'The "Manufacture" of Mental Defectives', pp. 73, 103.

29. *GACDFMC Report for 1909*, GCA, T-PAR 1.14, p. 485.

30. Case Book, NHSGGCA, HB 20 3/10: Miss M until 1913, Miss B until 1923, Miss C until 1948.

31. *GACDFMC Report for 1917*, GCA, T-PAR 1:30, p. 1295.

32. Minutes, NHSGGCA, HB 20 5/33, 1930, f. 25. *GACDFMC Report for 1910*, GCA, T-PAR 1.16, p. 526.

33. Admissions, Waverley Park, 1906–1947, NHSGGCA, HB 20 2/56, No. 56; *GACDFMC Report for 1916*, GCA, T-PAR 1. 30, p. 1332. There were fourteen inmates registered under the Children Act and fifty-nine under the Mental Deficiency Act, of ninety in total.

34. *GACDFMC Report for 1912*, GCA, T-PAR 1.20, p. 97.

35. *GACDFMC Report for 1916*, GCA, T-PAR 1.30, p. 1332.

36. Humphries, *Hooligans*, p. 212; P. Dale, 'Tension in the Voluntary-Statutory Alliance: "Lay Professionals" and the Planning and Delivery of Mental Deficiency Services, 1917–1945', in Dale and Melling (eds), *Mental Illness*, pp. 154–78, on pp. 155–6; *GACDFMC Report for 1916*, GCA, T-PAR, 1.30, p. 1331.

37. *GACDFMC Report for 1920*, GCA, T-PAR 1.33, p. 978.

38. *GACDFMC Report for 1919*, GCA, T-PAR 1.32, p. 1047 and *Report for 1920*, GCA, T-PAR 1.33, p. 977; *Twelfth Annual Report of the Board of Control*, 1926, p. xliv.

39. Minutes, NHSGGCA, HB 20 5/34, 23 February 1933, f. 149 and HB 20 5/36, 17 March 1948, f. 10.

40. Minutes, NHSGGCA, HB 20 5/35, 18 April 1945, f. 120.

41. See http://www.archives.gla.ac.uk/gghb/collects/hb20.html [accessed 23 November 2012].

42. Admissions, Waverley Park, 1906–1947, NHSGGCA, HB 20 2/56.

43. The Glasgow School Board accommodated 632 mentally defective children in 1908, 740 in 1909, 833 in 1909–10, with 154 imbeciles in institutions: *School Board of Glasgow-Annual Report, 1908–9*, GCA, D-ED 9/1/33, p. 15.

44. Case Books, NHSGGCA, HB 20 3/10–16. As case notes are closed for seventy years, subjects are identified by fictitious names; case note numbers only are given in the endnotes. Thomson, *The Problem of Mental Deficiency*, pp. 13–16, 33–9.

45. Most female cases identified by Thomson had been referred for this reason: Thomson, *The Problem of Mental Deficiency*, pp. 248–52; Egan, 'The "Manufacture" of Mental Defectives', p. 103; Case Book, NHSGGCA, HB 20 3/10, Nos. 84, 195 and 201.

46. Case Books, NHSGGCA, HB 20 3/10, No. 142 and HB 20 3/11, No. 245.

47. For sexual proclivities, see Case Books, NHSGGCA, HB 20 3/10, Nos. 123, 140, 169, 209 and HB 20 3/11, No. 324. For relatives' desire for supervision, see HB 20 3/11, Nos. 243, 285, 286, 290 and 349; for similar examples, see Egan, 'The "Manufacture" of Mental Defectives', p. 245.

48. Case Book, NHSGGCA, HB 20 3/11, No. 275, 3 September 1936, No. 325, 25 September 1941, No. 383, 1 November 1944 and No. 384, 2 November 1944.

49. For other uses of case notes, see G. Davis, *The Cruel Madness of Love: Sex, Syphilis, and Psychiatry in Scotland, 1880–1930* (Rodopi: Amsterdam, 2008), pp. 20–3 and J. Goodman, 'Reflections on Researching an Archive of Disability: Sandlebridge, 1902–1935', *Educational Review*, 55:1 (2003), pp. 47–54.

50. For a similar point, see Hutchison, *A History of Disability*, p. 30.

51. Case Book, NHSGGCA, HB 20 3/13, No. 363, December 1945; see also HB 20 3/11, Nos. 334, 3 July 1942 and 437, 23 January 1947.

52. 'Inquiry into Matters Arising out of the Methods of Discipline used at Waverley Park Certified Institution' (typed report, 10 June 1938) by Aidan Thomson and Dr Kate Fraser, and 'Reply to Report on Inquiry Into Matters arising out of the Methods of Discipline used at Waverley Park Certified Institution' (typed report) from W. Hill, Secretary, GACDFMC, 24 October 1938, NHSGGCA, HB 20 4/13 (Hereafter Inquiry Report and Reply). Inquiry Report, NHSGGCA, 10 June 1938, p. 7.

53. Humphries, *Out of Sight*, pp. 92–7.

54. Cox, *Gender*, p. 89.

55. *GACDFMC Report for 1909*, GCA, T-PAR, 1.14, p. 484.

56. *GACDFMC Report for 1912*, GCA, T-PAR, 1.20, p. 99.

57. Minutes, NHSGGCA, HB 20 5/33, 27 February 1931, f. 49.

58. Minutes, NHSGGCA, HB 20 5/34, 3 November 1938, f. 145.

59. *GACDFMC, Annual Report*, 1912, GCA, T-PAR 1.20, p. 99.

60. Minutes, NHSGGCA, HB 20 5/34, 28 August 1937, f. 28.

61. Minutes, NHSGGCA, HB 20 5/33, 10 August 1934, f. 219.

62. Minutes, NHSGGCA, HB 20 5/34, f. 91. On 25 October 1937, ninety-nine were 'actively occupied' including forty-two children on the school roll.

63. Case Books, NHSGGCA, HB 20 3/12, No. 79, December 1926 and HB 20 3/14, No. 60, December 1939.

64. Case Books, NHSGGCA, HB 20 3/12, No. 58, June 1924 and HB 20 3/13, No. 362, June and December 1947.

65. Case Book, NHSGGCA, HB 20 3/14, No. 314, December 1943.

66. Ibid., No. 58, December 1941, July–December 1942.

67. Case Book, NHSGGCA, HB 20 3/12, No. 58, June 1937.

68. Case Book, NHSGGCA, HB 20 3/14, No. 276, July 1942.

69. *Sixteenth Annual Report of the General Board of Control for Scotland for the year 1929* (Edinburgh: 1930), NHSGGCA, HB 13B/14/71, p. xliv.

70. *GACDFMC Report for 1917*, GCA, T-PAR 1.30, pp. 1293–5.

71. Daily Register, NHSGGCA, HB 20 2/88, 3 June 1933 and HB 20 2/89.

72. Minutes, NHSGGCA, HB 5/34, 25 October 1937, f. 91.

73. Ibid., HB 20 5/33, 20 February 1935, f. 239, HB 20 5/34, 24 March 1937, f. 60 and HB 20 5/35, 9 May 1940, f. 98; Daily register, NHSGGCA, HB 20 2/88, 2/89; Case Book, NHSGGCA, HB 20 3/12, No. 69, December 1926; Case Book, NHSGGCA, HB 20 3/14, No. 55, December 1941.

74. P. Cox, 'Girls, Deficiency and Delinquency', in Wright and Digby (eds), *Idiocy to Mental Deficiency*, pp. 184–206, on p. 199.

75. *GACDFMC Report for 1912*, GCA, T-PAR 1:20, p. 99.

76. Minutes, NHSGGCA, HB 20 5/34, 3 November 1938, f. 145.

77. *GACDFMC Report for 1920*, T.PAR 1: 33, p. 981; Minutes, NHSGGCA, HB 20 5/34, 25 November 1936, f. 38.

78. H. Burdett, *Burdett's Hospitals and Charities Annual: A Year Book of Philanthropy* (London: Scientific Press, 1925), p. 661.

79. Cox, *Gender*, pp. 90–2.

80. Egan, 'The "Manufacture" of Mental Defectives', pp. 95–6.

81. *GACDFMC Report for 1909*, GCA, T-PAR 1.14, p. 484.

82. *GACDFMC Report for 1912*, GCA, T-PAR 1:20, p. 101; Minutes, NHSGGCA, HB 20 5/34, 25 October 1937, f. 91.

83. Dale, 'Special Education', p. 42.

84. *GACDFMC Report for 1912*, GCA, T-PAR 1.20, p. 100 and *Report for 1920*, T-PAR 1.33, p. 977.

85. *GACDFMC Report for 1916*, GCA, T-PAR 1.30, p. 1332.

86. Minutes, NHSGGCA, HB 20 5/34, 25 October 1937, f. 91.

87. Daily Register, NHSGGCA, HB 20 2/89, 18 September 1943.

88. Case Book, NHSGGCA, HB 20/3/11, No. 276, December 1943; Minutes, HB 20 5/33, 23 December 1931, f. 90, HB 20 5/34, 28 August 1936, f. 29, 18 January 1939, f. 145; *Twelfth Annual Report of the Board of Control*, 1926, p. lxiv.

89. Inquiry Report, NHSGGCA, HB 20 4/13, 24 October 1938, p. 13; Minutes, HB 20 5/34, 16 February 1938, ff. 107–13.

90. Inquiry Report, NHSGGCA, HB 20 4/13, p. 13.

91. Ibid., 'Reply', p. 3.

92. Inquiry Report, p. 22.

93. Ibid., p. 13.

94. 'Reply', p. 4.

95. Inquiry Report, pp. 4–5.

96. Minutes, NHSGGCA, HB 20 5/34, 16 March 1938, f. 113.

97. Case Book, NHSGGCA, HB 20 3/12, No. 185, February 1929.

98. Ibid., No. 221, December 1939.

99. Ibid., No. 195, May 1931.

100. Inquiry Report, NHSGGCA, HB 20/4/13, p. 6.

101. Case Book, NHSGGCA, HB 20 3/14, No. 314, June 1947.

102. Case Book, NHSGGCA, HB 20 3/12, No. 104, 24 February 1926.

103. Case Book, NHSGGCA, HB 20 3/10, No. 137, 25 July 1925.

104. Daily Register, NHSGGCA, HB 20 2/88, 15 December 1934.

105. Register of absence on licence or temporarily without licence, Book 2, NHSGGCA, HB 20/2/68, No. 199, 19/6/37; reported returned 20/8/37.

106. Daily Registers, NHSGGCA, HB 20 2/88 and HB 20 2/89.

107. Cox, *Gender*, p. 97. For resistance, see Humphries, *Out of Sight*, pp. 92–6; Borsay, *Disability*, p. 105 and A. Clark, 'Wild Workhouse Girls and the Liberal Imperial State in

Mid-Nineteenth-Century Ireland', *Journal of Social History*, 39:2 (Winter 2005), pp. 384–409. For bullying, see Clarke, 'Wild Workhouse Girls', p. 392 and Abrams, *The Orphan Country*, p. 110.

108. Daily Register, NHSGGCA, HB 20 2/88, 5 October 1935 and 12 September 1936.

109. Case Book, NHSGGCA, HB 20 3/12, No. 94, December 1927.

110. Case Book, NHSGGCA, ibid., HB 20 3/13, No. 363, December 1945, September 1945, June 1946, June 1947 and June 1948.

111. Case Book, NHSGGCA, HB 20 3/14, No. 314, December 1943.

112. Ibid., No. 268, February 1944.

113. Case Book, NHSGGCA, HB 20 3/12, No. 11, January 1931.

114. Case Book, NHSGGCA, HB 20 3/14, No. 300, 17 January 1943.

115. Case Book, NHSGGCA, HB 20 3/12, No. 56, June and October 1930.

116. Ibid., No. 196, June 1931.

117. Case Book, NHSGGCA, HB 20 3/14, No. 300, August 1942.

118. Ibid., No. 243, July 1941.

119. Ibid., No. 268, April 1944.

120. Case Book, NHSGGCA, HB 20 2/13, No. 224, December 1936.

121. Ibid., HB 20 3/12, No. 268, 4 August 1941.

122. Inquiry Report, 1938, NHSGGCA, HB 20 4/13, p. 13; Minutes, HB 20 5/34, 16 November 1938, f. 139.

123. L. Walsh, '"The Property of the Whole Community": Charity and Insanity in Urban Scotland: The Dundee Royal Lunatic Asylum, 1805–1850', in Melling and Forsythe (eds), *Insanity*, pp. 180–99, on pp. 180–4.

124. *GACDFMC Report for 1920*, GCA, T-PAR 1.33, p. 979.

125. Register of official visits, 1907–80, NHSGGCA, HB 20 2/76, 9 March 1909 , 27 April, 15 August 1911.

126. Davis, *The Cruel Madness*, p. 68; G. Hutton, *Woodilee Hospital: 125 Years* (Glasgow: GGCMH Services NHS Trust, 1997), pp. 26–7, 73; Atkinson and Williams (eds), *Know Me as I Am*, p. 201.

127. Register of official visits, 1907–80, NHSGGCA, HB 20 2/76, e.g. 1911.

128. *GACDFMC, Report for 1920*, GCA, T-PAR 1.33, p. 979.

129. *GACDFMC, Report for 1921*, GCA, T-PAR, 1.34, p. 882.

130. Minutes, NHSGGCA, HB 20 5/34, 20 December 1939, f. 181.

131. Ibid., HB 20 5/34, 1935, f. 29, 28 August 1936.

132. Ibid., HB 20 5/34, 24 March 1937, f. 58.

133. Case Book, NHSGGCA, HB 20 3/15, No. 159, August 1945.

134. Minutes, NHSGGCA, HB 20 5/34, 24 March 1937, ff. 58–71.

135. Minutes, NHSGGCA, HB 20 5/34, 21 June 1939, f. 167.

136. Minutes, NHSGGCA, HB 20 5/33, 27 February 1931, f. 49.

137. Thomson, *The Problem of Mental Deficiency*, pp. 34–5, 170–1 and 302–4.

138. Case Book, NHSGGCA, HB 20 3/12.

139. Case Book, NHSGGCA, HB 20 3/14, No. 250, December 1940.

140. Minutes, NHSGGCA, HB 20 5/33, August 1930, f. 22.

141. Ibid., 25 September 1935, f. 264.

142. Ibid., 20 February 1935, f. 238, 18 December 1935, ff. 276–7.

143. Case Book, NHSGGCA, HB 20 3/13, No. 243, September 1942.

144. Absence on licence, Waverley Park, 1918–1937, 1937–60, NHSGGCA, HB 20 2/67, f. 68.

145. Licence Book, NHSGGCA, HB 20 2/67, No. 7, 9 April 1918.
146. Minutes, NHSGGCA, HB 20 5/34, 16, 19 June, 25 August 1937, ff. 72–3 and 76.
147. Admissions Book, 1906–47, NHSGGCA, HB 20 2/56; *GACDFMC Report for 1920*, GCA, T-PAR 1.33, p. 979 and T-PAR 1.34, p. 882.
148. There were forty-eight deaths. Discharges and Removals from Waverley Park, 1916–1955, NHSGGCA, HB 20 2/62; see http://www.archives.gla.ac.uk/gghb/collects/hb20.html [accessed 23 November 2012].
149. Minutes, NHSGGCA, HB 20 5/34, 21 June 1939, f. 165.
150. Inquiry Report, NHSGGCA, HB 20 4/13, 10 June 1938, f. 22.
151. Ibid., 'Reply' ff. 1–5, 24 October 1938; Borsay, *Disability*, p. 103.
152. Cox, 'Girls', p. 104; P. Dale, 'Training for Work: Domestic Service as a Route out of Long-Stay Institutions before 1959', *Women's History Review*, 13:3 (2004), pp. 387–405; A. Hughes, *Gender and Political Identities in Scotland, 1919–1939* (Edinburgh: Edinburgh University Press, 2010), pp. 30, 18, 21, 116, 130.
153. Minutes, NHSGGCA, HB 20 5/34, 24 March 1937, f. 56 and 21 April 1937, f. 64, and 18 December 1940, f. 218.
154. Ibid., 8 July 1940, f. 208 and HB 20 5/35, 17 June 1942, f. 10.
155. Minutes, NHSGGCA, HB 20 5/35, 18 June 1944, f. 88.
156. J. Melling and P. Dale, 'The Politics of Mental Welfare: Fresh Perspectives on the History of Institutional Care for the Mentally Ill and Disabled', in Dale and Melling (eds), *Mental Illness*, pp. 1–23, on pp. 6–7.
157. Case Book, NHSGGCA, HB 20 3/11, No. 431, 2 August 1945.
158. Case Book, NHSGGCA, HB 20 3/12, No. 257 and HB 20 3/11, No. 405.
159. Licence Book 2, NHSGGCA, HB 20/2/68, 19 July 1937.
160. School Board Minutes, Glasgow, Monday 16 January 1911, GCA, D-ED 1/1/1/14, p. 562.
161. Register of deaths, 1959–1984, NHSGGCA, HB 20, 2/66.
162. Case Book, NHSGGCA, HB 20 3/14, No. 129, born 1916, entered 1922.
163. Minutes, NHSGGCA, HB 20 5/34, 8 January 1938, f. 101.
164. Ibid., 9 Mar 1937, f. 58 and 24 March 1937, f. 61; HB 20 5/35, 6 October 1942, f. 20.
165. *GACDFMC Report for 1918–19*, GCA, T-PAR 1.32, p. 1046. Case Books, NHSGGCA, 3/10–16.
166. See note 86 above.
167. Inquiry Report, NHSGGCA, HB 20/4/13, p. 22.
168. 'Reply', NHSGGCA, HB 20/4/13, pp. 2, 7.
169. Case Book, NHSGGCA, HB 20 3/12, No. 268, 4 August 1940.
170. Case Books, NHSGGCA, HB 20 3/15, No. 159, December 1943 and HB 20 3/14, No. 343, 1 January 1949.
171. Case Book, NHSGGCA, HB 20 3/14, No. 250, December 1941 and No. 349, 10 January 1950.
172. Minutes, NHSGGCA, HB 20 5/33–36.
173. Lennox Castle Hospital, Female Patient Visitors' Books, 1958–83, NHSGGCA, HB 20 2/31–33; Cox, *Gender*, p. 98; Woodilee Asylum Admissions and Discharge Book, 1902–39, NHSGGCA, HB 10/23, No. 14747, admitted 24 February 1926, discharged 5 March 1927.
174. Lennox Castle Hospital, Discharges and Removals, 1930–54, NHSGGCA, HB 20/2/16.
175. Discharge Book, NHSGGCA, HB 2/62, No. 91, f. 129.

5 Boulton and Black, 'Paupers and their Experience of a London Workhouse: St Martin-in-the-Fields, 1725–1824'

1. D. R. Green, '"Icons of the New System": Workhouse Construction and Relief Practices in London under the Old and New Poor Law', *London Journal*, 34:3 (2009), pp. 264–9.

2. T. Hitchcock, 'Paupers and Preachers: The SPCK and the Parochial Workhouse Movement', in L. Davison, T. Hitchcock, T. Keirn and R. B. Shoemaker (eds), *Stilling the Grumbling Hive: The Response to Social and Economic Problems in England, 1689–1750* (Stroud and New York: St Martin's Press, 1992), pp. 145–66.

3. D. R. Green, *Pauper Capital: London and the Poor Law, 1790–1870* (Farnham: Ashgate, 2010); T. V. Hitchcock, 'The English Workhouse (a Study in Institutional Poor Relief in Selected Counties, 1696–1750)' (DPhil Dissertation, Oxford University, 1985); A. Levene, 'Children, Childhood and the Workhouse: St Marylebone, 1769–1781', *London Journal*, 33:1 (2008), pp. 41–59; J. Boulton and L. Schwarz, '"The Comforts of a Private Fireside"? The Workhouse, the Elderly and the Poor Law in Georgian Westminster: St Martin-in-the-Fields, 1725–1824', in J. McEwan and P. Sharpe (eds), *Accommodating Poverty: The Households of the Poor in England, c. 1650–1850* (Basingstoke: Palgrave Macmillan, 2011), pp. 221–45; K. Siena, 'Hospitals for the Excluded or Convalescent Homes?: Workhouses, Medicalization and the Poor Law in Long Eighteenth-Century London and Pre-Confederation Toronto', *Canadian Bulletin of Medical History/Bulletin Canadien D'histoire de la Médecine*, 27:1 (2010), pp. 5–25.

4. A. Tomkins, *The Experience of Poverty, 1723–82* (Manchester: Manchester University Press, 2006), pp. 36–78.

5. Green, *Pauper Capital*, p. 63; J. S. Taylor, 'The Unreformed Workhouse 1776–1834', in E. A. Martin (ed.), *Comparative Development in Social Welfare* (London: George Allen and Unwin, 1972), p. 61. The mean national size in 1803 was just 22: ibid., p. 63. London parish workhouses were actually roughly the same size as those serving provincial towns and cities: Tomkins, *The Experience of Poverty*, p. 38.

6. See Hitchcock, 'The English Workhouse', pp. 133–65.

7. J. McMaster, *A Short History of the Royal Parish of St Martin-in-the-Fields* (London: G. Holder & Sons, 1916), p. 222; L. MacKay, 'Moral Paupers: The Poor Men of St. Martin's, 1815–1819', *Histoire Sociale/Social History*, 67 (2001), pp. 115–31; L. MacKay, 'A Culture of Poverty? The St. Martin in the Fields Workhouse, 1817', *Journal of Interdisciplinary History*, 26 (1995), pp. 209–31.

8. P. Hoare, 'Archbishop Tenison's Library at St Martin in the Fields: The Building and its History', *London Topographical Record*, 29:165 (2006), pp. 127–50; P. Hoare, 'Hemmings Row and Castle Street', *Survey of London: vol. 20: St Martin-in-the-Fields, pt III: Trafalgar Square & Neighbourhood* (1940), pp. 112–4: http://www.british-history.ac.uk/report.aspx?compid=68424 [accessed 12 October 2011].

9. H. Simpson, *"Our Parish": Being an Outline of the History of the Parish of St. Martin-in-the-Fields; With a Comparative Statement of all Monies Received and Disbursed for and on Account of its Poor for the Last Six Years, etc* (London, 1836), p. 29.

10. Dimensions of the institution's sick wards in 1866 are given in *Report of the Committee Appointed to Consider the Cubic Space of Metropolitan Workhouses* (London, 1867), pp. 100–2; available online at: http://hdl.handle.net/2027/uc2.ark:/13960/t2m61sc2s [accessed 5 November 2012].

11. The Rocque and Horwood maps of London can be viewed in digital editions at http://www.motco.com/map/81002/ and http://www.motco.com/map/81005/ [accessed 5 November 2012].

12. St Martin-in-the-Fields Parish Vestry Minutes, 2 February 1740 to 20 April 1778, City of Westminster Archives Centre (hereafter COWAC), F2007/397.

13. P. Fisher, 'Houses for the Dead: The Provision of Mortuaries in London, 1843–1889', *London Journal*, 34:1 (2009), pp. 1–15; J. Boulton, R. Davenport and L. Schwarz, 'These ANTE-CHAMBERS OF THE GRAVE?: Mortality, Medicine and the Workhouse in Georgian London (1725–1824)', in J. Reinarz and L. Schwarz (eds), *Medicine and the Workhouse* (Rochester: Rochester University Press, forthcoming, 2013).

14. These images can be viewed at http://research.ncl.ac.uk/pauperlives/workhouseimages.htm. Thomas Hosmer Shepherd's picture of Archbishop Tenison's School and Library and the 1871 picture by Richardson are reproduced in Hoare, 'Archbishop Tenison's Library', pp. 128 and 136.

15. Hoare, 'Archbishop Tenison's Library', pp. 127–150.

16. MacKay, 'Moral Paupers', pp. 115–31.

17. See also *A Plan & Section of the Workhouse in the Parish of St George Hanover Square* (London, c. 1725–30); Hitchcock, 'Paupers and Preachers', p. 160; *Rules, Orders and Regulations for the Government of the Workhouse Belonging to that Part of the Parish of St. Andrew Holborn, which Lies above the Bars, in the County of Middlesex, and the Parish of St. George the Martyr, in the Said County* (London, 1791), p. 38.

18. J. Hanway, *The Citizen's Monitor* (London, 1780), p. 127; 'Double beds agreeable to the Plan suggested by Sir James Earle' were provided in the workhouse in 1813, COWAC F2076, 261.

19. K. Siena, *Venereal Disease, Hospitals and the Urban Poor: London's 'Foul Wards,' 1600–1800* (Rochester, NY: University of Rochester Press, 2004), pp. 135–80; Siena, 'Hospitals for the Excluded', pp. 5–25; Tomkins, *The Experience of Poverty*, pp. 120–62.

20. J. Boulton, 'The Parish Nurse in Early Modern London', *Family and Community History*, 10:2 (2007), pp. 127–52.

21. See Boulton, Davenport and Schwarz, 'These ANTE-CHAMBERS OF THE GRAVE?'; J. Boulton and L. Schwarz, 'The Parish Workhouse, the Parish and Parochial Medical Provision in Eighteenth-Century London', this article may be viewed at http://research.ncl.ac.uk/pauperlives/workhousemedicalisation.pdf; J. Boulton and J. Black, '"Those, that Die by Reason of Their Madness": Dying Insane in London, 1629–1830', *History of Psychiatry*, 23:1 (March 2012), pp. 27–39.

22. For a useful definition of the 'casual' poor, see Green, *Pauper Capital*, pp. 41–2.

23. D. R. Green, 'Pauper Protests: Power and Resistance in Early Nineteenth-Century London Workhouses', *Social History*, 31:2 (2006), pp. 137–59. See St Martin-in-the-Fields Workhouse Sub-committee's Reports, 17 May 1817 to 29 September 1822, COWAC, F3914. See also A. R. Neate, *The St. Marylebone Workhouse and Institution 1730–1965*, St Marylebone Society Publication No. 9 (1967), p. 8; MacKay, 'A Culture of Poverty?', pp. 215–18.

24. See COWAC, F2077 and F3914.

25. M. Barker-Read, 'The Treatment of the Aged Poor in Five Selected West Kent Parishes From Settlement to Speenhamland (1662–1797)' (PhD Dissertation, Open University, 1988), pp. 225, 234; S. and B. Webb, *English Local Government: English Poor Law History: Part 1. The Old Poor Law* (London: Longmans, Green & Co, 1927), pp. 221–39.

26. See M. A. Crowther, *The Workhouse System 1834–1929: The History of a Social Institution* (Athens, GA: University of Georgia Press, 1982), pp. 229–32; N. Goose, 'Workhouse Populations in the Mid-nineteenth Century: The Case of Hertfordshire', *Local Population Studies*, 62 (1999), p. 65; A. Hinde and F. Turnbull, 'The Populations of two Hampshire Workhouses, 1851–1861', *Local Population Studies*, 61 (1998), pp. 43–5.
27. See St Martin-in-the-Fields Workhouse Accounts and Workhouse Day Books, 1725–1819, COWAC F2212; F2213; F4003; F4004; F4005; F4006; F4008; F4009; F4010; F4011; F4012; F4013; F4014; F4016; F4017; F4018; F4019; F4020; F4021; F4023; F4024; F4025; F4026.
28. Green, 'Pauper Protests', p. 143.
29. Boulton and Schwarz, 'The Comforts of a Private Fireside', pp. 227–8.
30. Webb and Webb, *English Local Government*, p. 218; Crowther, *The Workhouse System*, pp. 37–9; Hitchcock, 'The English Workhouse', pp. 194–6. See also Tomkins, *The Experience of Poverty*, pp. 46–50.
31. These figures were calculated from some 86,000 dates of admission and discharge given in the following St Martin-in-the-Fields workhouse registers: COWAC, F4002; F4003; F4004; F4005; F4007; F4008; F4009; F4022; F4073; F4074; F4075; F4076; F4077; F4078; F4079; F4080; F4081.
32. See Levene, 'Children, Childhood and the Workhouse', pp. 49–50; Hitchcock, 'The English Workhouse', pp. 195–207.
33. For Berwick's pauper career see St Martin-in-the-Field Settlement Examinations and Workhouse Day Books, COWAC, F5036/173; F5053/324; F5058/459; F4074; F4076/20, 22–5, 27–35; F4077/33, 36, 39, 40, 42, 45–8, 54, 55–6, 60, 67–9, 73–4, 377 and 379; F4078/13, 14, 17, 27 and 29; F561(1772).
34. Green, 'Pauper Protests', pp. 152–3. See also, MacKay, 'A Culture of Poverty?', pp. 226–8; Crowther, *The Workhouse System*, p. 231.
35. See also Mackay, 'A Culture of Poverty?', p.218.
36. Hitchcock, 'The English Workhouse', p. 194; Tomkins, *The Experience of Poverty*, pp. 47–50.
37. Green, 'Pauper Protests', p. 159.
38. See *Regulations Agreed upon and Established this Twelfth Day of July 1726 by the Gentlemen of the Vestry then Present, for the Better GOVERNMENT and MANAGEMENT of the WORK-HOUSE belonging to the Parish of St. Giles in the Fields* (London, 1726); *Rules, Orders, and Regulations, for Maintaining, Governing, Employing, and Regulating, The Poor of the Parishes of St. Giles in the Fields and St. George Bloomsbury* (London, 1781); Hitchcock, 'The English Workhouse', pp. 104–32, 228–42; Barker-Read, 'Treatment of the Aged Poor', pp. 236–9. Parish officers also occasionally returned paupers who had run away from other workhouses; see St Martin-in-the-Fields Alphabetical Lists of Paupers Admitted into the Workhouse, 1746–1753 and 1811–1821, COWAC, F4081/212, 232, 449, 457; F4007/120.
39. See St Martin-in-the-Fields Churchwardens' and Overseers' Orders, 19 March to 17 May 1772, COWAC, F2072/32r–34r.
40. See MacKay, 'Moral Paupers', p. 120.
41. See Tomkins, *The Experience of Poverty*, p. 64. See also Deeds Relating to Property in St Marylebone, 1725–1908, COWAC, F2073.
42. *Rules and Regulations for the Government of the Workhouse, of the Parish of St. Martin in the Fields, and of the Infant Poor-House at Highwood-Hill* (London, 1828). For similar

establishments elsewhere in London, see Webb and Webb, *English Local Government*, p. 300.

43. *Rules and Regulations*, pp. 8–9.
44. Simpson, 'Our Parish', p. 38.
45. See Hitchcock, 'The English Workhouse', pp. 167–74.
46. Green, 'Pauper Protests', p. 146. See also, Hitchcock, 'The English Workhouse', pp. 177–8.
47. Webb and Webb, *English Local Government*, pp. 242–3, n. 5, pp. 250–1.
48. For workhouse discipline see also, Hitchcock, 'The English Workhouse', pp. 182–91.
49. See St Martin-in-the-Fields Officers of the Parish Minutes, 4 January 1792 to 20 June 1804 and 4 July 1804 to 28 December 1815, COWAC, F2075/, 203, 253, 222, 265, 269, 309, 383; F2076/311.
50. See also MacKay, 'Moral Paupers', p. 129.
51. COWAC, F2072/180.
52. See also Hitchcock, 'The English Workhouse', pp. 215–7.
53. For these cases see COWAC, F4081/55, 296, 255, 324, 348; F4080/97.
54. For the trial of William Nicholls, 28 April 1742 see Old Bailey Proceedings, London Lives, 1690–1800, t17420428-19, www.londonlives.org [accessed 12 October 2011]. For documentation relating to Waldron and others, see St Martin-in-the-Fields Churchwardens' and Overseers' Accounts, 1741–1742, COWAC, F511/193, 230. See also COWAC, F5026/150; F5038/266; F5032/45; F4073; F4074; F2222; and M. Ingram, 'Child Sexual Abuse in Early Modern England', in M. J. Braddick and J. Walter (eds), *Negotiating Power in Early Modern Society: Order, Hierarchy and Subordination in Britain and Ireland* (Cambridge: Cambridge University Press, 2001), pp. 63–84.
55. See J. Black, 'Illegitimacy, Sexual Relations and Location in Metropolitan London, 1735–85', in T. Hitchcock and H. Shore (eds), *The Streets of London: From the Great Fire to the Great Stink* (London, Sydney and Chicago, IL: Rivers Oram Press, 2003), pp. 101–18, 228–31.
56. COWAC, F4080/101; F4022/51, 147, 286 and 458.
57. COWAC, F4081/375.
58. COWAC, F2075/99. For a corrupt porter, see COWAC, F2072/36r.
59. See Green, *Pauper Capital*, pp. 151–5; E. Murphy, 'Mad Farming in the Metropolis, Part 1: A Significant Service Industry in East London', *History of Psychiatry*, 12:3 (2001), pp. 245–82; E. Murphy, 'Mad Farming in the Metropolis, Part 2: The Administration of the Old Poor Law of Insanity in the City and East London 1800–1834', *History of Psychiatry*, 12:4 (2001), pp. 405–30; E. Murphy, 'The Metropolitan Pauper Farms, 1722–1834', *London Journal*, 27:1 (2002), pp. 1–18. For Bazing's history see COWAC F4022/51, 55, 56, 57, 58, 60, 62 and 65. For a discussion of the freedom to come and go in workhouses and other aspects of pauper agency see Hitchcock, 'The English Workhouse', pp. 189–92, 214–16.
60. See G. Mooney and J. Reinarz (eds), *Permeable Walls: Historical Perspectives on Hospital and Asylum Visiting* (Amsterdam: Rodopi, 2009).
61. COWAC, F2072/16v; F2072/62v; F2076/18.
62. COWAC, F2076/203.
63. See, for example, COWAC, F2072/33v; 36r; F2075/308.
64. COWAC, F2076/18.
65. See J. Feltham, *The Picture of London, for 1803; being a Correct Guide to All the Curiosities, Amusements, Exhibitions, Public Establishments, and Remarkable Objects, In and*

Near London (London, 1802), p. 171. See also COWAC, F2077/21 February 1817. For Hanway's visit, see Hanway, *Citizen's Monitor*, pp. 173–4.

66. See especially L. Smith, '"The Keeper Must Himself be Kept": Visitation and the Lunatic Asylum in England, 1750–1850', and K. Siena, 'Stage-Managing a Hospital in the Eighteenth Century: Visitation at the London Lock Hospital', in Mooney and Reinarz (eds), *Permeable Walls*, pp. 175–222.

6 Hamlett and Preston, '"A Veritable Palace for the Hard-Working Labourer?" Space, Material Culture and Inmate Experience in London's Rowton Houses, 1892–1918'

1. H. Denham, 'Sketches in a Sixpenny Hotel', *London Society* (February 1898), pp. 151–63, on p. 152.
2. 'Death of Lord Rowton', *The Times*, 10 November 1903, p. 14.
3. R. Farrant, 'Lord Rowton and Rowton Houses', *Cornhill*, 16 (January–June 1904), pp. 835–44, on p. 835.
4. L. Davidoff and C. Hall, *Family Fortunes: Men and Women of the English Middle Class 1780–1850* (London: Hutchinson, 1987); criticized by Amanda Vickery: see A. Vickery, 'Golden Age to Separate Spheres? A Review of the Categories and Chronology of English Women's History', *Historical Journal*, 36:2 (1993), pp. 383–414.
5. D. Cohen, *Household Gods: The British and their Possessions* (New Haven, CT: Yale University Press, 2006); M. Ponsonby, *Stories from Home: English Domestic Interiors, 1750–1850* (Aldershot: Ashgate, 2007).
6. J. Hamlett, *Material Relations: Middle-Class Families and Domestic Interiors in England, 1850–1910* (Manchester: Manchester University Press, 2010).
7. M. J. Daunton, 'Public Place and Private Space: The Victorian City and the Working-Class Household', in D. Fraser and A. Sutcliffe (eds), *The Pursuit of Urban History* (London: Edward Arnold, 1983), pp. 212–33; G. Crossick, 'The Labour Aristocracy and its Values: A Study of Mid-Victorian Kentish London', *Victorian Studies*, 19:3 (1978), pp. 301–28; V. Kelley, *Soap and Water: Cleanliness, Dirt and the Working Classes in Victorian and Edwardian Britain* (London: I. B. Tauris, 2010).
8. Q. Colville, 'The Role of the Interior in Constructing Notions of Class and Status: Case Study of Britannia Royal Naval College Dartmouth, 1905–39', in S. McKellar and P. Sparke (eds), *Interior Design and Identity* (Manchester: Manchester University Press, 2004), pp. 114–32; A. Milne-Smith, 'A Flight to Domesticity? Making a Home in the Gentleman's Clubs of London, 1880–1914', *Journal of British Studies*, 45:4 (2006), pp. 796–818.
9. See L. Taylor, *The Study of Dress History* (Manchester: Manchester University Press, 2002), pp. 64–89; J. Hamlett, 'The British Domestic Interior in Cultural and Social History: Review Essay', *Cultural and Social History* 6:1 (2009), pp. 97–107; K. Harvey (ed.), *History and Material Culture: A Student's Guide to Approaching Alternative Sources* (London and New York: Routledge, 2009).
10. J. Attfield, *Wild Things: The Material Culture of Everyday Life* (Oxford: Berg, 2000), p. 75.
11. D. Miller, *Acknowledging Consumption: A Review of New Studies* (London: Routledge, 1995), p. 1.

12. T. Hitchcock, P. King and P. Sharpe, 'Introduction', in Hitchcock, King and Sharpe, *Chronicling Poverty: The Voices and Strategies of the English Poor, 1640–1840* (Basingstoke: Macmillan Press, 1997), p. 2.

13. John Styles explores the relationship between material culture and agency in his study of eighteenth-century London lodgings: J. Styles, 'Lodging at the Old Bailey: Lodgings and their Furnishing in Eighteenth-Century London', in J. Styles and A. Vickery (eds), *Gender, Taste, and Material Culture in Britain and North America, 1700–1830* (New Haven, CT: 2006), pp. 61–80. Vickery examines how lodgers sought privacy through locking, separation and concealment in eighteenth- and early nineteenth-century lodgings: A. Vickery, 'An Englishman's Home is His Castle? Thresholds, Boundaries and Privacies in the Eighteenth-Century London House', *Past & Present*, 99:1 (2008), pp. 147–73.

14. R. O'Day, 'Caring or Controlling? The East End of London in the 1880s and 1890s', in C. Emsley, E. Johnson and P. Spierenburg (eds), *Social Control in Europe: Vol. 2, 1800–2000* (Columbus, OH: Ohio State University Press, 2004), pp. 149–66.

15. S. Koven, *Slumming: Sexual and Social Politics in Victorian London* (Princeton, NJ and Oxford: Princeton University Press, 2004).

16. R. Livesey, 'Women Rent Collectors and the Rewriting of Space, Class and Gender in East London, 1870–1900', in E. Darling and L. Whitworth (eds), *Women and the Making of Built Space in England, 1870–1950* (Aldershot: Ashgate, 2007), pp. 87–106.

17. M. J. Daunton, *House and Home in the Victorian City: Working-Class Housing 1850–1914* (London: Edward Arnold, 1983), pp. 192–4; for the debate on philanthropic housing movements see J. White, 'Business out of Charity', in J. Goodwin and C. Grant (eds), *Built to Last: Reflections on British Housing Policy* (Nottingham: Russell Press, 1996), pp. 9–16 and P. Malpass, 'The Discontinuous History of Housing Associations in England', *Housing Studies*, 15:2 (2000), pp. 195–212. For a discussion of early model lodging houses see B. Trinder, 'The Model Lodging House: Window onto the Underworld', in F. Bosbach and J. R. Davis (eds) *The Great Exhibition and its Legacy* (Munich: K. G. Saur, 2002), pp. 223–42.

18. For the richest account of life for working-class families in a London tenement building, see J. White, *Rothschild Buildings: Life in an East End Tenement Block 1887–1920* (London: Routledge, 1980). For a spatial analysis of a settlement house in early twentieth-century New York, see A. Blunt, 'The "Skyscraper Settlement": Home and Residence at Christodora House', *Environment and Planning A*, 40:3 (2008), pp. 550–71.

19. E. Gee, 'Where Shall She Live? The History and Designation of Housing for Working Women in London 1880-1925', *Journal of Architectural Conservation*, 2:15 (July 2009), pp. 27–46; M. Sheridan, *Rowton Houses 1892–1954* (Southampton: Rowton Houses Ltd, 1956). On how Rowton Houses were used after 1918, see M. Houlbrook, *Queer London: Perils and Pleasures in the Sexual Metropolis, 1918–1957* (Chicago, IL: University of Chicago Press, 2005).

20. For a more sympathetic account of common lodging-house life, see R. Samuel, 'Comers and Goers', in H. J. Dyos and M. Wolff (eds), *The Victorian City: Images and Realities*, 2 vols (London: Routledge & Kegan Paul, 1973), vol. 1, pp. 123–60. See also A. Owens, N. Jeffries, K. Wehner and R. Featherby, 'Fragments of the Modern City: Material Culture and the Rhythms of Everyday Life in Victorian London', *Journal of Victorian Culture*, 15:2 (2010), pp. 212–25.

21. On his approach to the *Morning Post* and *Lloyd's News*, see Lord Rowton to Oliver Borthwick, 1 July 1899, Brotherton Library (University of Leeds), Glenesk-Bathurst

Papers, MS Dept 1990/1/1956 and T. Catling, *My Life's Pilgrimage* (London: John Murray, 1911), pp. 207–8.

22. 'Our London Correspondence', *Manchester Guardian*, 30 January 1896, p. 5.
23. 'The Manchester Sanitary Committee in London', *Manchester Guardian*, 24 September 1896, p. 10.
24. 'Private Action in Respect of Common Lodging-Houses, No. I', *Lancet*, 29 April 1893, p. 1019.
25. 'Private Action in Respect of Common Lodging-Houses, No. II', *Lancet*, 28 March 1896, p. 867.
26. E. R. Younghusband, 'Notes & Memoranda', *Economic Review*, 3:4 (1893), pp. 569–73, on p. 570.
27. 'A Poor Man's Palace', *East London Observer*, 9 August 1902, p. 1.
28. W. A. Somerville, 'Rowton Houses – From A Resident', *Nineteenth Century*, 46:271 (1899), pp. 445–54, on p. 452.
29. 'Municipal and Other Lodgings', *All the Year Round*, 25 March 1893, p. 279.
30. London County Council (General Powers) Bill, *Hansard*, vol. 137, 29 June 1904, cc. 90–9; S. Barnett, 'The Abodes of the Homeless', *Cornhill*, 7 (July 1899), p. 58.
31. 'Private Action II', p. 869.
32. H. Long, *The Edwardian House: The Middle-Class Home in Britain, 1880–1914* (Manchester: Manchester University Press, 1993), pp. 170–5.
33. Denham, 'Sketches', p. 153.
34. 'The New Rowton House', *Standard*, 30 January 1896, p. 6.
35. 'Notes from Fleet Street: Lodging House or Hotel?', *Newcastle Weekly Courant*, 12 August 1899, p. 4.
36. 'In the Poor Man's Hotel, London', *Chambers's Journal*, 25 March 1899, p. 259.
37. 'Rowton House', *British Medical Journal*, 25 February 1893, p. 426.
38. 'Lord Rowton's Model Lodging House', *London*, 25 July 1895, p. 596, we are grateful to Peter Higginbothom of www.workhouses.org.uk for this reference.
39. T. Crook, 'Power, Privacy and Pleasure: Liberalism and the Modern Cubicle', *Cultural Studies*, 21:4 (2007), pp. 549–69.
40. For an examination of earlier nineteenth-century ideas of male comfort associated with the dining room and public house, see L. Hoskins, 'Reading the Inventory: Household Goods, Domestic Cultures and Difference, 1841–1881' (PhD dissertation, University of London, 2011), pp. 122–4.
41. 'Private Action II', p. 868.
42. 'Private Action I', p. 1018.
43. T. W. Wilkinson, 'London's Model Lodging-Houses', in G. R. Sims (ed.), *Living London*, 3 vols (London: Cassell & Company, 1902–3), vol. 3, pp. 172–8.
44. For 'slumming' literature, see Koven, *Slumming*; F. Driver, *Geography Militant: Cultures of Exploration and Empire* (Oxford: Blackwell, 2001); M. Freeman, '"Journeys into Poverty Kingdom": Complete Participation and the British Vagrant, 1866–1914', *History Workshop Journal*, 52 (2001), pp. 99–121; E. Schocket, 'Undercover Explorations of the "Other Half" or the Writer as Class Transvestite', *Representations*, 64 (Autumn 1998), pp. 109–33.
45. *Review of Reviews*, 20 July 1899, p. 68.
46. RG13/418 110, pp. 1–22.
47. One resident in 1907 recalled 'the great number of criminals that were continually in the Police courts giving that address', so that lodgers had their correspondence addressed to

local shops: W. H. Davies, *The Autobiography of a Super-Tramp* (London: A. C. Fifield, 1908), p. 175.

48. Walk with Sergeant Sales, 12 June 1899, LSE Booth Archive, Police Notebook B365, District 34, pp. 13–14.

49. For the later nineteenth century, the indictments of the Central Criminal Court, held at the National Archives (PRO CRIM 44/1090) provide details of perpetrators, offences and the parish where they were committed but do not give precise locations for the crime. Detailed notes as well as basic registers are available for some of the local police courts, which are held at City of London, London Metropolitan Archives. However, these records only survive for our period in Clerkenwell (Rowton House, King's Cross): LMA/PS/CLE/B1 and B2. These notes, clearly an aide memoire for the clerk who compiled the registers, are often idiosyncratic and light on geographical detail.

50. H. B. Measures, 'The Rowton House, Newington Butts', *British Architect*, 22 March 1901, p. 211.

51. J. H. Richardson, 'A Visit to "the Dossers"', *Quiver*, 28:301 (1893), pp. 668–72, on p. 671; Sheridan, *Rowton Houses*, p. 31.

52. 'Yesterday's Police', *Lloyd's Weekly Newspaper*, 16 October 1898, p. 3.

53. *Old Bailey Proceedings Online* (www.oldbaileyonline.org, version 7.0; hereafter *OBP*), June 1908, trial of WILSON, Charles (25, stoker) (t19080623-57).

54. 'An American Consul's Death', *The Times*, 10 January 1913, p. 11.

55. Somerville, 'Rowton Houses', pp. 450, 452.

56. L. James, *Times of Stress* (London: John Murray, 1929), p. 96.

57. C. Noel, *An Autobiography*, ed. S. Dark (London: J. M. Dent, 1945), p. 41.

58. 'Private Action II', p. 870.

59. Houlbrook, *Queer London,* pp. 119–20.

60. For a full discussion of the problems involved with this, see H. G. Cocks, *Nameless Offences: Homosexual Desire in the Nineteenth Century* (London: I. B. Tauris, 2010).

61. J. Smithers, *The Early Life and Vicissitudes of Jack Smithers* (London: Martin Secker, 1939), p. 75.

62. *OBP*, October 1893, trial of EDWARDS, George (55) (t18931016-932).

63. Anon., 'Rowton House, by an Inmate', *Charity Organisation Review* (October 1898), pp. 192–202, on p. 195; F. Hastings, 'A Night in Rowton House', *Leisure Hour* (June 1905), pp. 633–6, on p. 635; Somerville, 'Rowton Houses', p. 450.

64. Noel, *An Autobiography*, p. 41.

65. James, *Times of Stress*, p. 98.

66. P. Gibbs, *England Speaks* (London: William Heinemann Ltd, 1935), p. 39; James, *Times of Stress*, p. 95.

67. 'Old Bailey Trials', *Lloyd's Weekly Newspaper*, 1 July 1900, p. 17.

68. 'Death at a Rowton House', *Leicester Chronicle*, 30 June 1900, p. 2.

69. 'Yesterday's Police', *Lloyd's Weekly Newspaper*, 16 October 1898, p. 3.

70. Minutes of Evidence taken by the Departmental Committee on Vagrancy, vol. 2, *House of Commons Parliamentary Papers* (Cd. 2891), 1906, p. 290.

71. 'The Police Courts', *The Times*, 25 December 1906, p. 8.

72. T. Horsley, *The Odyssey of an Out-of-Work* (London: John Lane the Bodley Head Limited, 1931), p. 119.

73. 'The Rowton House. Is it a Boon or a Bane?', *Penny Illustrated Paper*, 17 December 1910, p. 786.

74. Noel, *An Autobiography*, p. 41.

75. 'Rowton House, by an Inmate'.
76. Mackenzie, *Rowton House Rhymes*, pp. 56–61.
77. Smithers, *The Early Life and Vicissitudes of Jack Smithers*, p. 74.
78. 'Our London Letter', *Sheffield & Rotherham Independent*, 31 July 1900, p. 5.
79. Hastings, 'Night in Rowton House', p. 635; Smithers, *The Early Life and Vicissitudes of Jack Smithers*, p. 72.
80. James, *Times of Stress*, p. 98.

7 Soanes, '"The Place was a Home from Home": Patient Identity and Belonging in the English Cottage Home for Convalescing Psychiatric Patients, 1910–1939'

1. J. Adams, 'The Last Years of the Workhouse, 1930–1965', in J. Bornat, R. Perks, P. Thompson and J. Walmsley (eds), *Oral History, Health and Welfare* (London and New York: Routledge, 2000), pp. 75–97, on p. 100.
2. E. Shorter, *A History of Psychiatry* (New York: John Wiley, 1997), p. 133.
3. G. Wagner, *Barnardo* (London: Weidenfeld & Nicolson, 1979), pp. 79–82.
4. The chapter does not cover private homes or convalescent villas built within mental hospitals. For more discussion of these developments, see S. Soanes, 'Rest and Restitution: Convalescence and the Public Mental Hospital in England' (PhD dissertation, University of Warwick, 2010), ch. 1, and Louise Hide's chapter in the present volume.
5. Mental After Care Association (hereafter MACA), Press Cuttings from Albums, 1897–1927, Wellcome Library for the History and Understanding of Medicine (hereafter WLHUM), SA/MAC/H.1/2–4.
6. MACA, Council Minutes, 25 April 1918, WLHUM, SA/MAC/C.2/1/2.
7. Ibid., 31 December 1928.
8. MACA Annual Report, 1936, WHLUM, SA/MAC/B.1/48, pp. 10–11.
9. Ibid.
10. The first of the MACA's published aims was to 'bridge over the difficult period that follows discharge from a mental hospital': 'The Mental After-Care Association', *Journal of Mental Science* (hereafter *JMS*), 72 (July 1926), p. 443.
11. J. Walton, 'Casting Out and Bringing Back in Victorian England: Pauper Lunatics, 1840–70', in W. F. Bynum, R. Porter and M. Shepherd (eds), *Madness: Essays in the History of Psychiatry, Volume II: Institutions and Society* (London: Tavistock, 1985), pp. 132–46; D. Wright, 'Getting Out of the Asylum: Understanding the Confinement of the Insane in the Nineteenth Century', *Social History of Medicine* (hereafter *SHM*), 10:1 (1997), pp. 137–55.
12. A. Suzuki, 'Enclosing and Disclosing Lunatics within the Family Walls: Domestic Psychiatric Regime and the Public Sphere in the early Nineteenth Century', in P. Bartlett and D. Wright (eds), *Outside the Walls of the Asylum: A History of Care in the Community* (London and New Brunswick, NJ: Athlone, 1999), pp. 115–31.
13. J. Welshman, 'Inside the Walls of the Hostel, 1940–74', in P. Dale and J. Melling (eds), *Mental Illness and Learning Disability since 1850* (Basingstoke, Hants and New York: Routledge, 2006), pp. 200–23, on pp. 219–20.
14. On the scope and functions of the MACA's aftercare activities, see S. Strong, *Community Care in the Making: A History of MACA, 1879–2000* (London: MACA, 2000); V.

Long, 'Changing Public Representations of Mental Illness in Britain, 1870–1970' (PhD dissertation, University of Warwick, 2004), ch. 4.

15. L. Wannell, 'Patients' Relatives and Psychiatric Doctors: Letter Writing in the York Retreat, 1875–1910', *SHM*, 20:2 (2007), pp. 297–313; L. Smith, '"Your Very Thankful Inmate": Discovering the Patients of an Early County Lunatic Asylum', *SHM*, 21:2 (2008), pp. 237–52; G. Mooney and J. Reinarz (eds), *Permeable Walls: Historical Perspectives on Hospital and Asylum Visiting* (Amsterdam and New York: Rodopi, 2009).

16. D. Bennett, 'The Drive Towards the Community', in G. E. Berrios and H. Freeman (eds), *150 Years of British Psychiatry, 1841–1991* (London: Gaskell, 1991), pp. 321–32, on p. 323; H. Freeman and D. Bennett, 'Origins and Development', in D. Bennett and H. Freeman (eds), *Community Psychiatry* (London: Churchill Livingstone, 1991), pp. 40–70, on pp. 41–2; K. Jones, *Asylums and After* (London: Athlone, 1993), p. 128.

17. Welshman, 'Inside the Walls of the Hostel', pp. 204, 220.

18. Figures are not available for cottage-home admissions prior to the 1930s. Nevertheless, the fact that the MACA's work with convalescence in the 1930s exceeded the sum of all its activities in the 1910s indicates the extent of growth in its cottage-home referrals over these decades.

19. H. Hawkins, 'After Care', *JMS*, 24 (October 1879), p. 364.

20. MACA, Annual Reports, 1919, p. 5, WLHUM, SA/MAC/B.1/32.

21. Ibid., 1930, p. 5, WLHUM, SA/MAC/B.1/42.

22. Hawkins, 'After Care', p. 362.

23. [Editorial] '"After-Care" Association', *JMS*, 27 (October 1881), p. 477; '"After-Care" Anniversary', *JMS*, 30 (October 1885), p. 448.

24. E. G. Gardiner, *Convalescent Care in Great Britain* (Chicago, IL: University of Chicago Press, 1935), pp. 61–3; J. Cronin, 'The Origins and Development of Scottish Convalescent Homes, 1860–1939' (PhD dissertation, University of Glasgow, 2003), p. 165.

25. MACA, Annual Reports, 1924, pp. 4–5, WLHUM, SA/MAC/B.1/43.

26. Cronin, 'Origins and Development of Scottish Convalescent Homes', p. 289; MACA, Case Agenda Books, 1910–1924, WLHUM, SA/MAC/G.2.

27. 'Mental After Care', *Mental Welfare*, 11:2 (15 May 1930), p. 44.

28. MACA, Annual Reports, 1890/1–1920, WLHUM, SA/MAC/B.1/4–33.

29. Hawkins, 'After-Care', pp. 358–9.

30. H. Rayner, 'After-Care of Male Patients Discharged from Asylums', *JMS*, 38 (October 1891), pp. 535–6 and 539.

31. MACA, Annual Reports, 1931–1938 (cf. 1931, pp. 6–7), WLHUM, SA/MAC/B.1/42–50.

32. MACA, Council Minutes, 9 July 1931, WLHUM, SA/MAC/C.2/1.

33. MACA, Annual Reports, 1926, p. 4 and 1936, pp. 10–11, WLHUM, SA/MAC/B.1/37,47; C. Philo, *A Geographical History of Institutional Provision for the Insane from Medieval Times to the 1860s in England and Wales* (Lampeter, Ceredigion, and New York: Edwin Mellen Press, 2004), p. 612.

34. MACA, Annual Reports, 1931, p. 12; 1936, p. 11, WLHUM, SA/MAC/B.1/43, 47.

35. Ibid., 1931, p. 3; R. P. Smith (Chairman, MACA), cited in WLHUM, MACA, Scrapbooks, 'Plight of the Mentally Afflicted', *City Press*, 22 March 1929; Cronin, 'Origins and Development of Scottish Convalescent Homes', pp. 191–6.

36. MACA, Publicity and Information Sheets, [untitled] *c.* 1938, WLHUM, SA/MAC/H.2/1.

37. MACA, Annual Report, 1937, p. 2, WLHUM, SA/MAC/B.1/48.

38. D. Gittins, *Madness in its Place: Narratives of Severalls Hospital, 1913–1997* (London and New York: Routledge, 1998), p. 128.

39. Gardiner, *Convalescent Care*, p. 85.

40. MACA, Scrapbooks, Reginald Worth, 'After-Care of Mental Patients', paper presented to the Central Association for Mental Welfare Public Health Congress, 1934, WLHUM, SA/MAC/H.1/5.

41. H. Bond, 'After-Care in Cases of Mental Disorder, and the Desirability of its More Extended Scope', *JMS*, 60 (April 1913), p. 285.

42. MACA, Scrapbooks, [no title] *Essex County Chronicle*, 5 November 1897, WLHUM, SA/MAC/H.1/3.

43. Ibid., 'Mental After-Care Association', *City Press*, 6 June 1930. MACA, Annual Report, 1914, p. 5 (marginalia on article in *Life of Faith*, 16 July 1915), WLHUM, SA/MAC/B.1/27.

44. P. Nolan, *A History of Mental Health Nursing* (Cheltenham: Stanley Thornes, 1998), p. 81.

45. MACA, Scrapbooks, Reginald Worth, 'After-Care of Mental Patients', paper given to Central Association for Mental Welfare Public Health Congress, 1934, WLHUM, SA/MAC/H.1/5.

46. *Minutes of Evidence Taken before the Royal Commission on Lunacy and Mental Disorder* (London: H. M. Stationery Office, 1927), Ethel Vickers, 13 January 1925, pp. 310–1.

47. MACA, Propaganda Committee Minute Book, 'Rules for Matrons for Cases on Trial', *c.* 1914, WLHUM, SA/MAC/C.4/4.

48. MACA, Case Files, 4897 (Edith V. E.), 23 November 1916, WLHUM, SA/MAC/G.3/30; J. Melling and B. Forsythe, *The Politics of Madness: The State, Insanity and Society in England, 1845–1914* (Abingdon and New York: Routledge, 2006), pp. 26–7.

49. R. Porter, 'Madness and its Institutions', in A. Wear (ed.), *Medicine in Society: Historical Essays* (Cambridge: Cambridge University Press, 1992), pp. 277–301, on p. 294; A. Rogers and D. Pilgrim, *Mental Health Policy in Britain* (Basingstoke and London: Macmillan, 1996), p. 61.

50. MACA, Annual Reports, 1926, p. 4, WLHUM, SA/MAC/B.1/38.

51. Bond, 'After-Care in Cases of Mental Disorder', p. 278; Board of Control, *Annual Report for 1924* (London: H. M. Stationery Office, 1924), p. 27.

52. MACA Annual Report, 1936, pp. 10–11, WLHUM, SA/MAC/B.1/48.

53. MACA, Agenda Case Books, 31 January 1918, WLHUM, SA/MAC/G.2/3.

54. Gittins, *Madness in its Place*, pp. 128–33; A. Shepherd, 'The Female Patient Experience in Two Late-Nineteenth-Century Surrey Asylums', in J. Andrews and A. Digby (eds), *Sex and Seclusions, Class and Custody: Perspectives on Gender and Class in the History of British and Irish Psychiatry* (Amsterdam: Rodopi, 2004), pp. 223–48, on p. 244.

55. MACA, Agenda Case Books, 31 January 1918 and 30 December 1920, WLHUM, SA/MAC/G.2/3–4.

56. MACA, Case Files, 4118 (Ernest S.), 4 and 18 December 1914, WLHUM, SA/MAC/G.3.

57. A. Beveridge, 'Life in the Asylum: Patients' Letters from Morningside, 1873–1908', *History of Psychiatry*, 9 (1998), pp. 431–69, on p. 462; Smith, 'Your Very Thankful Inmate', p. 250.
58. Gittins, *Madness in its Place*; Shepherd, 'Female Patient Experience'.
59. Bartlett and Wright (eds), *Outside the Walls of the Asylum*.
60. Walton, 'Casting Out'; Wright, 'Getting Out'; Suzuki, 'Enclosing and Disclosing'.

8 Johansen, '"The Father and Mother of the Place": Inhabiting London's Public Libraries, 1885–1940'

1. Chiswick Free Public Library, Minute Book 1, 30 September 1890, Hounslow Archives and Local Studies (hereafter HALS), 027.405.
2. 'Tabulation of returns obtained by the town clerk as to the salaries &c. of librarians in Greater London', 1906, Bishopsgate Institute Archives (hereafter BI), London Collection, A3, Box 2/1.
3. P. Cowell, *Public Library Staffs* (London: Simpkin, Marshall, Hamilton, Kent & Co., 1893), p. 15; J. J. Ogle, 'The Free Library: Its History and Present Condition', in R. Garnett (ed.), *The Library Series* (London: George Allen, 1897), pp. 134–56.
4. T. Kelly, *A History of Public Libraries in Great Britain 1845–1975* (London: Library Association, 1977), pp. 3–15; A. Black, S. Pepper and K. Bagshaw, *Books, Buildings and Social Engineering* (Surrey: Ashgate, 2009), pp. 28–32. For a discussion of rational recreation, see P. Bailey, *Popular Culture and Performance in the Victorian City* (Cambridge: Cambridge University Press, 1998), pp. 21–6.
5. S. Hales, *Working Men and Free Public Libraries* (London: W. Reeves, 1889), p. 1.
6. Librarians lived across London in districts ranging from Shoreditch, Whitechapel, Limehouse, Poplar, East Ham and Leyton in the east, to Chelsea, Fulham, Chiswick, Hammersmith, Paddington, Ealing, Richmond and Westminster in the west and West End, from Newington, Lambeth, Camberwell, Woolwich, Bermondsey and Battersea in the south, to Harlesden, Willesden Green, Walthamstow, Kilburn and Stoke Newington in the north.
7. C. Steedman, *Past Tenses: Essays on Writing, Autobiography and History* (London: Rivers Oram Press, 1992), p. 179. See also the introduction to R. Samuel and P. Thompson (eds), *The Myths We Live By* (London: Routledge, 1990), p. 6; T. K. Hareven, *Family Time and Industrial Time* (Cambridge: Cambridge University Press, 1982), pp. 355–82.
8. No study to date has considered the issue of residency. Brief contemporary commentary can be found in A. L. Champneys, *Public Libraries: A Treatise on their Design, Construction and Fittings* (London: B. T. Batsford, 1907), pp. 110–11. For confirmation that the notion of living-in was outmoded by the inter-war period, see W. A. Briscoe, *Library Planning* (London: Grafton & Co., 1927).
9. M. Johansen, 'The Public Librarian in Modern London (1890–1914): The Case of Charles Goss at the Bishopsgate Institute' (PhD dissertation, University of East London, 2006), pp. 27–9, 61–2.
10. East Ham Urban District Council, Minutes and Reports, 1897–1901, 8 July 1898, Newham Archives and Local Studies Library. Emphasis added.
11. C. Hammond, *Chiswick Library: One Hundred Years of Service to the Community* (London: Hounslow Leisure Services, 1991), p. 2; A. W. Ball, *The Public Libraries of London: A Pictorial History 1856–1914* (London: Library Association, 1977), p. 7.

12. J. Tosh, *A Man's Place* (New Haven, CT and London: Yale University Press, 1999), pp. 43–50, 172–4; see also Harlesden Public Library Committee, Minute Book 1905–1922, Special Meeting of the Harlesden Public Library Committee, 14 November 1906, 31 January 1907, Brent Archives (hereafter BA).

13. Hammersmith Library Committee, Minute Book 1, 6 October 1896 to 30 October 1900, Hammersmith & Fulham Archives and Local History Centre (hereafter HFA), PAH/2/40; Chiswick Free Public Library, Minute Book 1, 14 November 1892, HALS, 027.405.

14. Commissioners of Public Libraries and Museums of the Parish of St Giles, Minute Book 1, 1888–1893, 2 October 1889 and 11 November 1889, Southwark Local Studies Archive (hereafter SLS), 2775; Borough of Stepney, Borough Librarians' Reports, 1900 to 31 March 1914, year ended 31 March 1906, Tower Hamlets Local History Library and Archive (hereafter THLH).

15. 'Mr Chennell's Career: His Life is the Story of the Libraries', *Willesden Chronicle*, 12 November 1937, and 'Farewell to Borough Librarian', *Willesden Chronicle*, 29 October 1937, BA, Library Press Cuttings, Frank Chennell.

16. Kenneth Rogers to Charles Goss, 24 November 1940, BI, Correspondence and Institute Papers, 1940–2, Box 16; see also 'Presentation to Mr A. Cawthorne', *East London Observer*, 6 June 1936, THLH, Whitechapel Library, Albert Cawthorne, classes 100, 850, 850.11.

17. *Library*, 1:1 (1889), pp. 274–5.

18. J. Hamlett, *Material Relations: Domestic Interiors and Middle-Class Families in England, 1850–1910* (Manchester and New York: Manchester University Press, 2010), pp. 90–1; see also pp. 40–3, 90–6.

19. Champneys, *Public Libraries*, p. 111.

20. S. Muthesius, *The English Terraced House* (New Haven, CT and London: Yale University Press, 1982), p. 62.

21. 'Bermondsey Public Library', *South London Press*, 23 January 1892, SLS, Bermondsey Central Library Press Cuttings Miscellaneous, 1881–1929, PC.021. Emphasis added.

22. H. Long, *The Edwardian House: The Middle-Class Home in Britain 1880–1914* (Manchester: Manchester University Press, 1993), p. 11; see also A. A. Jackson, *The Middle Classes 1900–1950* (Great Britain: David St John Thomas Publisher, 1991), p. 41.

23. Hugh Smith to William Benson Thorne, 24 October 1946, BI, The Thorne Collection, Library Association Archive, facsimile copy, Charles Goss Papers, GOSS/2/6.

24. J. Rose, *The Intellectual Life of the British Working Classes* (New Haven, CT and London: Yale University Press, 2001), pp. 43–9, 189.

25. *Library*, 1:1 (1889), pp. 350, 211; see also untitled newspaper fragment by S. Martin in Samuel Martin Biographical Folder, HFA, H920 MAR.

26. Ball, *The Public Libraries of Greater London*, pp. 57–71; A. Cotgreave, *Views and Memoranda of Public Libraries* (London: Library Aids Co., 1901).

27. A. Black, *A New History of the English Public Library* (London: Leicester University Press, 1996), pp. 230–1.

28. A. Milne-Smith, 'A Flight to Domesticity? Making a Home in the Gentlemen's Clubs of London, 1880–1914', *Journal of British Studies* (hereafter *JBS*), 45:4 (October 2006), pp. 796–818, on pp. 801–3.

29. First Minute Book 1895–1897, 13 November 1895, 4 November 1896, 1 June 1897, BI, Society of Public Librarians Archive, SPL/1.

30. C. P. Hosgood, '"Doing the Shops" at Christmas: Women, Men and the Department Store in England *c*.1880–1914', in G. Crossick and S. Jaumain (eds), *Cathedrals of Consumption* (Aldershot and Vermont: Ashgate, 1999), pp. 97–115, on p. 99; Milne-Smith, 'A Flight to Domesticity?', pp. 801–3.

31. D. Rubinstein, *Victorian Homes* (Newton Abbot: David & Charles, 1974), p. 13.

32. Cowell, *Public Library Staffs*, pp. 20–3; 'Tabulation of returns obtained by the town clerk as to the salaries &c. of librarians in Greater London', BI.

33. F. D. Klingender, *The Condition of Clerical Labour in Britain* (London: Martin Lawrence, 1935), pp. 11–12.

34. M. Heller, *London Clerical Workers, 1880–1914* (London: Pickering & Chatto, 2011), pp. 17–20.

35. L. Young, *Middle-Class Culture in the Nineteenth Century* (Basingstoke: Palgrave Macmillan, 2002), p. 55; Tosh, *A Man's Place*, pp. 19–20.

36. P. Bailey, 'White Collars, Gray Lives? The Lower Middle Class Revisited', *JBS*, 38:3 (July 1999), pp. 273–90.

37. H. Perkin, *The Rise of Professional Society* (London: Routledge, 1989), pp. 8–9; J. Harris, *Private Lives, Public Spirit* (Oxford: Oxford University Press, 1993), pp. 6–11; D. Cannadine, *Class in Britain* (New Haven, CT and London: Yale University Press, 1998), pp. 15–23; Bailey, *Popular Culture and Performance in the Victorian City*, pp. 2–6; Young, *Middle-Class Culture*, pp. 5–19.

38. D. Garrison, *Apostles of Culture* (Madison, WI: University of Wisconsin, 1979), pp. xiii–xiv.

39. Some of the arguments introduced in this paragraph are unpacked in Bailey, *Popular Culture and Performance in the Modern City*, pp. 30–46 and Johansen, 'The Public Librarian in Modern London', pp. 5–17, 174–83.

40. B. Fletcher, *Model Houses for the Industrial Classes* (London: Longmans, Green & Co., 1871), pp. 17–21, 47; J. Burnett, *A Social History of Housing 1815–1985* (London and New York: Methuen, 1986), pp. 148–51.

41. Perkin, *The Rise of Professional Society*, pp. 95–101.

42. T. S. Jones, *The Moral Side of Living-in* (London: Shop Assistant Publishing Company, 1907), pp. 11, 37.

43. C. Hosgood, 'Mercantile Monasteries: Shops, Shop Assistants, and Shop Life in Late-Victorian and Edwardian Britain', *JBS*, 38:3 (July 1999), pp. 322–52.

9 Robert, '"Discipline with Home-Like Conditions": The Living Quarters and Daily Life of the Women's Army Auxiliary Corps in First-World-War Britain and France'

1. The corps was renamed Queen Mary's Army Auxiliary Corps in March 1918, but remained popularly known as WAAC.

2. For press reports, see Imperial War Museum (hereafter IWM), Women at Work Collection (hereafter WWC), SUPP. 32/4–7, 17–18, 26–7, 34–5, 38–9, 41, 47–9, 51, 59–65 and 138; for photographs, recruiting posters and art, see nn. 32 and 58; IWM, ART, PST, 13167; B. Lithiby, *The Camp in the Orchard*, IWM, ART 2896, at http://www.iwm.org.uk/collections/item/object/16863 [accessed 19 June 2012]; J. Lavery, *QMAAC Camp*, 1918, private collection, at http://www.artvalue.com/auctionresult-

-lavery-john-1856-1941-united-k-qmaac-camp-1476519.htm [accessed 17 September 2012].

3.   Compare the recruiting poster in n. 2 with IWM, PST 3283, 5471, 5996, 5489, 2766 and 0325.
4.   For membership numbers, see A. Conway, 'Women's War Work', *The Encyclopaedia Britannica*, 12th edn (London: EB Company, 1922), vol. 36, pp. 1054–65, on p. 1056.
5.   D. Shaw, 'The Forgotten Army of Women: Queen Mary's Army Auxiliary Corps', in H. Cecil and P. Liddle (eds), *Facing Armageddon: The First World War Experienced* (London: Leo Cooper, 1996), pp. 365–79; E. Crosthwait, '"The Girl Behind the Man Behind the Gun": The Women's Army Auxiliary Corps, 1914–18', in L. Davidoff and B. Westover (eds), *Our Work, Our Lives, Our Worlds: Women's History and Women's Work* (Totowa, NJ: Barnes & Noble, 1986), pp. 161–81; A. Woollacott, *On Her Their Lives Depend: Munitions Workers in the Great War* (Berkeley, CA and London: University of California Press, 1994), pp. 50–7.
6.   Q. Colville, 'The Role of the Interior in Constructing Notions of Class and Status: Case Study of Britannia Royal Naval College Dartmouth, 1905–39', in S. McKellar and P. Sparke (eds), *Interior Design and Identity* (Manchester: Manchester University Press, 2004), pp. 114–32; and Q. Colville, 'Corporate Domesticity and Idealised Masculinity: Royal Naval Officers and Their Shipboard Homes, 1918–39', *Gender & History*, 21 (2009), pp. 499–519.
7.   J. Hamlett, '"Nicely Feminine, Yet Learned": Student Rooms at Royal Holloway and the Oxford and Cambridge Colleges in Late-Nineteenth-Century Britain', *Women's History Review*, 15 (2006), pp. 137–61.
8.   J. Watson, *Fighting Different Wars: Experience, Memory, and the First World War in Britain* (Cambridge: Cambridge University Press, 2004); L. Noakes, *Women in the British Army: War and the Gentle Sex* (London and New York: Routledge, 2006).
9.   J. Hamlett, *Material Relations: Domestic Interiors and Middle-Class Families in England, 1850–1919* (Manchester: Manchester University Press, 2010).
10. H. Rappaport, *No Place for Ladies: The Untold Story of Women in the Crimean War* (London: Aurum, 2007), p. xv.
11. A. Summers, *Angels and Citizens: British Women as Military Nurses, 1854–1914* (Newbury: Threshold Press, 2000), pp. xiii, 63–4, 80–2, 90.
12. W. Burdett-Coutts, 'Our Wars and Our Wounded', *The Times*, 29 June 1900; Summers, *Angels*, pp. 174–7, 181–2.
13. Ibid., pp. 155–60; *Nursing Record and Hospital World*, 31 March 1894, p. 205.
14. J. Cowper, *A Short History of Queen Mary's Army Auxiliary Corps* (Guildford: WRAC Association, 1967), pp. 10–26.
15. Conway, 'Women's War Work', p. 1059.
16. See Summers, *Angels*, pp. 87–8, 152–3, 249–50 and Watson, *Fighting*, pp. 71–104, about nurses' semi-professional and voluntary status.
17. The National Archives, NATS1/109; IWM, Art IWM, PST 13171.
18. Watson, *Fighting*, pp. 30–41.
19. H. Gwynne-Vaughan, *Service with the Army* (London and New York: Hutchinson, 1942), p. 26.
20. See articles in IWM, WWC, SUPP. 32/4–8, 38–9, 41, 44, 51 and 59–64.
21. 'City Depot for Women Recruits', *The Times*, 21 May 1917; 'The Women's Army', *The Times*, 28 August 1917; 'Women March to Armageddon', *Weekly Dispatch*, 2 September 1917.

22. *Lady's Pictorial*, 28 July 1917; Private W.A.A.C. on Active Service, *The Letters of Thomasina Atkins* (New York: George H. Doran, 1918), pp. 42–3; The Diary of Mrs Gwynne-Vaughan re her visit to France, IWM, WWC, Army 3.10/2; F. T. Jesse, *The Sword of Deborah: First-Hand Impressions of the British Women's Army in France* (New York: George H. Doran, 1919), pp. 65–7.

23. Private, *Letters*, pp. 42–3; 'Women of the Army', *Daily Telegraph*, 19 November 1917.

24. *The Work of the Royal Engineers in the European War, 1914–1919. Work Under the Director of Works (France)* (Chatham: W. & J. Mackay, 1924), pp. 40, 70 and plate II; Lithiby, *Princess Beatrice Camp*, IWM, ART 2905, at http://www.iwm.org.uk/collections/item/object/16872 [accessed 19 June 2012].

25. *Work of the Royal Engineers*, pp. 6–9, 19–23, 40.

26. P. Simkins, *Kitchener's Army: The Raising of the New Armies, 1914–1916* (Manchester: Manchester University Press, 1988), pp. 191–211, 231–9, 240–50.

27. *Work of the Royal Engineers*, pp. 6, 19, 53, 64, 66.

28. Ibid., p. 70.

29. 'Women and Army Work', *Daily Telegraph*, 13 August 1917.

30. 'Happy War Girls', *Daily Mail* (Dundee), 19 June 1917; 'Women in France', *Westminster Gazette*, 18 June 1917; 'Women Army Clerks', *Yorkshire Observer*, 11 July 1917.

31. 'The Women's Army', *Evening News*, 15 October 1917.

32. IWM, Department of Photographs (hereafter DP), Q5748, Q5756, Q5751.

33. IWM, WWC, SUPP. 32/4, 44 and 51.

34. Violet Markham, the deputy director of the WS, had protested repeatedly against militarism in women's war organisations.

35. Gwynne-Vaughan, *Service*, p. 26.

36. Ibid., p. 36.

37. V. Rumbold, IWM, Department of Sound Records (hereafter DSR), 576/7.

38. D. Pickford to her sister, 15 July, 1918, IWM, DD, 11301; M. Hay, *On Waactive Service* (Plymouth: Plymouth Press, 1932), pp. 43, 58–9.

39. M. Mullins, 1998-01-83, National Army Museum (hereafter NAM).

40. General Instructions No. 1, Gwynne-Vaughan, *Service*, pp. 157–8.

41. Hay, *Waactive*, pp. 24, 33, 150–4.

42. Ibid., p. 147; L. Parfitt, 1998-01-87, NAM.

43. Hay, *Waactive*, pp. 147–8; E. Shepherd, IWM, DSR, 579/12; V. Newing, 1998-01-84, NAM.

44. Hay, *Waactive*, pp. 146–7.

45. Ibid., pp. 158–9; R. Ord, IWM, DSR, 44/05.

46. Rumbold, IWM, DSR, 576/7.

47. 'The Women's Army', *The Times*, 18 September 1917 and *Glasgow Herald*, 15 September 1917.

48. For recruiting estimates, see D. Lamm, 'Emily Goes to War: Explaining the Recruitment to the Women's Army Auxiliary Corps in World War I', in B. Melman (ed.), *Borderlines: Genders and Identities in War and Peace, 1870–1930* (New York and London: Routledge, 1998), pp. 377–95.

49. Gwynne-Vaughan, Diary, 26 May 1917, 1994-253-2067, NAM; *Service*, p. 53.

50. Ibid., pp. 12–13, 28–31 and 71–2; Watson, *Fighting*, p. 33.

51. Gwynne-Vaughan, *Service*, p. 28.

52. Ibid., p. 25.

53. K. Robert, "'All that is Best of the Modern Woman'? Representations of Female Military Auxiliaries in British Popular Culture, 1914–1919', in J. Meyer (ed.), *British Popular Culture and the First World War* (Leiden and Boston, MA: Brill, 2008), pp. 97–122.
54. Gwynne-Vaughan, *Service*, pp. 25, 26, 27; O. Jordan to Mrs Hubbard, 8 October 1917, 1998-01-75, NAM.
55. M. Trevor, *Military Barracks* (Princes Risborough, Buckinghamshire: Shire, 2002), pp. 12–20; A. Service, *Edwardian Interiors: Inside the Homes of the Poor, the Average and the Wealthy* (London: Barrie & Jenkins, 1982), pp. 46–56; H. Long, *The Edwardian House: The Middle-Class Home in Britain, 1880–1914* (Manchester: Manchester University Press, 1993), pp. xiii, 33, 83.
56. K. Mellory and A. Ottar, *Walls of War: A History of Military Architecture in North West Europe, 1900–1945* (London: Astragal, 1979), pp. 73–7.
57. *Work of the Royal Engineers*, pp. 51, 70.
58. IWM, DP, Q8120, Q9303, Q9306; Pickford, 14 February, 14 March 1918, IWM, DD, 11301.
59. A. Martin, IWM, DSR, 42/3; J. Swann, IWM, DD, 9373; 'Khaki Girls in France', *Daily Mail*, 19 November, 1917.
60. Gwynne-Vaughan, *Service*, p. 41; Pickford, 24 January, 7 February 1918, IWM, DD, 11301; Lithiby, *The Workers' Quarters*, IWM, ART, 2904 at http://www.iwm.org.uk/collections/item/object/16871 [accessed 19 June 2012].
61. Q8042, Q7952, IWM, DP; Hay, *Waactive*, p. 169; Lithiby, *YWCA Hut*, IWM, ART 2907 at http://www.iwm.org.uk/collections/item/object/16874c [accessed 19 June 2012].
62. A. Kimber, 1998-01-76; E. Cooper, IWM, DSR, 3137/02.
63. M. Gibson, 17 September 1917, IWM, DD, 86/19/1.
64. Private, *Letters*, p. 26; Hay, *Waactive*, pp. 45, 101–3; Summary of Hygienic methods in Hostels, IWM, WWC, Army 3.30/6.
65. Hay, *Waactive*, pp. 45–46, 59, 65, 105.
66. Ibid., pp. 84, 155; Private, *Letters*, pp. 59, 78; A. Anderson, *'Johnny' of Q.M.A.A.C.* (London: Heath Cranton, 1922), pp. 94–5.
67. Robert, "'All that is Best'", pp. 112–15.
68. 'The Transition of Eve', *Lady's Pictorial*, 22 September 1917; 'Making Soldiers of Girls', *Daily Chronicle*, 1 October 1917.
69. 'The Women's Army', *Scotchwoman*, November, 1917, IWM, SUPP. 32/41.
70. 'TommyWaacs', *Everyweek*, 28 February 1918; 'The Bristol Unit of the WAAC', *Bristol Times*, 5 October 1917.
71. C. Hambleton, 8888/2; Cooper, 3137/2; Anon., 7444/2; Anon., 7448/1; N. Barker, 9731, all IWM, DSR.
72. Pickford, 24 January, 23 April, 2 and 5 May 1918, IWM, DD, 11301.
73. Martin, IWM, DSR, 42/3; O. Castle, IWM, DD, 9190.
74. E. Waller, IWM, DD, 10232; Hay, *Waactive*, pp. 51–2.
75. Cooper, IWM, DSR, 3137/2; Pickford, 5 January, 4, 7, 14 and 24 February 1918, IWM, DD, 11301; Johnston to Hastie, 1 May 1918, E. Hastie, IWM, DD, 1719.
76. Out of 57,200 women about 17,000 served in France, see Shaw, 'Forgotten Army', p. 365; Hay, *Waactive*, pp. 56–7, 107, 129–30; Cooper, 3157/2; I. Kewley, 3154/2, both IWM, DSR.
77. Parfitt, 1998-01-87, NAM; Mullins, 1998-01-83, NAM; G. Ottoway, IWM, DSR, 7486/1.

78. Gibson, IWM, DD, 86/19/1; 'Khaki Girls in France', *Daily Mail*, 19 November, 1917.

79. Cooper, 3137/2; Kewley, 3154/2; Ord, 44/5; Rumbold, 576/7, all IWM, DSR.

80. Gwynne-Vaughan, *Service*, pp. 39, 41; Pickford, 24 January 1918, IWM, DD, 11301.

81. Gwynne-Vaughan, *Service*, p. 39.

82. Gibson, 17 September 1917, IWM, DD, 86/9/1; Pickford, 22 July and 27 August 1918, IWM, DD, 11301.

83. Gwynne-Vaughan, *Service*, p. 39; Pickford, 15 July 1918, IWM, DD, 11301.

84. Ibid., 15 July, 22 July, 29 July and 11 August 1918.

85. Private, *Letters*, 62 and 90; D. Philp, 1998-01-92, NAM; Pickford, 7 February 1918, IWM, DD, 11301; Cooper, IWM, DSR, 3137/2; Martin, IWM, DSR, 42/3.

86. Ibid.; Ord, 44/5, Cooper, 3137/2, both IWM, DSR; Hay, *Waactive*, pp. 52, 170–74 and 176–7.

87. Ibid., p. 101; Ord, IWM, DSR, 44/5.

88. Ibid.; Hay, *Waactive*, pp. 116–17.

89. Ibid., pp. 175–6, 179, 188–9; Private, *Letters*, pp. 59, 80–1, 151; Pickford, 20 January and 17 November 1918, IWM, DD, 11301.

90. Parfitt, 1998-01-87, NAM; Hay, *Waactive*, pp. 169, 188.

91. O. Taylor, IWM, DD, 4181; F. Parrott, IWM, DSR, 8857/3.

92. Taylor, IWM, DD, 4181.

93. M. Holme, 1998-01-70, NAM; Mullins, 1998-01-83, NAM; Castle, 9190; Swann, 9373; Taylor, 4181, all IWM, DD; Anon., 7448/1; Parrott, 8857/3, both IWM, DSR.

94. Ibid.; Castle, 9190; Taylor, 4181, both IWM, DD.

95. Holme, 1998-01-70, NAM; Castle, IWM, DD, 9190.

96. E. Quinlan, IWM. DD, 11315; Hay, *Waactive*, p. 89; Private, *Letters*, p. 71.

97. Swann, 9373; Castle, 9190, both IWM, DD; E. Shepherd, 579/12, IWM, DSR; O. Graham, 1998-01-59, NAM; Kimber, 1998-01-76, NAM; Hay, *Waactive*, pp. 13, 38, 20, 57, 79; Pickford, 4 February and 28 August 1918, IWM, DD, 11301.

98. Castle, IWM, DD, 9190; Gwynne-Vaughan, Diary, 12 April 1917, 1994-253-266, NAM.

99. Gibson, 16 September 1917, 86/19/1; C. Wagstaff, 4273; Miscellaneous, 1917; G. Heaney, 88/27/1; Pickford, 14 and 28 February 1918, 11301, all IWM, DD.

100. Pickford, 5 and 19 December 1918, IWM, DD, 11301; Hay, *Waactive*, pp. 210–13.

101. Gwynne-Vaughan, *Service*, pp. 41, 34, 49–50; Cowper, *A Short History*, pp. 65–6.

10 Whyte, 'Halls of Residence at Britain's Civic Universities, 1870–1970'

1. H. Silver, 'The Universities' Speaking Conscience: "Bruce Truscot" and Redbrick University', *History of Education*, 28 (1999), pp. 173–89. See also A. L. Mackenzie and A. R. Allan (eds), *Redbrick University Revisited* (Liverpool: Liverpool University Press, 1996) and H. C. Dent, 'Bruce Truscot', *Universities Quarterly*, 7 (1952–3), pp. 326–32.

2. B. Truscot [E. A. Peers], *Red Brick University*, 2nd edn (1943; London: Pelican, 1951), pp. 17, 33–4.

3. See, for example, B. Simon, *A Student's View of the Universities* (London and New York: Longmans, Green, 1943); C. Forrester-Paton, *Universities Under Fire* (London: SCM, 1946); Nuffield College, *The Problem Facing British Universities* (London: Oxford University Press, 1948); W. Moberly, *The Crisis in the University* (London: SCM, 1949).

4. The definition of a Redbrick University is broad, but owes much to W. H. Armytage, *Civic Universities: Aspects of a British Tradition* (London: Benn, 1955). See also T. W. Heyck, 'The Idea of a University in Britain, 1870–1970', *History of European Ideas*, 8 (1987), pp. 205–19.

5. D. R. Jones, *The Origins of Civic Universities: Manchester, Leeds, and Liverpool* (London and New York: Routledge, 1988).

6. For a good concise introduction, see S. J. M. M. Alberti, 'Civic Cultures and Civic Colleges in Victorian England', in M. Daunton (ed.), *The Organisation of Knowledge in Victorian Britain* (Oxford: Oxford University Press, 2005), pp. 337–56.

7. *First Congress of the Universities of the Empire* (London: Hodder & Stoughton, 1912), p. 3.

8. Though the second wave were also known as Whitetile universities, following the term coined by John Osborne: J. Osborne, *Look Back in Anger* (London: Evans Brothers, 1957), p. 34.

9. C. H. Shinn, *Paying the Piper: The Development of the University Grants Committee, 1919–1946* (London: Falmer, 1986).

10. W. Whyte, 'Private Benefit, Public Finance? Student Funding in Britain, 1960–1998', in L. Goldman and S. Jones (eds), *Welfare and Social Policy in Britain Since 1870* (forthcoming, 2014).

11. *Sheffield Daily Telegraph*, 7 January 1913.

12. Quoted in H. J. W. Hetherington, 'The History and Significance of the Modern Universities', in H. Martin (ed.), *The Life of the Modern University* (London: Student Christian Movement Press, 1930), pp. 9–20, 12.

13. For especially good institutional histories see, for example, E. Ives, D. Drummond, and L. Schwartz (eds), *The First Civic University: Birmingham, 1880–1980* (Birmingham: Birmingham University, 2000); T. Kelly, *For Advancement of Learning: the University of Liverpool, 1881–1981* (Liverpool: Liverpool University Press, 1981); H. Mathers, *Steel City Scholars: the Centenary History of the University of Sheffield* (London: James and James, 2005).

14. M. Sanderson, *The Universities and British Industry, 1850–1970* (London: Routledge and Kegan Paul, 1971); M. Sanderson, 'The English Civic Universities and the 'Industrial Spirit', 1870–1914', *Historical Journal*, 61 (1988), pp. 90–104.

15. S. V. Barnes, 'England's Civic Universities and the Triumph of the Oxbridge Ideal', *History of Education Quarterly*, 36 (1996), pp. 271–305, on p. 305.

16. E. J. Morse, 'English Civic Universities and the Myth of Decline', *History of Universities*, 9 (1992), pp. 177–204, on p. 183.

17. Though see H. Silver, '"Residence" and "Accommodation" in Higher Education: Abandoning a Tradition', *Journal of Educational Administration and History*, 36 (2004), pp. 123–33.

18. *Oxford University Extension Gazette*, 4 (1893–4), p. 122.

19. P. Raymont, 'An Analysis of the Significance of Halls of Residence in the British University During the Late-Nineteenth and Early-Twentieth Centuries' (PhD Dissertation, Cambridge University, 2005) uses the example of a single Leeds hall; C. Dyhouse, *No Distinction of Sex? Women in British Universities 1870–1939* (London: UCL Press, 1995), ch. 3, explores women's experiences of residence. See also M. B. Vickery, *Buildings for Bluestockings: The Architecture and Social History of Women's Colleges in Late Victorian England* (London: AUP/University of Delaware Press, 2000). For Oxbridge, see P. R. Deslandes, *Oxbridge Men: British Masculinity and the Undergraduate Experience,*

1850–1920 (Bloomington, IN and Indianapolis: Indiana University Press, 2005), pp. 62–82.

20. See especially A. Duke, *Importing Oxbridge: English Residential Colleges and American Universities* (New Haven, CT and London: Yale University Press, 1996); H. L. Horowtiz, *Alma Mater: Design and Experience in the Women's Colleges from Their Nineteenth-Century Beginnings to the 1930s* (Boston, MA: Beacon Press, 1984); L. Wilkie, *The Lost Boys of Zeta Psi: a Historical Archaeology of Masculinity at a University Fraternity* (Berkeley, CA: University of California Press, 2010).

21. R. A. Lowe and R. Knight, 'Building the Ivory Tower: the Social Functions of Late-Nineteenth-Century Collegiate Architecture', *Studies in Higher Education*, 7 (1982), pp. 81–91, on p. 88.

22. A. H. Halsey, 'Oxford and the British Universities', in B. Harrison (ed.), *The History of the University of Oxford vol. viii: the Twentieth Century* (Oxford: Oxford University Press, 1994), pp. 577–606, on p. 597. See also A. H. Halsey and M. A. Trow, *The British Academics* (London: Faber & Faber, 1971), p. 80, and J. Brothers and S. Hatch, *Residence and Student Life: a Sociological Enquiry into Residence in Higher Education* (London: Tavistock, 1971).

23. See also J. Abbott, *Student Life in a Class Society* (Oxford: Pergamon Press, 1971), pp. 102–3 for a useful contemporary reflection on this theme.

24. Committee of Vice Chancellors and Principals (CVCP), *The Planning of University Halls of Residence* (Oxford: Clarendon Press, 1948), pp. 10, 46.

25. G. A. Sutherland, *Dalton Hall: A Quaker Venture* (London: Bannisdale Press, 1983).

26. T. E. Lawrenson, *Hall of Residence: Saint Anselm Hall in the University of Manchester, 1907–1957* (Manchester: Manchester University Press, 1957).

27. H. H. Bellot, *University College, London, 1826–1926* (London: University of London Press, 1929), p. 58.

28. Miss Hutchinson, quoted in J. N. Harding (ed.), *Aberdare Hall, 1885–1985* (Cardiff: University College, Cardiff Press, 1986), p. 5.

29. M. Tylecote, *The Education of Women at Manchester University* (Manchester: Manchester University Press, 1941).

30. *University College Liverpool Hall of Residence for Women Students* (Liverpool: Liverpool University College, 1900), p. 8.

31. Dyhouse, *No Distinction of Sex*, ch. 3.

32. W. M. Childs, 'A New Residential University', *University Bulletin*, 3:1 (June 1924), pp. 92–4, on p. 93.

33. University Grants Committee (hereafter UGC), *Report of the Sub-Committee on Halls of Residence* (London: HMSO, 1957), p. 5.

34. *The History of Loughborough College, 1915–1952* (Loughborough: Past Students Association, 1957), p. 24. See also, for example, *The Opening of Highfield Hall by the Duke of York* (1930), 1/7/292/26, University of Southampton Archives.

35. Raymont, 'Halls of Residence', pp. 190–1, 215; P. Geddes, W. W. Seton, J. W. Graham, A. C. Ward, W. McDougall and T. B. Whitson, *Halls of Residence for University Students* (Edinburgh: Geddes and Colleagues, 1906).

36. National Union of Students, *The Challenge to the University* (London: National Union of Students, 1938), p. 44.

37. J. A. Brennan, *Redbrick University: A Guide for Parents, Sixth-Formers and Students* (Oxford: Pergamon Press, 1969), p. 10. See also W. Whyte, 'The Modernist Moment

at the University of Leeds, 1957–1970', *Historical Journal*, 51 (2008), pp. 169–93, on p. 183.

38. H. C. G. Herklots, *The New Universities: An External Examination* (London: Benn, 1928), pp. 50, 49, 54, 121–6.

39. B. Dobrée, *The Universities and Regional Life* (Newcastle: King's College, Newcastle, 1943), p. 16.

40. B. Wilson, 'The Needs of Students', in M. Reeves (ed.), *Eighteen Plus: Unity and Diversity in Higher Education* (London: Faber & Faber, 1965), p. 45.

41. CVCP, *Planning of University Halls of Residence*, p. 6.

42. This bears comparison with P. Bourdieu, *The State Nobility: Elite Schools in the Field of Power*, trans. L. C. Clough (Oxford: Polity Press, 1996).

43. UGC, *Halls of Residence*, p. 12.

44. P. Goldberger, 'James Gamble Rogers and the Shaping of Yale in the Twentieth Century', in V. Scully, C. Lynn, E. Vogt, and P. Goldberger (eds), *Yale in New Haven: Architecture and Urbanism* (New Haven, CT: Yale University, 2004), pp. 263–92; J. G. Seasonwein, *Princeton and the Gothic Revival 1870–1930* (Princeton, NJ: Princeton University Art Museum, 2012); W. Whyte, '"Redbrick's Unlovely Quadrangles": Reinterpreting the Architecture of the Civic Universities', *History of Universities*, 21 (2006), pp. 151–77.

45. The Principal, 'Rutland Hall', *Limit*, 14 (1931–32), pp. 55–6, on p. 55.

46. W. Whyte, 'Georgian: The Other Style in British University Architecture', in J. Holder and E. McKellar (eds), *Re-Appraising the Neo-Georgian 1880–1970* (forthcoming, 2014); A. P. Fawcett and N. Jackson, *Campus Critique: The Architecture of the University of Nottingham* (Nottingham: University of Nottingham, 1998), ch. 4.

47. Though see R. Proctor, 'Social Structure: Gillespie, Kidd, and Coia's Halls of Residence at the University of Hull', *Journal of the Society of Architectural Historians*, 67 (2008), pp. 106–29.

48. R. Gardener-Medwin, 'University of Liverpool: HALLS OF RESIDENCE RESEARCH (1959)', University of Liverpool Special Collections, 728.54(427.21)M49.

49. Buildings Advisory Committee, 3 November 195, Leicester University Archive, uncatalogued.

50. A. M. Shorto, 'The First Hall' (1941) and A. J. Walker, 'Halls of Residence' (1941), Devon County Record Office (hereafter DCRO), Exeter University Archive, 26/10b.

51. Notes on the Residential System at the University College of the South West. Exeter (?1935/6), DCRO, University of Exeter Archive, 26/10b.

52. A. Giddens, 'Aspects of the Social Structure of a University Hall of Residence', *Sociological Review*, 8 (1960), pp. 97–108.

53. M. Punch, 'The Student Ritual', *New Society*, 10 (1967), pp. 811–13.

54. CVCP, *The Planning of University Halls of Residence*, p. 46.

55. Inventory of Furniture at Dalton Hall (1897–1905), University of Manchester Archive (henceforth UMA), HDH/9/1.

56. R. Hoggart, 'Higher Education and Personal Life: Changing Attitudes', in W. R. Niblett (ed.), *Higher Education: Demand and Response* (London: Tavistock, 1969), pp. 211–30, on p. 214.

57. UGC, *Halls of Residence*, p. 12.

58. Inventory of Furniture at Dalton Hall (1897–1905), UMA, HDH/9/1; Wilkie, *Lost Boys of Zeta Psi*, pp. 184–95.

59. Notes on the Residential System at the University College of the South West. Exeter (?1935/6), University of Exeter Archive, DCRO, 26/10b.

60. *Keele in Ten Years* (Keele: University College of North Staffordshire, 1961), p. 22; Giddens, 'University Hall of Residence', p. 105.

61. See http://www.keele.ac.uk/alumni/thekeeleoralhistoryproject/ [accessed 3 September 2012].

62. Brothers and Hatch, *Residence and Student Life*, p. 207.

63. Lawrenson, *Hall of Residence*, p. 65.

64. E. Huxley, quoted in Dyhouse, *No Distinction of Sex*, p. 120.

65. *Ripple*, 1 October 1968, p. 3.

66. UGC, *Halls of Residence*, p. 12.

67. Punch, 'The Student Ritual', p. 812.

68. Giddens, 'University Hall of Residence', p. 100.

69. S. W. Town, 'Letter', *New Society*, 10 (1967), p. 908.

70. Brothers and Hatch, *Residence and Student Life*, pp. 191, 314, 323.

71. *Ripple*, 25 February 1964, p. 1.

72. M. J. Crossley Evans and A. Sulstan, *A History of Wills Hall, University of Bristol* (Bristol: University of Bristol Press, 1994), pp. 49–50; Mathers, *Steel City Scholars*, p. 197.

73. *Sphinx*, January 1964, p. 12.

74. *Select Committee on Education and Science: Report on Student Relations*, PP 1968-9 (449-I), vol. 1, p. 100.

75. *Gair Rhydd*, May [1973], p. 1.

76. I. McPhail, 'Hall Marked', *Guerilla*, 18 March 1969, p. 8.

77. M. C. Albow, 'The Influence of Accommodation upon 64 Reading University Students – an Ex Post Facto Experiment Study', *British Journal of Sociology*, 17 (1966), pp. 403–18.

78. J. M. Kolbert, *Keele: The First Fifty Years, a Portrait of the University 1950–2000* (Keele: Melandrum Books, 2000), p. 65.

79. Punch, 'Student Ritual', p. 812.

80. Harding (ed.), *Aberdare Hall*, p. 47.

81. J. Dundonald, *Letters to a Vice-Chancellor* (London: Edward Arnold, 1962), pp. 57–8.

82. C. G. Robertson, *The British Universities* (London: Ernest Benn, 1930), p. 69; M. Skene, 'Development of a Modern University: Bristol', *Universities Quarterly*, 2 (1947–8), pp. 83–90.

83. UGC, *University Development 1947–1952*, Cmnd. 8875 (1953), p. 30.

84. W. G. de Burgh, 'Wantage Hall', *Reading University College Review*, 1 (1908–9), pp. 24–37, on p. 27.

85. W. M. Childs, 'The Essentials of a University Education', *Hibbert Journal*, 10 (1912), pp. 581–98, on p. 595.

86. P. Allen, quoted in S. Smith, 'Wantage Hall, 1927–1933', p. 25, unpublished MS, Reading University Archives.

87. W. Dibelius, *England*, trans. M. A. Hamilton (1922; London: Jonathan Cape, 1930), p. 438.

88. Quoted in Brothers and Hatch, *Residence and Student Life*, p. 135.

89. UGC, *University Development 1952–57*, Cmnd. 534 (1958), p. 39.

90. Notes on the Residential System at the University College of the South West. Exeter (?1935/6), DCRO, University of Exeter Archive, 26/10b.

91. Quoted in Harding, *Aberdare Hall*, p. 5.

92. Notes on the Residential System at the University College of the South West. Exeter (?1935/6), DCRO, University of Exeter Archive, 26/10b.

93. UGC, *Halls of Residence*, p. 7.

94. Halsey, 'Oxford and the British Universities', p. 597.
95. Truscot, *Red Brick University*, pp. 48–9.
96. Ibid., p. 34.
97. *University College Liverpool Hall of Residence*, p. 7.
98. E. Ashby, 'A Note on an Alternative to Halls of Residence', *Universities Quarterly*, 5 (1950–51), pp. 150–4.
99. Quoted in Brothers and Hatch, *Residence and Student Life*, p. 135.
100. Quoted in Mathers, *Steel City Scholars*, pp. 177–9.
101. I explore this more fully in W. Whyte, '"You are Doing a Funnerful Groovey Thing": Student Life and Student Protest in 1960s Britain', in M. Grimley (ed.), *Bulletin of the John Rylands Library: Sixties Britain Reassessed* (forthcoming, 2015).
102. Hoggart, 'Higher Education and Personal Life', p. 214.

INDEX